"Narayan wakes in me a spring of gratitude, for he has offered me a second home. Without him I could never have known what it is like to be an Indian."
—Graham Greene

R. K. NARAYAN's novel *The Guide* won the National Prize of the Indian Literary Academy, his country's highest literary honor. His other works include *Waiting for the Mahatma, The Man-Eater of Malgudi, The Vendor of Sweets,* and most recently, *Under the Banyan Tree.* His writing is marked by a genial humor and tenderness, and an elegance and simplicity of style. He is recognized as one of the finest Indian authors of his generation, and lives and writes in Mysore, India.

Bantam Classics
Ask your bookseller for these other World Classics

GREEK DRAMA, edited by Moses Hadas

THE COMPLETE PLAYS OF SOPHOCLES

TEN PLAYS, Euripides

THE DIALOGUES OF PLATO

THE COMPLETE PLAYS OF ARISTOPHANES

PLAUTUS: THREE COMEDIES (translated by Erich Segal)

THE AENEID, Virgil (translated by Allen Mandelbaum)

THE BHAGAVAD-GITA (translated by Barbara Stoller Miller)

GODS, DEMONS, AND OTHERS, R. K. Narayan

INFERNO, Dante (translated by Allen Mandelbaum)
PURGATORIO, Dante (translated by Allen Mandelbaum)
PARADISO, Dante (translated by Allen Mandelbaum)

THE PRINCE, Machiavelli

CANDIDE, Voltaire

FAUST, Johann Wolfgang von Goethe

THE COUNT OF MONTE CRISTO, Alexandre Dumas
THE THREE MUSKETEERS, Alexandre Dumas

THE HUNCHBACK OF NOTRE DAME, Victor Hugo

MADAME BOVARY, Gustave Flaubert

FATHERS AND SONS, Ivan Turgenev

ANNA KARENINA, Leo Tolstoy
THE DEATH OF IVAN ILYICH, Leo Tolstoy

THE BROTHERS KARAMAZOV, Fyodor Dostoevsky
CRIME AND PUNISHMENT, Fyodor Dostoevsky
THE IDIOT, Fyodor Dostoevsky
NOTES FROM UNDERGROUND, Fyodor Dostoevsky

CYRANO DE BERGERAC, Edmond Rostand

20,000 LEAGUES UNDER THE SEA, Jules Verne
AROUND THE WORLD IN EIGHTY DAYS, Jules Verne

FOUR GREAT PLAYS, Henrik Ibsen

FIVE MAJOR PLAYS, Anton Chekhov

THE METAMORPHOSIS, Franz Kafka

Gods, Demons, and Others
by R. K. Narayan

BANTAM BOOKS

TORONTO · NEW YORK · LONDON · SYDNEY · AUCKLAND

GODS, DEMONS, AND OTHERS

*A Bantam Book / published by arrangement with
the author*

PRINTING HISTORY

Gods, Demons, and Others was
first published in 1964
Bantam Classic edition / August 1986

*Cover painting, Krishna Slays Vatsasura, by an unknown artist
of the Malwa School, circa 1640, used by kind permission of
Dr. Alvin O. Bellak.*

ISBN 0-553-21240-0

Published simultaneously in the United States and Canada

Bantam Books are published by Bantam Books, Inc. Its trademark, consis-
ting of the words "Bantam Books" and the portrayal of a rooster, is Regis-
tered in U.S. Patent and Trademark Office and in other countries. Marca
Registrada. Bantam Books, Inc., 666 Fifth Avenue, New York, New York
10103.

PRINTED IN THE UNITED STATES OF AMERICA

O   0 9 8 7 6 5 4 3 2 1

Several of the stories in this volume are based on the *Mahabharata:* "Yayati," "Draupadi," "Nala," "Savitri," "Shakuntala," "Harischandra," and "Sibi"; three are from the *Ramayana:* "Viswamitra," "Ravana," and "Valmiki." The source of "Lavana" and "Chudala" is the *Yoga-Vasishta;* of "Devi," the *Devi Bhagavatam;* and of "Manmata," the *Shiva Purana.* "The Mispaired Anklet" is from the Tamil epic *Silapadikharam.*

CONTENTS

THE WORLD OF THE
STORYTELLER

HE IS PART and parcel of the Indian village community, which is somewhat isolated from the main stream of modern life. The nearest railway station is sixty miles away, to be reached by an occasional bus passing down the highway, which again may be an hour's marching distance from the village by a shortcut across the canal. Tucked away thus, the village consists of less than a hundred houses, scattered in six crisscross streets. The rice fields stretch away westward and merge into the wooded slopes of the mountains. Electricity is coming or has come to another village, only three miles away, and water is obtainable from a well open to the skies in the center of the village. All day the men and women are active in the fields, digging, ploughing, transplanting, or harvesting. At seven o'clock (or in the afternoon if a man-eater is reported to be about) everyone is home.

Looking at them from outside, one may think that they lack the amenities of modern life; but actually they have no sense of missing much; on the contrary, they give an impression of living in a state of secret enchantment. The source of enchantment is the storyteller in their midst, a grand old man who seldom stirs from his ancestral home on the edge of the village, the orbit of his movements being the vegetable patch at the back and a few coconut palms in his front yard, except on some very special occasion calling for his priestly services in a village home. Sitting bolt upright, cross-legged on the cool clay-washed floor of his house, he may be seen any afternoon poring over a ponderous volume in the Sanskrit language mounted on a wooden reading stand, or tilting towards the sunlight at the doorway some old palm-leaf manuscript. When people want a story, at the end of their day's labours in the fields, they silently assemble in front of his home, especially on evenings when the moon shines through the coconut palms.

On such occasions the storyteller will dress himself for the part by smearing sacred ash on his forehead and wrapping himself in a green shawl, while his helpers set up a framed picture of some god on a pedestal in the veranda, decorate it with jasmine garlands, and light incense to it. After these preparations, when the storyteller enters to seat himself in front of the lamps, he looks imperious and in complete control of the situation. He begins the session with a prayer, prolonging it until the others join and the valleys echo with the chants, drowning the cry of jackals. Time was when he narrated his stories to the accompaniment of musical instruments, but now he depends only on himself. "The films have taken away all the fiddlers and crooners, who have no time nowadays to stand at the back of an old storyteller, and fill his pauses with music," he often comments. But he can never really be handicapped through the lack of an understudy or assistants, as he is completely self-reliant, knowing as he does by heart all the 24,000 stanzas of the *Ramayana,* the 100,000 stanzas of the *Mahabharata,* and the 18,000 stanzas of the *Bhagavata*. If he keeps a copy of the Sanskrit text open before him, it is more to demonstrate to his public that his narration is backed with authority.

The Pandit (as he is called) is a very ancient man, continuing in his habits and deportment the traditions of a thousand years, never dressing himself in more than two pieces of cotton drapery. (But sometimes he may display an amazing knowledge of modern life, acquired through the perusal of a bundle of old newspapers brought to him by the "weekly" postman every Thursday afternoon.) When he shaves his head (only on days prescribed in the almanac), he leaves just a small tuft on the top, since the ancient scriptures, the shastras, prescribe that a man should wear his hair no thicker than what could pass through the silver ring on his finger; and you may be sure he has on his finger a silver ring, because that is also prescribed in the shastras. Every detail of his life is set for him by what the shastras say; that is the reason why he finds it impossible to live in a modern town—to leave his home where his forefathers practiced unswervingly the codes set down in the shastras. He bathes twice daily at the well, and prays thrice, facing east or west according to the hour of the day; chooses his food according to the rules in the almanac, fasts totally one day every fortnight, breaking his fast with greens boiled in salt water. The hours that he does not spend in contemplation or worship are all devoted to study.

His children could not, of course, accept his pattern of life and went their ways, seeking their livelihood in distant cities. He himself lives on the produce of his two acres and the coconut garden; and on the gifts that are brought him for storytelling—especially at the happy conclusion of a long series, or when God incarnates himself as a baby of this world or marries a goddess in the course of a story. He is completely at peace with himself and his surroundings. He has unquestioned faith in the validity of the *Vedas*, which he commenced learning when he was seven years old. It took him twelve years to master the intonation of the *Vedas*. He had also to acquire precise knowledge of Sanskrit grammar, syllabification, meaning of words.

Even his daily life is based on the authority of the *Vedas*, which have in them not only prayer and poetry, but also guidance in minor matters. For instance, whenever he finds his audience laughing too loudly and protractedly at his humour, he instantly quotes an epigram to show that laughter should be dignified and refreshing rather than demonstrative. He will openly admonish those who are seen scratching their heads, and quote authority to say that if the skin itches it should be borne until one can retire into privacy and there employ the tip of a stag-horn, rather than fingernails, for the purpose. He has no doubt whatever that the *Vedas* were created out of the breath of God, and contain within them all that a man needs for his salvation at every level.

Even the legends and myths, as contained in the puranas, of which there are eighteen major ones, are mere illustrations of the moral and spiritual truths enunciated in the *Vedas*. "No one can understand the significance of any story in our mythology unless he is deeply versed in the *Vedas*," the storyteller often declares. Everything is interrelated. Stories, scriptures, ethics, philosophy, grammar, astrology, astronomy, semantics, mysticism, and moral codes—each forms part and parcel of a total life and is indispensable for the attainment of a four-square understanding of existence. Literature is not a branch of study to be placed in a separate compartment, for the edification only of scholars, but a comprehensive and artistic medium of expression to benefit the literate and the illiterate alike. A true literary composition should appeal in an infinite variety of ways; any set of stanzas of the *Ramayana* could be set to music and sung, narrated with dialogue and action and treated as the finest drama, studied analytically for an understanding of the subtleties of language and grammar, or distilled finely to yield esoteric truths.

The characters in the epics are prototypes and moulds in which humanity is cast, and remain valid for all time. Every story has implicit in it a philosophical or moral significance, and an underlining of the distinction between good and evil. To the storyteller and his audience the tales are so many chronicles of personalities who inhabited this world at some remote time, and whose lives are worth understanding, and hence form part of human history rather than fiction. In every story, since goodness triumphs in the end, there is no tragedy in the Greek sense; the curtain never comes down *finally* on corpses strewn about the stage. The sufferings of the meek and the saintly are temporary, even as the triumph of the demon is; everyone knows this. Everything is bound to come out right in the end; if not immediately, at least in a thousand or ten thousand years; if not in this world, at least in other worlds.

Over an enormous expanse of time and space events fall into proper perspective. There is suffering because of the need to work off certain consequences, arising from one's actions, in a series of births determined by the law of Karma. The strong man of evil continues to be reckless until he is destroyed by the tempo of his own misdeeds. Evil has in it, buried subtly, the infallible seeds of its own destruction. And however frightening a demon might seem, his doom is implied in his own evil propensities—a profoundly happy and sustaining philosophy which unfailingly appeals to our people, who never question, "How long, oh, how long, must we wait to see the downfall of evil?"

The events in Indian myths follow a calendar all their own, in which the reckoning is in thousands and tens of thousands of years, and actions range over several worlds, seen and unseen. Yet this immense measure of time and space does not add up to much when we view it against the larger timetable of creation and dissolution. Brahma, the four-faced god and Creator of the Universe, who rests on a bed of lotus petals in a state of contemplation, and by mere willing creates everything, has his own measure of night and day. In his waking half-day he creates the Universe, which passes through four well-defined epochs, called *yugas*.* Then Brahma falls asleep, and there is a total dissolution of everything. Brahma sleeps for twelve hours, wakes up, and the business of creation begins all over again and lasts another full cycle of four epochs.

Brahma's own life span is a hundred celestial years,† at the end of which he himself is dissolved, and nothing is left of creation or the Creator. The sun and the stars are put out and the oceans rise in gigantic waves and close over the earth. Ultimately even the waters from this deluge evaporate and are gone. A tremendous stillness, darkness, and vacuity occur. Beyond this cosmic upheaval stands a supreme God, who is untouched by time and change, and in whose reckoning creation and dissolution have occurred in the twinkling of an eye. He is the ultimate Godhead, called Narayana, Iswara, or Mahashakti. From this Timeless Being all activity, philosophy, scripture, stories, gods and demons, heroes and epochs, emanate, and in Him everything terminates.

For certain purposes this Timeless Being descends to the practical plane in the form of a trinity of gods, Brahma, Vishnu,

---

* Each *yuga* lasts for 3000 years, by celestial measurements; but one celestial year is the equivalent of 3600 years of human time, so that the four *yugas* cover a span of 43,200,000 mortal years. Each of the four *yugas*, *Krita*, *Treta*, *Dwapara*, and *Kali*, possesses special characteristics of good and evil. In *Kritayuga* righteousness prevails universally. In *Tretayuga* righteousness is reduced by one quarter, but sacrifices and ceremonies are given greater emphasis. Men act with certain material and other objectives while performing the rites, no longer doing them with a sense of duty. There is a gradual decrease in austerity. In *Dwaparayuga* righteousness is diminished by half. Some men study four *Vedas*, some three, others one, and others none. Ceremonies are multiplied as goodness declines, and diseases and calamities make their appearance. In *Kaliyuga* righteousness, virtue, and goodness completely disappear. Rites and sacrifices are abandoned as mere superstitions. Anger, distress, hunger, and fear prevail, and rulers behave like highwaymen, seizing power and riches in various ways.

† The equivalent of 311,040,000,000,000 mortal years.

and Shiva, each of whom has his specific function. Brahma is the creator, Vishnu is the protector, and Shiva is the destroyer; and all of them have important roles in mythological stories, along with a host of minor gods (whom Indra heads) and an even larger host of evil powers broadly termed demons—*asuras* and *rakshasas;* added to these are the kings and sages of this earth. The pressures exerted by these different types of beings on each other, and their complex relationships at different levels, create the incidents and patterns of our stories.

The narratives may be taken to have come down to us mostly by word of mouth, at first, and were also recorded in the course of centuries. Each tale invariably starts off when an inquiring mind asks of an enlightened one a fundamental question. The substance of the story of the *Ramayana* was narrated by the sage Narada when Valmiki (who later composed the epic) asked, "Who is a perfect man?" Narada had heard the story from Brahma, and Brahma heard it from the Great God himself at a divine council. And so each tale goes back and further back to an ultimate narrator, who had, perhaps, been an eye-witness to the events.* The report travels, like ripples expanding concentrically, until it reaches the storyteller in the village, by whom it is passed to the children at home, so that ninety per cent of the stories are known and appreciated and understood by every mortal in every home, whether literate or illiterate (the question does not arise).

Everyone knows what the hero achieves by God's grace, and also what the end of the demon is going to be. The tales have such inexhaustible vitality in them that people like to hear them narrated again and again, and no one has ever been known to remark in this country, "Stop! I've heard that one before." They

---

* Fixing the date of the *Ramayana,* the *Mahabharata,* or the puranas—the source books of all legendary tales—involves one in calculations of geological rather than historical proportions. The *Vedas* are believed to have existed eternally—to have taken shape, as mentioned above, out of the breath of God; they had no beginning and will have no end. The antiquity of the puranas may be judged from the fact of their being mentioned in the *Vedas.* A certain historian of Sanskrit literature fixes the date of the *Mahabharata* at 3000 B.C., and of the *Ramayana* earlier.

are heard or read and pondered over again and again, engendering in the listener an ever-deepening understanding of life, death, and destiny.

Most narratives begin in a poetic setting, generally a cool grove on the banks of a river or a forest retreat, in which are assembled sages at the end of a period of fruitful penance. A visitor comes from afar. After honouring the guest, the sages will ask, "Where are you coming from? What was noteworthy at such-and-such a king's sacrifice? Tell us whatever may be worth hearing." And the visitor will begin his tale. Thus did Sauti, a wandering scholar, narrate the story of the *Mahabharata* at a forest retreat, when questioned by the sages. Sauti also mentions that Vyasa (the author of the *Mahabharata*) dictated the whole of it, his amanuensis being no less a personage than Ganesha, the elephant-faced god, who agreed to take down the story provided the author did not falter or pause in his narration. Vyasa accepted this condition and commenced dictating so fluently that the elephant god had to break off one of his ivory tusks and use it as a stylus for etching the text on a palm-leaf. Even today the image of the elephant god is represented as possessing only a vestige of a tusk on the right-hand side of his trunk.

All the tales have certain elements in common, namely: Sages spend their lives in the forest, seeking a life of illumination through austerity and concentrated meditations (called *tapas*). Demoniacal creatures also undertake intense penance, acquire strange, unlimited powers, and harass mankind and godkind alike until a redeemer appears and puts them out. In the stories that follow, the demon Ravana, and Taraka in "Manmatha," are such creatures.

The kings in the tales are men of action, waging war and expanding their empires, which is their legitimate public activity. The king rules his subjects strictly according to the code of conduct set for him in the shastras. Sometimes he slips and goes through great tribulations (gambling is the weakness of the Pandavas, in "Draupadi," and of the hero of "Nala"). Sometimes the king goes out hunting, strays away from his companions, and steps right into a set of circumstances which prove a turning point in his life, as in "Harischandra" and "Shakuntala."

Another common element in the tales is the Swayamwara ceremony, the outstanding event in a palace, by which a princess, when she comes of age, can select a husband. Proclamations go out far and wide that the princess is about to choose her husband. Eligible princes arrive at the capital from all directions and fill the galleries in the assembly hall. At a given moment the princess appears in the middle of the hall, bearing a flower garland, looks about, and gives it to the one she finds acceptable. Swayamwara figures with some importance in the stories "Draupadi," "Valmiki," and "Nala."

While the evil-minded pursue power and the acquisition of riches, there are idealists who renounce everything, including the ego, in their search for an abiding reality, as in "Chudala" and "Yayati." Renunciation is ever a desirable means of attaining a higher life, and at some stage every character of goodness adopts it.

Since didacticism was never shunned, every story has implicit in it a moral value, likened to the fragrance of a well-shaped flower.

In the following pages, I have included only stories which revolve around outstanding personalities. I believe that, though circumstances and details may vary, it is personality alone that remains unchanging and makes sense in any age or any idiom, whether the setting is 3000 B.C. or 2000 A.D. I have aimed at assembling as large a variety of characters as possible, so that taken together they may provide the readers of this book with a total picture of Indian mythology. The stories are grouped, as the introductory note for each of the five parts indicates, according to certain common themes, or the treatment of certain typical figures, as the ideal king or the virtuous wife.

Although I have made my selection after listening to the narratives of several storytellers such as I have described, and checking them again by having the originals read out to me by a Sanskrit scholar, and although I have tried to follow closely the course of the original narratives, these stories in no sense should be taken as translations. For one thing, I have had to avoid many theological or didactic interludes that considerably held up the narrative, sometimes for two or three days, as the storyteller halted at a particular point and went off at a tangent to criticize modern attitudes or to expound a philosophy; I had to keep my focus on the sheer narrative value and omit all else, if for no other reason, to confine this volume to its present dimensions. My method has been to allow the original episodes to make their impact on my mind, as a writer, and rewrite them in my own terms, from recollection, just as I would write any of my other stories normally out of the impact of life and persons around me. In keeping with the traditional method, I have retained the narrator in the background, who occasionally comes forward with an explanation or an introduction.

THE GODS OF THE STORIES

Iswara, Narayana, Mahashakti: the supreme God who is beyond all creation and dissolution, and beyond change, is called by one of three names. The descent of this Supreme Being to a practical plane establishes the Trinity:

1. *Brahma:* The Creator, father of all creatures, whose vehicle is a swan, and whose consort is Saraswati, the goddess of learning. Brahma's progeny are numerous, but among them the most distinguished are the Seven Sages; Brihaspati, the god of wisdom; Prajapati; and Daksha.

2. *Vishnu:* The Protector, who resides in Vaikunta. His spouse is Lakshmi, the goddess of wealth. Whenever the world is threatened with extinction by evil powers, Vishnu incarnates himself (each incarnation is known as an avatar). According to mythology, Vishnu descended as an avatar nine times and saved humanity; among the most important of his avatars should be mentioned Rama, hero of the *Ramayana,* and Krishna, who supported the Pandavas, heroes of the *Mahabharata,* against their evil cousins. Krishna's birth and earlier life are chronicled in the *Bhagavata.*

3. *Shiva:* An austere god whose function is broadly termed "destruction." His spouse is Parvati, and he resides on the Kailas mountain. Shiva's two sons are Subramanya, who destroyed the demon Taraka, and Ganesha, the god with an elephant's head, prayer to whom is said to remove all obstacles, who wrote down the *Mahabharata* at the dictation of Vyasa.

Indra: Chief among the minor gods, or *devas,* who number thirty-three million.

Varuna: Lord of oceans, atmosphere, and water.

Agni: The god of fire.

Yama (also known as *Yama Dharma*): The god of death and justice.

Surya: The sun god.

The Aswinis: Twin sons of the sun or the sky, ever young, handsome, and bright.

Vayu: The god of wind, father of Bhima (in the *Mahabharata*) and of Hanuman (in the *Ramayana*).

Kama (*Manmata*): The god of love.

Kali and *Dwapara:* Minor deities, each presiding over an epoch, or *yuga,* bearing his name.

ONE

LAVANA

CHUDALA

YAYATI

In these three stories concerning the "Others," in the title *Gods, Demons, and Others*, we note the least interference from gods. Each story is concerned with a discovery in the realm of the spirit: "Lavana" explores the nature of time; "Chudala" deals with the unfoldment of the psyche; "Yayati," in part, examines the age-old quest for perpetual youth.

LAVANA

THE PANDIT THIS afternoon was reading a newspaper instead of his usual palm-leaf. The afternoon was still, blue and bright, and his favourite calf, tethered to a post within his view, had eaten from a small bundle of dry grass he had placed for it in a trough. He put away the newspaper, took off the glasses on his nose, and said, "I took a little time to read the account of the man who has been flung into the regions of the upper air and has circled the earth—strange experiments people of the Western world attempt. Such a man does not wait for the earth to turn towards the sun or away from it, but himself goes round and creates his own night and day. So between two dawns he does not pass through twenty-four hours as we do, but through a half-day or two days, who can say which? All this makes one think again and again of the nature of time. What is a day? What are two days? What is a lifetime? I am going to tell you the story of Lavana to illustrate this."

Once (he said) there was an ancient kingdom called Uttar Pandava, of which Lavana was the ruler. This was a rich and beautiful country. The king was pleased with his subjects, and the subjects were equally pleased with their ruler. His daily routine consisted in meeting at his assembly hall, every afternoon, his ministers, secretaries, visitors, and petitioners. One day at the assembly hall, a stranger arrived. He was a bare, gaunt man; his forehead was blazoned with holy marks and his shawl was a rare Kashmir one, declaring to one and all that he was an honoured man. On his wrist gleamed a gold band inset with gems; at his throat was an impressive rosary strung on a gold chain; his head, covered with white hair falling on his nape, struck awe in anyone beholding him. They seated him amidst learned men.

The king could not take his eyes off him. He asked the minister, "Who is he?"

"A magician, wants an audience."

"Let him come forward."

The magician came up with a flourish. The king asked, "What can you do? Let it be something new," and the magician said, "I want to perform a feat which none else could have thought of."

Lavana smiled cynically and said, "I've seen a mango tree develop fully under a towel. I don't want to see it again."

"This will be different, my lord."

"I don't want to see a rope crawl up into mid-air with someone climbing it."

"That's a tiresome, banal trick. I won't inflict it on Your Majesty."

"I have often witnessed the dead skins of a cobra and a mongoose coming to life and fighting."

"I performed that when I was a boy of eight. I would not inflict such a worn-out entertainment on this august assembly."

"Would you do something new? I cannot tolerate the sight of any woman being sawn in half, nor anyone rising from the floor and floating to the roof: I'm sick and tired of all that show."

"Your Majesty may order my head to be cut off if I do no more than that."

"Why? Have you so little use for your head, that you wish to forfeit it so cheaply?"

"Your Majesty, I know I can perform something different."

"If you succeed, you may ask for the highest reward. Now proceed. Bring out your bag."

"I have no bag."

"That is a good sign. No bag of tricks. Then what have you?"

"Only these," said the magician, indicating his own eyes and opening them wide.

"Only what?" asked the king, looking up. When his eyes met the other's eyes—everything changed. The prime minister, who always stood on his right, faded out of view; the durbar hall with its golden pillars and carpets dissolved. The very seat on

which the king had been sitting was gone. He found himself all
alone in a wide field, on which grazed a horse of pitch-black
colour with a flowing mane and a tail brushing the earth. It
rolled its eyes wildly and foamed at the mouth. It bounced,
capered, and dug the earth with its hoofs. The king felt challenged. He caught himself muttering, "If I can't seize and break
that horse, I shall be worth nothing."

He approached it cautiously, but it shied away, tossing its
head haughtily, awaited his approach, and bounded off again and
again. The king enjoyed the thrill of the chase and did not notice
how far he had strayed. The horse drew him after it into strange
regions. At length he became infuriated and, springing forward
suddenly, seized its shaggy mane and heaved himself onto its
back. And the horse flew. It whizzed through the air, racing and
galloping as if the earth, air, trees, fields, and other impediments
were just not there. It cut through the air, jungles, trees, and
hedges and valleys and meadows.

Lavana found himself blinded and breathless as he clung to
its back. He dug his heels in its flanks, circled its neck with his
arms, and flattened himself on its back. The horse moved not
only horizontally, but also vertically through the air, and the
branches of trees hit him on the head. He shot out his arm to
ward off a bough that threatened to scratch his face and suddenly
found himself dangling in mid-air, clutching it for dear life.

What terrible things have come upon me, Lavana thought.
Where am I? There was nothing but a green abyss under his feet,
and if he dropped down he could not say where he would be
landing. He heaved himself onto the cross-arms of the tree and sat
there, he knew not how long. He looked up and saw, above, a
family of monkeys. The father lay on his back; the mother was
searching his coat for lice, and the little one was capering up and
down, restrained often by one or the other of the parents, who
pulled him back by the tail to safety. Suddenly all of them
stood arrested and kept watching him. Their eyes seemed to
mock him.

They are in their own world, and I have strayed in here by
mistake, he thought. Who am I anyway? I was a king. I had
authority, a palace, and so many who bowed deferentially when
I passed and disappeared when I looked severe, and now here I
am in a tree, verily like a monkey. Perhaps in a tree the monkey
is superior to the king, and I have to accept this status. If I

attempted to climb, I am sure the monkey would climb higher and still look down upon me. Before the situation worsens, let me get out of this place. I would rather perish in whatever may be awaiting me down there.

He looked down. Anything might be there in that wild greenery below! Beasts which might make a mouthful of him, or reptiles or wild men who might want to torture him. He let go his hold and went down, his fall cushioned by the foliage. His face bled from the scratches, his feet ached with the impact of the fall, but he felt happy to be back on firm earth, away from the flying horse, and away from the lofty monkeys. He did not know which direction to take, where to go. But he had to go somewhere. He paused for a moment and suddenly started walking.

He walked on and on. When night came, he lay on the ground and fell asleep. He could not judge how many days he spent thus or how far he had gone and from where. All that he was aware of was the path ahead and the pain at his joints; his clothing was ragged, he was covered with sores. Hunger and thirst racked him. When he could not move another step, he lay in a faint on the hard ground, hoping to be dead soon. But predicaments do not end so simply. He did not know how long he had lain unconscious, but when he opened his eyes he saw a young woman standing by and staring at him with curiosity. She had covered her body with a rag and carried a little basket in her hand. He asked, "Who are you?"

"Why?" she asked.

He said, "I am hungry, I am thirsty. What have you in that basket?"

She said, "Food which I am carrying to my father, who is chopping wood in the forest."

"What food is it?"

"The usual thing," she said. "Nothing for a feast."

"Oh, give it to me!" he cried. "Save me. I am dying; give me anything."

"It is for my father," said the girl firmly.

"Have you no heart?"

"No, I have no heart," she said. "Who are you?"

The king at this point still remembered who he was. He said, "I am a king . . . that is . . . I used to be a king. . . . Forget all that. Give me that food; I will reward you when I am back in my kingdom."

The woman said, "You may be a king, but I am not. . . . I am of the lowliest class. My father is a Chandala! We cannot give you any food. I would be committing a sin if I gave you the food contaminated by my touch. I do not want to commit this sin and go to hell. You belong to the Kshatriya caste. I belong to the lowliest Chandala caste."

The king said, "Forget that I mentioned the word king. I am a Chandala actually. I was joking with you. Do I look like a king?"

"I don't care what you look like," she said. "This is the flesh of a hog, which I have cooked with a little wild rice and greens gathered from the jungle."

As she went on describing the food, though it was an unsavoury combination of things, his mouth watered. He told her, "Please describe your food."

She described how they hunted the wild boar whose flesh she had cooked. How a number of persons from her hamlet went after the beast and speared it to death and brought home the remains and shared it among themselves, how she cooked it with wild grains found in the fields, and how she larded it, how she dried the flesh in the sun and preserved it in a pot buried underground.

The king felt desperate and said, "I am dying. Give me that food."

She said, "No, I am doing what is proper for my caste. I cannot violate the code which says that I should not feed someone of higher caste. I do not want to go to hell. If you are dying of hunger, I can't help you."

The king fell at her feet and said, "Take pity on me. Save me."

She said, "I can save you on condition that you do what I say. If you marry me you become my equal and then I can give you all the food you want. But first let me speak to my father."

The king thought it over; the proposal seemed simple, sound, and perfectly reasonable. He said, "All right, I will come with you to see your father; but I am unable to walk. I am very tired."

"If you are tired you will have to get more tired, that is all. If you want to make that an excuse not to marry me, you may die of hunger."

"Oh! Woman, you mistake me. I do want to marry you, I adore you. I will come with you."

When they reached the heart of the forest they found a shrunken old man chopping wood. The girl went close to him and explained the situation. The father asked the girl, with his eyes on the king, "You want to marry this man?"

The girl said, "I do not want to marry anyone, but he must be saved."

The father looked at the king and said, "Do you want to marry this dirty girl? She is hare-lipped, ugly, uncouth, she is a Chandala woman. She was born to a concubine of mine. I do not remember who her mother was. But if you want to marry her, I will not object."

The king blurted out, "I want food."

The woodcutter said, "You will get food when you have become her husband."

In course of time the king was quite well settled as the son-in-law of the old woodcutter and lived with the family in a hut which was roofed with coconut thatch. One evening the woodcutter died; the next day they buried him in their yard and the king became the head of the family. He speared the forest animals, skinned them with his own hands, and maintained the food supply at home. Sometimes he went into the forest to cut wood. In time he lost all memory of his identity. If anyone had asked him who he was, he would have said, "I am of course a hunter living in the forest, married to this lovely woman." He had become blind not only to his own identity, but also to that of the hare-lipped Chandala woman. He had become her slave and as years passed she bore him four sons. He clothed himself in tree bark, his hair was matted and long, and his nails were grown clawlike.

A great famine struck the land, and all vegetation dried up. All the water in the ponds was gone. Most of the animals went away, and the few that had been caught in this famine-stricken corner of the world lay dead and were so parched that there was no flesh on them to eat. The trees stood gaunt and bare, and one day a small fire started in a bamboo thicket and came raging across the entire area; Lavana with his family had to move off. The king carried on his head a basket filled with oddments of the household such as hunting knives, spears, and some dried skins and a few ragged clothes. His sons were fairly grown up now.

He told them, "My boys, I cannot support you any longer. You will have to fend for yourselves. Do not follow me, but go your own ways."

At this, the wife flew at him. "How dare you talk to the children in this manner! Have you no heart, you want to turn them out?"

"Children! Children!" the king cried. "They used to be children. They are old now. Do you not see that the oldest is middle-aged? Do they seem like children in your eyes?"

"Yes, they do!" said the woman. "And it is your business to keep them as long as they want to be with us. I want all my children to be with me."

The king detested his first three sons, who always seemed to sit around their mother and chatter away, looking to him to bring food and water. But he was deeply attached to his youngest son, who was now twenty. And so they moved on without breaking up.

They walked and walked without food or water until a time came when they could proceed no longer as a family.

One by one, the first three sons deserted when they found that their father could support them no more. The king became extremely weary, especially when nagged by his wife. "What a man you are! When you could not support a family, why should you have married? Did you think that you could throw away the children when they were born? Oh! You monster! You have driven away those three children. I do not know where they are."

The king bore it all patiently. He merely said, "We will come to rest somewhere. We cannot go on like this. There must be a green patch somewhere. When we get there and get settled, I will go back and search for the lost sons."

They went on and on until one day the king felt too tired to take another step, but he saw his son lying on the ground half dead. He bent over him and said, "Boy, be courageous! You will have something to eat soon."

The boy whispered, "Where is it? I see nothing. I want meat . . . cooked . . . some meat." He was nearly in a delirium.

The king said, "All right, I will cook you some. Wait. . . ." He went over to his wife as she lay in a drowse under a tree and said, "I will provide meat for you and for that child of ours. Stay here for half an hour and then look behind yonder rock.

You will find meat, cooked and ready to be eaten. If you have any salt, sprinkle it on it and eat.''

"What about you?" she asked.

He was touched by her concern for him. For the first time in many days she was showing consideration for his feelings. "Do not worry about me. I will manage. But on no account should you stir before I am ready. You will soon notice a fire on the other side; when it subsides, come and find your food ready. Meanwhile, sleep." He patted his son and said, "You will have food soon, my boy. Sleep in peace."

The king said, as he left, "Be sure to give this boy all the food he wants. All the meat he wants." Beyond the rock he gathered faggots and dry leaves, struck a flint,. and lit a fire. When it was satisfactorily crackling, he cried to his wife, "Do not move. Come when the fire has died down." So saying, he jumped into the fire, screaming, "Don't take out the meat before it is well cooked. Have your salt ready."

With that, the king woke up. He saw that he was still sitting in his usual seat in the assembly. The ministers were around him. He looked about him and said, "Have you been here all this time?"

The ministers said, "Yes, Your Majesty. We have not moved."

Lavana said, "I don't understand. How long has it been?"

The minister said, "Your Majesty?"

"How long did I sleep?"

"Well, perhaps a minute or two, Your Majesty; not more than that."

The king cried, "But I passed through seventy years. I passed through a whole lifetime of seventy years. Did I not?" He looked about and cried, "Where is that magician?"

And everyone looked about, but the magician was gone.

CHUDALA

SIKHI-DHVAJA WAS a young prince, greatly interested in games and sports and in the exercise of arms. At sixteen he undertook various military expeditions and enlarged his father's empire. Wherever he went he was received with honours and acknowledged as a conqueror, and where he was not thus received he forced the people to accept his superiority.

Preoccupied with all this activity, he was totally blind to the charms of women. But when he was eighteen he became aware of the subtleties of the seasons and their influence, watched, and understood the language of birds when they uttered their love calls. Noticing his new interest, his father arranged for him to marry a princess from the Saurashtra country, whose name was Chudala. Finding them happy in each other's company, the king transferred all his authority to the prince and retired into the forest.

Now began a life of the utmost felicity for the prince. Chudala was very accomplished, beautiful, full of youth and charm. They travelled to beautiful spots, listened to music, and visited waterfalls, mountains, and rivers together; when they were in each other's company the beauties of nature seemed to be enhanced a thousandfold, and all the sweet qualities of existence too. All this delightful experience seemed to produce only one result—to bring them closer and to involve them in endless lovemaking and a search for further enjoyment.

Thus passed many years, and they became suddenly dissatisfied with their life. They said to each other, "How long are we to go on like this, enjoying and enjoying, what is the end of it? This is all a manifestation of youth, but youth itself ebbs away every second. It is time to turn our minds to other things." They both resolved in a mood of grand renunciation and satiety to turn over a new leaf in their lives.

Chudala spent all her time in study, in inquiry into the nature of the self and the ultimate, and by disciplining her mind she progressed quickly to a life of illumination and self-knowledge. A great serenity came upon her, and a new lustre shone in her face. Sikhi-Dhvaja was struck by this change in her and asked, "What is this new radiance that I see in your face? Are you no longer my wife but someone else?"

She replied, "I look at myself in a mirror now and then but see no change. I see the same mask covering me. But I see more clearly something that you don't see, that is my inner self, which is no different from the illumination that you see in the sun or the soul that moves even the smallest creature. And that gives me a sense of peace and oneness with every being; the joy that I feel at the sight of a cloud is the inner joy that is ever there within the cloud itself and within every creature on earth." Thus she went on, and stopped short only when she saw that her husband could not follow her speech. She realized that, although both of them had decided to pursue a life of self-illumination, he had remained undeveloped.

Sikhi-Dhvaja proved a good and conscientious king and ruled his subjects justly, but his spiritual development was stunted, and that made Chudala sad. She performed all her duties as a wife correctly. Still her secret grief was her husband's crassness. He took her every word literally. But she did not despair. She knew that sooner or later he would attain understanding. When he remarked, as was his wont, "I see a new look in you," she felt happy that perhaps he was becoming perceptive. But then, when he spoiled it all by adding, "I was wondering if you have discovered some new cosmetic," she would ignore the frivolity of his remark and speak of serious matters. Sometimes he boasted, "I am an independent thinker. I like to arrive at my own conclusions. When you mention 'truth,' you must consider its implications in a rational manner," and he would launch into banal logic and argumentativeness and try to exhaust her. But she always listened to his nonsense with forbearance and silently prayed for the dawn of wisdom in him.

One day he suddenly lost his complacency. The perennial cravings of the physical self and its propitiation began to weary him. He became restless and unhappy and wailed, "I am not able to meditate, I am not able to contemplate, everything seems unreal.'' He sought comfort in listening to the reading of the scriptures, he gathered learned men about him and encouraged them to discuss philosophy in his presence, he ordered elaborate rituals and sacrificial feasts and noisy chanting of sacred verse. But when the effect of it all wore off he was back in his solitude, fumbling for security. This condition became intolerable, and one day Sikhi-Dhvaja told his wife, ''This is no place for me, I have no peace here. Let me retire into the forest and meditate.''

Chudala said, ''What you cannot attain here, you will never attain in a forest. What makes you think that you will be better off there? Moreover, you have your duties as a king, you cannot abandon them so summarily.'' She dissuaded him again and again. Finally one morning, waking up, she found his half of the bed vacant; he was gone.

In spite of her wisdom and understanding, she felt distraught at this separation. She wept and lamented in secret, but, since she was an adept in various psychic techniques, she could follow him through her subtle perceptions as he wandered in far-off forests and mountains. It saddened her to see him in this plight, but she realized that he had to go through his spiritual explorations in his own way.

In the king's absence Chudala ruled the country.

She had mastered the art of assuming any form she chose, and presently she took the shape of a young ascetic and appeared before her husband as he loitered madly in the wilderness, searching for inner peace.

''Who are you?'' he asked the moment he saw the young ascetic.

''My name is Kumbha,'' he replied. ''I am an adept, having practised spiritual austerities under rare masters. I understand your problem. Your aim is sound but you are struggling because you have no guru. Under the guidance of a proper guru you can achieve your purpose.''

''Where am I to find that guru?''

''Here and now, he stands before you. Make use of him.''

''You mean yourself?''

''Yes, I am here to help. I will be with you as long as you want me. Will you follow my advice?''

Sikhi-Dhvaja immediately engaged the young man as his friend, philosopher, and guide, and attained spiritual benefits in

the course of time. Kumbha explained that renunciation of exter-
nal possessions alone would not help. One had also to cultivate
perfect detachment, which led to a well-poised mind, unaffected
by opposites such as good and evil, pain and pleasure, loss and
gain, and when one ceased to identify one's real inner soul with
extraneous impacts and experiences, one attained equanimity,
calmness, and imperturbability. Now and then Kumbha left his
ward alone on the pretext of having to go somewhere on an
errand, returned to the capital, and, assuming her queenly form,
attended to state duties.

Once, on returning to the forest, Chudala found her husband
in samadhi, a state of trance, with his body completely emaciated. Although she knew that this state signified an inner ripen-
ing, as a seed hardens within a shrivelling, drying fruit, she felt
harrowed by the spectacle. She tried to awaken him, but could
not. She went back to the capital and returned a few days later,
to find him still in samadhi. At this she created with her subtle
breath *simha nada,* that is, a roar sounding like a lion that
reached to the skies and reverberated through the forests, frightening wild animals into a stampede. The king's samadhi, however, remained undisturbed.

Chudala was pleased, but at the same time she wanted to
awaken him. She shook him vigorously, but it was like shaking
dead wood. She now tried a last remedy. She left her own body
and transmigrated into his and awoke him from within. He opened
his eyes little by little. Chudala went back to her own body and,
assuming again the form of Kumbha, sat at a distance away and
sang the *Sama* tune, that rare melody, and it soothed and pleased
the king as he gradually came back to the mundane world.
Kumbha said, "You were in deep meditation and I am pleased
with your development. Do you feel assured that you will never
more be affected by *kama, krodha,* and *moha*?"*

"Yes," said Sikhi-Dhvaja. "I am above all passions now. I
have complete confidence in myself. I feel my soul pervading
the entire universe. I find myself in a state of bliss at all times."

Kumbha said, "You have nothing to fear any more. Now
let us travel and see the world."

---

* Passion, resentment, and attraction, three of the four cardinal
  sins, the fourth being *lobha,* acquisitiveness, from which Sikhi-
  Dhvaja freed himself at the beginning.

They visited different countries, forests, and deserts. When they relaxed in some ideal romantic surrounding, Chudala felt an overwhelming love for her husband and desired his company as a woman. But she could not reveal herself to him yet without spoiling the fruits of their labours.

Kumbha took leave of the king on the pretext of having to visit the world of the god Indra on an urgent summons and, as Chudala, went back to the capital to attend to state matters; she returned to him in two days, as Kumbha, but with a sad face. "I notice a lack of joy in your face," said Sikhi-Dhvaja. "Something has, perhaps, made you unhappy. May I know what it is?"

Kumbha said, "A dreadful thing has happened to me. You are, after all, a friend of mine and I cannot hide anything from you. While returning from Indra Loka I met the sage Durvasa. He was wearing rather flashy robes, as it seemed to me, and I could not help cracking a joke with him. I said, 'O Sage, you are dressed like a damsel going in search of her lover. How is that?' I should not have joked with a person like Durvasa, whose bad temper is known in all the worlds. His eyes blazed with anger and he said, 'Young fellow, you are frivolous and silly. Normally I would not have noticed you, but today you have forced yourself on my attention and uttered insulting words. For this you are going to pay a price. Since damsels seem to be so much on your mind, you shall be transformed into a damsel at sunset each day and regain your manhood at daybreak, for the rest of your life,' and he was gone after uttering this curse. Now what shall I do?"

"You have helped me through my troubled times," the king said. "It will be my turn to help you now. Do not worry. Nothing is lost by this curse. I shall always treat you as my guru and friend, whatever may be your form."

"It is a great consolation that you will not mind it," said Kumbha.

"Let nothing worry you," said the king, and he elaborated a philosophy of acceptance.

As the evening wore on and dusk came, Kumbha excused himself from continuing in the presence of the king. He half withdrew behind a partition and cried pathetically, "O King, the curse is taking effect. Long tresses have appeared on my head, with flowers and scent."

Unperturbed by this information, the king continued his

meditation. "Where there was a flat chest," began Kumbha—"I am shy to mention it, but you are my friend—breasts, firm and round, have appeared."

"Yes, all that must happen as expected," said the king without any emotion, coldly.

"Ornaments have appeared, sparkling with gems, around my neck. I wish you could see me."

"It is all a part of the mask," said Sikhi-Dhvaja. "What do the details matter? All that will last until the morning. You will get used to the change."

"My clothes have grown longer and drape me."

"You should have expected it."

"My voice has changed, do you not notice it?"

"Yes, I do. Naturally you should have the appropriate voice for your changed state," the king said without turning.

"My hips have grown wider, and—oh, friend, this is indeed frightening—I am a complete woman now. I am no longer Kumbha. I repeat, I am a complete woman now. May I come before you?"

"Certainly, I never told you to go into concealment."

And now Chudala emerged as a woman of great beauty. The king looked on this vision unemotionally. She said, "My name is Madanika."

"Yes?" said the king without any agitation.

As the night advanced, Madanika came closer to the king and put her arm around his neck. "Be my husband. If you don't take me someone else will, for that is the curse. What is wrong in your becoming my husband every night?" The king agreed, for it seemed to him all the same, whatever he did.

She said, "Let us marry this very minute, since this is an especially auspicious night. Let us spend the night as husband and wife." At that very hour they were married according to Gandharva rites, and that night and the following nights enjoyed the utmost conjugal bliss.

She found that the king, though responsive, remained untouched by any experience. He took no initiative at any stage, although he denied her nothing when she made a demand on him as a wife. Chudala felt happy that her husband had come through the first test successfully. He was so far advanced that he made no distinction between yielding and resisting; both seemed to him immaterial, since they happened outside him. Now she wanted to put him through a second test, to see how far he would yield to *bhoga,* pleasure and enjoyment.

She created through her magical powers an illusory Indra and set him to tempt Sikhi-Dhvaja. When the king was meditating, the illusory Indra stood before him and said, "Few have achieved your spiritual status, O King. Why don't you now turn to other things? Come to my world and be my guest. There you will have the maximum enjoyment. Every kind of pleasure and delight will be at your command; come with me, and spend a few years with me; my world is known for the beauty of its surroundings, the beauty of its men and women, the food and drink, and the comforts provided for sitting, lounging, sleeping, walking, travelling, or lovemaking; there is nothing in my world that is not perfect and unique. Why should you torment yourself any more? You have attained perfection; now it is for you to seek the comforts of life."

The king looked at Indra with amusement and asked, "Does one have to go so far to seek happiness? It seems to me that all one needs is where one is, and there is no need for one to go in search of anything. It will be like going out in search of my own heart or lungs." The "Indra" disappeared. Chudala felt triumphant that her husband had come successfully through the second test also. She planned for him a third trial.

She had tested his passion and his attitude to pleasure, and now she planned a third test to find out whether he had mastered *krodha,* or anger. At dusk one day while the king was away at the river for his evening prayers, Chudala converted herself, as usual, into Madanika and she also created a lover for herself out of thin air. When the king returned home Madanika was in the embrace of her lover. The king came in, saw them, and passed on without wasting any attention on the couple.

Madanika took her own time to free herself from her lover's embrace, sent him away, and came contritely before the king. He just looked at her and said nothing. She pretended to feel disappointed at his reaction and said, "Oh, that youth came in when you were away. He seemed so beautiful and strong, any woman would have succumbed to him. I resisted his advances as long as I could, but after all I am a woman with my own weaknesses, and I surrendered myself to him. Please forgive my lapse."

The king said, "You have followed your inclination, for which you are responsible, and I can have no voice in it."

"Will you still have me as your wife? Please don't abandon me. I promise I will never do it again."

"You don't have to beg my forgiveness."

"Will you still have me as your wife?" persisted Madanika.

The king thought it over for a minute and replied, "I do not know. Perhaps it is no longer necessary for us to continue as husband and wife. Be with me as Kumbha by day and Madanika by night. Whatever name and form you assume, you will always be dear to my heart."

But she could not long continue as Kumbha and Madanika. Presently she assumed her original form as Chudala and stood before the king. He rubbed his eyes and said, "I am greatly confused. Where is that great saviour of mine, Kumbha, where is that Madanika, and how do you come to be here?" Whereupon Chudala explained the whole tangle to him. The king burst out, "Man's truest guru is his wife!"

She said, "I have tried you in every way to see if you have attained ripeness and maturity. You have attained the stability of a rock, you are a *jivan mukta*. You have surpassed me in a hundred ways. Let me become again your humble wife."

Sikhi-Dhvaja said, "Let us renounce this world completely and spend the rest of our days in contemplation in one of those caves."

"This is just the stage at which you should return to your worldly duties as a king," said Chudala. "You have attained the perfections that will benefit humanity, which should be your chief concern now, rather than withdrawal."

A second coronation was held in the capital in grand style, the populace celebrating the rediscovery of their king and queen. It is recorded that Sikhi-Dhvaja ruled happily for ten thousand years.

YAYATI

IN THE PERPETUAL strife between the gods, led by Indra, and the *asuras,* or anti-gods, who were full of accomplishments and power, the gods were always losing. This caused much anxiety and self-examination in the world of gods. The worst of it was that when a demon was killed he revived quickly and got on his feet again, while a god who was killed was fit only for a funeral. The secret of survival of the *asuras* was puzzling, the more so because the gods were under the guidance of Brihaspati, the presiding god of wisdom and acumen.

Eventually the gods discovered the secret of their enemies: they survived because they were guided by Sukracharya, the great sage who had mastered the Sanjivini mantra, an esoteric incantation which could bring the dead back to life. There were hurried consultations among the gods. They felt doomed to extinction unless they too could learn this mantra. It was known only to Sukracharya, and he was not likely to respond to an invitation from the gods. The gods decided to send down a disciple who could learn the Sanjivini from the master. They chose young Kacha, son of Brihaspati. They sent him down to the country of the demon King Vrishaparva, where Sukracharya was kept as an honoured guest and teacher.

Sukracharya accepted young Kacha as his disciple, charmed by his humility and earnestness. The young man assured him that he would go through the novitiate, practise austerity, and adhere unwaveringly to a vow of celibacy. Sukracharya had a daughter named Devayani, who fell in love with Kacha. Kacha amused and enchanted her with music, stories, and talk, and she in turn attended to his needs, gave him fruit and flowers, sang songs and danced for him.

One day Kacha went into the forest to graze the cattle. The *asuras*, realizing that if Kacha learned the Sanjivini it might eventually lead to their own annihilation, attacked him fatally, cut his body into bits, and fed dogs and wolves with the flesh. When the cattle returned home in the evening without him, Devayani was distraught with grief. She told her father, "I tremble to think what might have happened to Kacha. I assure you that I cannot live without him." Her fond father immediately uttered the Sanjivini mantra and called the youth by name. At this call Kacha rent his way through the intestines of the dogs and wolves that had devoured him, became whole again, and joined Devayani.

Another day Kacha went into the forest to gather rare flowers that Devayani had asked him to fetch. The demons ambushed him, ground his body into a fine paste, and dissolved it in the sea. Once again Devayani appealed to her father, and he uttered the mantra and Kacha became whole again.

In their third attempt on Kacha, the demons burned his body, converted his ashes into a fine flourlike substance, and secretly dissolved it in wine that Sukracharya was about to consume. Sukracharya drained the cup and Devayani came again to implore him to find Kacha. Not knowing that the young man was in his stomach, he invoked the Sanjivini mantra and called Kacha aloud, whereupon Kacha answered from his bowels and explained how he had got there. Sukracharya was greatly upset at this callous, wanton murder that the *asuras* had repeatedly attempted, and swore that he would cease to be their patron if they misused their powers. But how to fetch the boy out? He told his daughter, "I can revive Kacha by uttering my mantra, but he can come out only by bursting my belly. If you want him back I shall have to give up my life."

Devayani said, "I cannot live without my father. I want both you and Kacha. You will have to think of a way."

Sukracharya thought of a way. "I cannot help dying when Kacha comes out, but I will teach him the Sanjivini so that he may revive me after coming out of my body." And so he called to the disciple in his stomach and taught him the formula. When he emerged from the belly of Sukracharya, Kacha uttered the mantra and made his master whole again. Sukracharya warned the demons, "You have been stupid and overreached yourselves. Now Kacha has learnt the rare mantra. He has acquired the necessary knowledge and will be my equal hereafter." The demons heard this and retreated in great bewilderment.

In course of time Kacha desired to go back to his own world, having completed his studies and training. When he approached his master for the final leavetaking, Devayani said, "Marry me, don't go. I can't live without you."

Kacha replied, "I am under an eternal vow of celibacy and I cannot marry you. Moreover, the daughter of one's guru can never be other than a sister."

She lamented. "Remember all the anxiety I have gone through for your sake whenever the demons tried to destroy you, and remember all the time we have spent together."

He merely repeated, "It's unthinkable. You are my sister forever; especially after, thanks to the demons, I was forced to sojourn within your father's belly—both of us are from his loins."

She pleaded again and again, remonstrated, threatened to kill herself, but Kacha remained firm. He made ready to soar to the higher world. At which she cursed him. "May the mantra you have learnt from my father prove ineffectual to you at all times!"

This was a terrible curse, frustrating his life's purpose. He was aghast at her viciousness. He merely said, "You are blinded by lust, O Devayani. I love you as a sister, but you will not have it, O creature with those beautiful brows, and face like the full moon! How can you be so irresponsible? You are the daughter of a sage. I have admired you, loved you endlessly, but not through your attraction as a woman; nothing was farther from my mind. You care nothing for my vow of celibacy, you care nothing for my mission, you don't value my affection for you, and you curse me out of blind rage from frustrated lust. So be it. Let me tell you that the Sanjivini may prove ineffectual when I utter it, but I can still impart it to others and use it through them. As for you, you will never attain the hand of a sage or find happiness in marriage."

So saying, he ascended to the higher realms, where he was welcomed by the gods. They rejoiced that he had brought with him the mantra that would save them from extinction. Now they felt that they should take the offensive and sent Indra down to the world of *asuras* in order to provoke them to a fight.

Indra planned first the disruption of the relationship between

Sukracharya and the demon king, and he achieved it in a curious, roundabout way. In a forest glade he saw women sporting
in a lovely little pool. Their clothes were on the bank. Indra
piled up the clothes, carried them to a distant spot, and left them
there. When they came ashore the women had to rush for their
clothes and found them in a bundle of confusion; each wrapped
herself in the first robe her hand fell on, not caring to whom it
belonged.

One such person was Sarmishta, daughter of Vrishaparva,
the king of the demons, on whose behalf Sukracharya was
employing his powers and talent. The sari that she picked up
belonged to Devayani. At this Devayani lost her temper and
cried, "How dare you clothe yourself in my sari? You are, after
all, in the position of a disciple and a subordinate to me, as your
father learns the art of war from my father. What foolhardiness
on your part to touch my clothes!"

Sarmishta replied, "Subordinate! We are the givers, you are
the receivers. You and your father have your palms out always to
receive the gifts we throw you in return for teaching. You teach
because you need our support. Whereas we are a class who never
ask support of anyone, we would rather die than ask a favour or
a gift of anyone, and you think you are so superior that I should
not touch your clothes even by mistake!"

At this Devayani swore. "Your clan would be extinct but
for my father's great help!"

Sarmishta cried, "Great! Do you know how servile your
father is when he stands before my father to ask for this and that,
and yet you talk! I will teach you what it is to talk thus to a
warrior girl." So saying, she wrenched her clothes from Devayani,
pushed her into a dried-up well, and returned to her palace
without once looking back, and with no remorse in her heart.

As Devayani stood at the bottom of the deep well, crying,
Prince Yayati, from the neighbouring country, came on horseback in search of a deer that he had been hunting. When he
peeped in, he cried, "O lovely one, who are you? How do you
come to be in this situation?"

She replied, "Whom the gods kill, my father revives with
his mantra. I am the daughter of Sukracharya."

He reached down, gave her a hand, and helped her out,
saying, "Now go where you like without any fear."

Devayani said, "Take me with you. You have clasped my

right hand, as you would during the wedding ceremony, and so you must become my husband."

The prince gently put her off. "I am a prince, of the ruling and fighting class," he said. "You are the daughter of a seer, a man who sees the events in all the worlds. I would not give him offence. I feel I am not worthy of you."

"If you will not accept me yourself, through my father I will attain you, be assured," she declared, and the prince went away. Then she stood under a tree, crying her heart out.

Sukracharya grew quite worried when Devayani failed to return home and sent out her personal attendant in search of her. After a long time, the attendant came back to report, "Devayani was assaulted and thrown into the well by Sarmishta, and she has vowed never to set foot in this city again." Sukracharya went after Devayani himself, consoled her, and explained to her the importance of forbearance and tried to persuade her to return home. But she was adamant. He then went to Vrishaparva and declared, "I feel I have made a mistake in supporting you and your clan. Your daughter called us beggars. My daughter will not set foot in this city again, and where my daughter is, is my place, none other. I must leave you to your own devices hereafter."

The king replied with a lot of feeling, "All that I own—palaces, wealth, treasures, elephants, and army—all are yours. You are truly the master of everything I possess and also master of me. I mean every word of what I say."

"If you mean it, declare this to my daughter and personally comfort her."

In response to the king's appeal, Devayani, who found it difficult to forgive the memory of the injury she had suffered, said, "I desire that Sarmishta should become my servant, and that when I marry, she should follow me."

The demon king said, "Oh, let someone fetch my daughter immediately. Let her implicitly obey this young woman hereafter. To save a family an individual must be sacrificed, for the welfare of a village one family may be sacrificed, to save a country one village may be sacrificed. Sarmishta must be brought here at once."

Sarmishta arrived, accompanied by a thousand servants of her own, and declared with all humility to Devayani, "With my own one thousand attendants, I come to you as your servant to do your bidding." And Devayani's shattered self-respect was now fully restored, and she consented to re-enter the city.

Months later Devayani went into the same glade to sport in the water and play games with her companions, her chief attendant this time being Sarmishta. While they were enjoying themselves there, once again, as before, Yayati appeared in search of a deer he had been chasing. He stood arrested by the spectacle before him—the battalion of beauties presided over by Devayani, and, sitting just a step below her, Sarmishta, whose beauty outshone that of the rest. He became involved in a conversation with Devayani, as he had before. At the end of it Devayani again proposed that he should marry her, as he had already grasped her hand.

He resisted the proposal, giving the same reason as before, namely, that she was too far above him in birth. Also, he felt drawn to Sarmishta. But he could not escape Devayani this time. She sent a messenger to fetch her father, explained the situation to him, and suggested that he should give her in marriage to this prince. Yayati accepted the situation, as all means of retreat were blocked. His last hope was that the father of the girl might object, but Sukracharya gave his blessing to the union, declaring that it was predestined and must be accepted without argument.

"You will be blessed in every way," said the seer. But he warned the prince, "This girl Sarmishta will also accompany my daughter. She is the king's daughter, and she will deserve all the honourable treatment you may provide for her, but take care of one thing; never call her into your sleeping chamber, and never seek to talk to her alone nor touch her. Devayani will be your wife and you will be blessed in every way."

Yayati took his wife, with her retinue, including Sarmishta, to his own country, of which he was now ruler. In a beautiful spot outside the capital he built a mansion for Sarmishta and equipped it for her comfort.

Presently a son was born to Devayani.

Sarmishta was not happy at heart. She brooded over her lonely lot and began to think to herself: I am of an age to have a husband and a child. But he who might have been my husband is monopolized by Devayani. I cannot think of any other man as my husband. Will he ever come this way? I am Devayani's slave and whatever belongs to her belongs to me. She has a son and I must have one too. What is the good of all these gardens and flowers and food and marble halls, in this terrifying solitude? O trees, tell me, when will the king be here?

Very soon the king, happening to pass that way, paused for a moment to have a word with Sarmishta. Straight away, as if to express herself fully before he should be gone, she confessed her love for him and demanded that he reciprocate.

He merely said, "Ever since I met you, I have carried your image in my heart, but I have promised my father-in-law that I will never speak to you alone."

Sarmishta replied, "A promise made in jest, or under extraordinary circumstances, or to save a life or property, may be broken without any moral consequences. Truth is something more than that, and for all such lapses there are extenuations."

The king was charmed with her speech. "Ask for any gift," he said. "You want wealth, you want a kingdom? Ask for it and it will be yours."

"O King, all such material gifts are of no value, they do not give one lasting satisfaction. I want a gift that will be a part of my body—that is, a child by you. It is said that a woman without a child goes to hell. Save me from hell. It is your duty. Devayani belongs to you, I belong to Devayani, whatever is a wife's may be freely used by the husband. Take me." The king's defences were completely broken by this time, and when they parted for the day he had fulfilled her desire.

Yayati began to find Devayani less and less interesting. He left her alone, ignored her, and took extreme measures to keep away from her, spending all his time with Sarmishta. Devayani was unhappy and sent a message to her father complaining that the king had grown cold towards her.

Yayati often reflected: It is my good fortune that Sarmishta has come into my possession. She is like rain for the crops and nectar for thirsting souls. Devayani looks to me fierce like a serpent.

Devayani was rather puzzled when she heard about the birth of a child to Sarmishta and went out one day to verify the fact. She confronted Sarmishta with her misgivings. "What is this you have done? I had always thought you were so pure and innocent!"

Sarmishta answered, "I am not the sort to run after mere pleasure. I came across a person of the utmost divinity and effulgence. I begged him to enrich me with a child, and he obliged me out of compassion; as anyone knows, it is proper and legitimate to acquire a child in this way when a noble soul acquiesces in it. The baby I have is a gift from a rare being.''

Devayani was somewhat appeased by this explanation, but she asked testily, "Can you tell me where this great being lives, his whereabouts and his name? I also would like to know him.''

Sarmishta rose to the occasion by answering, "His purity and spiritual eminence glowed like the sun, and I could not muster the courage to ask of him his name.'' Devayani was satisfied with the explanation and went back to her palace.

Yayati had a second son by Devayani. As time passed he encouraged her to drink a strange beverage that looked colourful and tasted sweet, but was intoxicating. She grew accustomed to this drink and fell into a perpetual state of inebriety. Often she wept, sang, or was lost in prolonged slumber; sometimes she even failed to recognize Yayati and warded him off as if he were a stranger come to molest her. The king spoke severely to her, ill-treated her in many ways, and finally surrounded her with a company of deformed freaks, eunuchs, and senile persons, and took himself off to Sarmishta and was lost in the Elysium of her company, night and day. She now had three sons by this king.

Once when Devayani had passed through a phase of inebriation, she asked Yayati to take her for a change to a lonely garden place outside the city; there she found lovely children playing. She asked her husband, "Who may these children be that have such a godly appearance and have some of your wonderful looks?'' So saying, she approached the children themselves and asked who their father was. She was so gentle, persuasive, and insistent that the children pointed their fingers at Yayati standing beside her. He turned pale and remained aloof, and the children burst into tears and ran to the side of their mother, who was standing a little distance away, her head bowed in shame.

But her abashment lasted only a little while, until it received the full blast of Devayani's indignation. Sarmishta retorted, "When I said my child was the gift of a person of great divinity I did not utter a falsehood, but meant it. Who could be more divine in appearance and accomplishments than the person at your side? When he accepted you, he accepted me too. When your worthy father gave you away, he gave me away to the same person. You and I have always shared everything.''

Devayani drew herself apart from the king, and declared to him, "Let it be so. You may live with her and enjoy all the pleasures that you seek. I cannot stay here any more." She plucked off her ornaments and threw them down and started to go back to her father. Yayati followed her, uttering many words of apology.

She reached her father's house and announced at the threshold, "I have been wronged. The daughter of the demon has betrayed her true quality." She concluded, "I have two sons by this king, Sarmishta has three. You may judge him for yourself."

Sukracharya told Yayati, "You are one well versed in ethics and morality, and yet you have committed the sin of infidelity. Old age will overtake you in a few minutes in retribution."

The king explained how he had come to have children by Sarmishta; he tried to represent it as an impersonal and altruistic act. Sukracharya was not taken in by this explanation; he merely said, "A man who keeps up an appearance of righteousness and performs misdeeds under a false cloak is no better than an ordinary thief. You are already suffering for this duplicity."

Even as they were talking, Yayati's appearance underwent a change. His flesh sagged, his hair turned white, he began to stoop. He cried, "Oh, forgive me, don't condemn me to senility. I still have longings and desires to fulfil."

Sukracharya took pity on him and uttered a condition: "If you find a youth who is prepared to take on your age, you will be free to effect the exchange. You shall have that power."

Yayati approached the eldest of his sons by Devayani and offered him the kingdom immediately in exchange for his years. The son said, "The senile man has no place in life; he is unable to enjoy anything in life, is laughed at by the servants and little girls. No, Father, let us keep our respective years to ourselves." Yayati cursed him for his selfishness. "You will never be a king."

He asked his second son by Devayani, who said, "Old age kills the power to love, to live, and it misshapes a man and destroys intelligence and judgment. No, I don't want old age yet." The king cursed him. "Your lineage will perish. You will find yourself leader of the lowest grade of human beings, those that eat carcass and offal, adulterous and bestial creatures."

Now he turned to his three sons by Sarmishta with the same

request. The first one said, "No," and the king cursed him. "Your lineage will perish and you will be the king of a desert, inaccessible by road, by water, or by a donkey-ride." The next son also declined to take on his years.

He then turned to his last son, named Puru, and asked him to make the exchange. The young man said, "I will do anything you like. All I have is yours, Father."

The father embraced him with joy and said, "I will give you back your youth in a thousand years."

Yayati attained Puru's youth in every detail. He settled down to a life of the utmost enjoyment, never missing even a single moment of delight; and since he had youth and energy he also proved a just and good ruler. He fostered learning, honoured the saints, never missed a sacrifice or ritual that would please the gods, succoured the poor and the suffering, and punished evil-doers fearlessly. In private life he pursued a life of uninhibited pleasure, with women, wine, gold, possessions, and comforts.

As he squeezed the utmost out of every second, a thousand years passed by uncounted, and suddenly, while enjoying the company of a semi-divine damsel, Yayati remembered that it was time to return his son his youth. He dropped the damsel abruptly and turned his back on the life of abandon. Returning the loan, he told Puru, "You have been a wonderful son to me. Become young again and rule this kingdom as long as you wish. I have tasted every pleasure in life, and what I have realized is that there is no end to desire: it grows and keeps growing; there is no such thing as satiety. Gold, cattle, women, and food, you seek and attain, but the satisfaction each affords is short-lived, since you lust for more and more of them. After a thousand years of enjoyment, the mind craves for further and fresh enjoyments. I want to end this phase of life and turn to God. I want to live without the duality in mind of victory and defeat, profit and loss, heat and cold, pleasant and unpleasant. These distinctions I shall eradicate from my mind, divest myself of all possessions, and live in the forests amidst nature, without fear or desire."

He kept his word. He was followed by his two wives. He ate the roots of plants and leaves; he overcame all desires and all moods and emotions, and his purity of mind helped him please the spirits of his ancestors as well as the gods. He lived on water alone for thirty years, completely controlling and suppressing his thoughts and words. One whole year he nourished himself by

swallowing air and nothing else; he stood on one leg and meditated, surrounding himself on all four sides with fire and the
blazing sun above.

By such austerities, Yayati attained enormous spiritual status and merit and was worthy of going to heaven in his physical
body. He was welcomed in heaven by Indra, seated in the place
of honour as befits a soul who has attained perfection, and was
asked, "You have attained salvation through great renunciation.
Who is your equal in spiritual prowess?"

"None," replied Yayati promptly. "Among men, gods,
saints, or divinities, I see none that has my attainments."

Indra replied, "Since you respect none, you shall fall back
to earth; the weight of your ego must necessarily pull you
back." In consideration of his attainments Indra added, "You
shall, however, fall amidst good folk and return here in the
ripeness of time."

Yayati began his great fall from the heavens. When he
reached the earth again, he was gently received by a group of
saints in the forest. They said, "Who may you be, resplendent
one? In the dark clouds of the sky you shone like a meteor
blazing down the path of the sun. May we know who you are?"
They surrounded him and questioned him eagerly about heaven
and hell, birth and death, and the good and bad life. After some
time he went back to heaven; this time, with his ego controlled,
he was fit not only to reach heaven but also to stay there.

TWO

DEVI

VISWAMITRA

MANMATA

Three stories depicting a process of sublimation: The Devi, personifying the highest form of beauty and energy, battles with and destroys the demon Mahisha, who symbolizes the unmitigated brute; the sage Viswamitra attains extraordinary powers, enough to be able to create a universe of his own, but remains restless and unhappy until he realizes that the exercise of his gifts must be for other ends than the gratification of his ego; and Manmata, the God of Love, undergoes an ordeal until he is burnt up physically and left to exist only in essence.

DEVI

EVERY DEMON, SAID the storyteller, as a general rule sought immortality after attaining the favour of a god, but even the most thoughtless boon-giving god always stopped short of granting absolute immortality. This precaution has saved the world from annihilation. As an alternative the demon would always decree that if he was to be destroyed it must be only under certain fantastic circumstances. Hiranya stipulated that his killer should be neither man nor god, at a spot which was neither earth nor heaven, neither inside nor outside, and so the god took as an avatar a lion, sat on a threshold, placed Hiranya on his thigh, and ripped him up with his claws (he could not be killed by any weapon), thus satisfying all the conditions. When the demons invent impossible and fantastic situations in order to remain alive, the gods have to match wits with them and find a way of ridding the world of troublemakers.

Of all the demonly requests, the strangest was that of Mahisha, who had prayed for a thousand years, asking of Brahma that he might continue to live until a woman appeared, capable of killing him in a fight. Thereby he felt that he had insured himself against mortality, as it seemed inconceivable there could ever appear a woman capable of attacking him.

His full name was Mahishasura. *Mahisha* means buffalo, and an *asura* is a demon. He was so named because his mother was a buffalo and his father a dreaded *asura*, who had stood for thousands of years in fire and prayed. The god of fire appeared and asked what he wanted. The *asura* said, "I want a son who will conquer all the worlds, possess extraordinary strength, and remain undefeated forever, and who can assume any form he fancies." The god of fire thought over it: he realized that the consequences of such a gift would be unfathomable and said, "Whomever you love and marry will be able to produce the son you desire and deserve," leaving the fulfilment to his own choice of wife.

The *asura* looked about; his nature led him to fall in love with nothing more ravishing than a she-buffalo grazing in a field. He married the she-buffalo and settled down in the nether worlds to a life of domestic peace and felicity. One day he noticed a male buffalo molesting his wife and tried to fight off the rival, but was gored to death in the encounter. When his body was cremated, the she-buffalo, unable to bear the grief, threw herself into the fire. Before being consumed in the flames, she gave birth to a child; and the *asuras* adopted him as their king and named him Mahisha, or buffalo.

The storyteller here paused to remark, "This looks rather fantastic, this union of an *asura* with a buffalo, but perhaps we may take the word for what it signifies, that is, qualities rather than an actual creature; the buffalo is slow-witted, thick-skinned, coarse, enjoys lounging in slush, and symbolizes a mere physical development, fit for the benighted nether worlds." After this preamble he proceeded with the story.

Mahisha grew up and proceeded to fulfil the ambitions of his father. He sent an emissary to Indra to say, "Why don't you hand over your kingdom to me and get out of sight somewhere or join my household as a servant?" After this suggestion he heaped abuses on Indra: "You were often defeated by my ancestors, you low-class fellow, who did not hesitate to assume the voice and form of the sage Gautama and ravish his wife in his absence!"* And he went on to recall many unsavoury details of

---

* The sage Gautama's wife was Ahalya, a woman of great beauty. To win her, Indra secured the help of the Moon, who assumed the form of a cock and crowed at midnight. Roused thus, Gautama rose from his bed and went out to the river for his morning ablutions, according to his daily practice. Indra assumed the form of Gautama, went in, and seduced Ahalya. When this trickery was discovered, Indra was cursed with disfigurement, and Ahalya was condemned to become a rock by the wayside—thus she remained until touched by Rama's feet, during his passage in the forest.

Indra's past, concluding his message with a command to him to surrender.

Indra told the emissary, "This grass-nibbling buffalo is your master! I am fully aware of his strength, which is concentrated in his horns, as befits his species; but tell him that I have adequate weapons to quell his conceit."

When the emissary went back and reported, Mahisha declared to his followers that Indra was lusting for war and declared, "I am capable of squeezing that Indra out of existence single-handed, that worthless fellow, the commander-in-chief of weaklings and doting women. I can also mangle the gods out of existence with my hoofs and horns, but I propose to confront them with an army, since that will be more in keeping with my status as a ruler of the three worlds. Let us all repair to heaven, drink the gods' store of nectar, seize their chariots, and enjoy the company of celestial women."

Indra had sent his spies into the enemy camp. The little hope that he had of peace was gone when the spies returned to report not only on the resources and organization of Mahisha, but also of the enormous enthusiasm of Mahisha's men for the expedition. Now Indra called a council of elders presided over by Brihaspati, the god of wisdom. Brihaspati said, "Indra, don't lose your courage. Success or defeat is no one's monopoly. We must strive our best. Only the effort can be ours, the result is God-given. Muster your army and prepare to fight."

Indra journeyed into the higher worlds to appeal for the support of the Big Three: Brahma the creator, Vishnu the protector, and Shiva the destroyer, and they arrived for the battle, each riding his own *vahana,* or live vehicle—Shiva on his bull, Vishnu on his eagle, and Brahma on his swan. All the minor gods also assembled, flourishing a variety of arms. A terrific conflict ensued, with elephants, horses, men, and gods clashing with the demons. Mahisha rushed into the midst of the gods with his mace and laid about with it blindly, until Indra repulsed the mace with his *vajra,* or diamond spike.

Mahisha now invoked the power of illusion and created a million Mahishas, all armed and terrible in action. The gods saw Mahisha here, there, and everywhere. Yama and Varuna and other lesser gods fled from this terrible multiple image. Vishnu sent his discus spinning and removed at one stroke the illusion created by Mahisha. Mahisha was enraged, gathered his com-

manders around, and opposed the Trinity. He maimed and put
out of action Vishnu's vehicle, Garuda the eagle. Vishnu hit
Mahisha with his dreaded mace, and Mahisha fell in a swoon but
recovered and attacked Vishnu with a rare weapon and the god
himself fell into a faint. Shiva advanced, aiming his trident at the
demon's heart. Mahisha warded it off and hit Shiva in the chest.

Vishnu recovered and resumed his attack, but presently
realized that this was an indefatigable monster, to be quelled
only to rise again with redoubled force; he realized the futility of
continuing the battle and withdrew to his own world, Vaikunta.
Shiva understood in a moment that the monster could never be
killed by a male and retreated to the security of his own world,
the Kailas. Brahma also retreated to his own Satya Loka. Now
only the lesser gods were left, and Mahisha routed them, invaded
the heavens, and placed his relatives and supporters in the seats
of the gods. The gods fled from the scene and hid themselves in
remote caves.

After remaining in hiding for many long years they went in
a secret deputation to Brahma and pleaded, "How long are we to
live in anonymity, away from our legitimate worlds and activities?" Brahma sympathized with them, but, realizing his own
helplessness, led them along to the worlds of Shiva and Vishnu,
where the gods recounted Mahisha's atrocities.

Vishnu cut them short, saying, "This is all known. Every
asura who acquires power goes through the same set of actions,
of tormenting the gods, encouraging evil, and enjoying the pleasures of the senses. In addition to all this, they are strong-
minded, intelligent, and capable of offering arguments to establish
that they are righteous, and all others are evil-minded.

"They succeed—but, as all the gods here are aware, only
for a while; sooner or later they are overcome. Otherwise we
should still have in our midst Taraka, Ravana, Bhasmasura, and
all the other demons that were ever born, each one of them
capable of putting out the sun."

Vishnu's words heartened the gods. He added, "Now we
must think of practical measures. First, remember that Mahisha
enjoys a boon, in that he can be killed only by a woman. Where
is that woman? Are any of our wives good for this task?"

They speculated. Brahma said, "My spouse Saraswati pre-
sides over learning. But I cannot imagine her facing Mahisha in
a fight."

"My wife Lakshmi is the goddess of wealth," said Vishnu. "Anyone here is free to go and suggest to her that she challenge Mahisha. I know what she will say."

Shiva said, "My wife Parvati may have the courage, but I doubt if she has the strength. I don't see why we should think of exposing our wives to this risk."

Vishnu remained in contemplation for a while and said, "The Great Source from whom we are all derived—the Great God, who is timeless and sexless, being neither man nor woman, but both—this is the time to call on this Great Being to come to our help." They all prayed intensely to the Highest Source for help; and Grace descended in the form of emanations from the face of each god: from Brahma's face a blood-red one, from Shiva a dazzling whiteness, from Vishnu a dark one. All these combined to form an effulgent female personality, the three colors sparkling as through a prism. The Devi,* as she was called, had eighteen arms.

The Trinity were dumbstruck by her beauty. The gods showered on her their best weapons and also the rarest of their jewellery. Presently she stood there clad in red robes, crowned with a sparkling diadem, and wearing a garland of unfading lotus around her neck; she bore in her arms mace, scimitar, shield, sword, and lance. An enormous lion stood beside her in readiness to carry her on its back. All the gods were moved to a supreme prayer at the vision before them.

The Devi assured them, "O gods, fear no more, I am here to end Mahisha's career. Victory and defeat follow in a cycle. No one can claim that he has finally vanquished God; gods may suffer defeat temporarily but God himself never. Now your turn of suffering is over," she cried, and laughed happily. The next moment she thought of Mahisha, and her body was convulsed with anger as she uttered a loud challenge, which reverberated through space and shook the worlds.

The gods cried, "Victory to you!"

All this hubbub reached Mahisha, who cried, "Who is making all this noise? Bring him before me. The *asuras* are under me and dare not create any disturbance, and the gods dare not squeal for fear of being discovered. So who is it that dares to make all this row in the universe? Search him out!"

---

* Meaning the Great Goddess.

His scouts returned to report, "The earth-shaking roar emanated from a most beautiful damsel. She has eighteen arms, and each one of the arms bears a different weapon. Her seat and vehicle is the back of a lion. Her face radiates light. We do not know who she is. We could not glimpse her face for more than a second, as it dazzled us, but that was enough for us to realize that it radiated the purest emotions of joy, anger, wonder, laughter, and compassion."

Mahisha softened on hearing the description. "You babble as if you had been seeing visions after becoming intoxicated. All right, let me see this beauty for myself." He dismissed his messengers, summoned his minister, and said, "Go and fetch this woman. Use all your tact and cunning, threats of force, and cajoling, and bring her here. I will make her my chief queen."

The minister approached the Goddess and said, "Our king is the mightiest in all the worlds. He loves you and wishes to marry you. If you so desire he is capable of assuming a human form too. Come with me."

The Goddess replied, "I am incarnated in order to destroy Mahisha. Tell him that he must at once take himself off to the nether world where he belongs. Let him clear out at once; otherwise, I will destroy him."

"O lady, you are betraying a woman's judgment. How dare you, a mere girl, challenge Mahisha, who heads a formidable army? How foolish you are! He can deal with you just as a wild elephant would deal with the tender *malati* creeper entangled at his feet. Since our king likes you, I am avoiding harsh words. For the sake of our king I ask you in all humility, please come with me and accept him as your lord."

"You are the minister of a buffalo, and you possess the same intelligence!" said the Goddess. "You remarked that I have betrayed a woman's judgment. Are you aware that I am neither man nor woman, and that I have assumed this form because your king's ambition seems to be to die at the hands of a woman? When the time comes, he will have to die. Not all his army can save him. No one has so far been able to avoid death because of an army."

The minister reported to Mahisha, "I dare not repeat all that the woman said. She seems to be a haughty sort, and talks strangely. Whether you should enter into a fight with her or go back to your own nether regions, as she suggests, must be a matter for your own judgment.''

Mahisha called a council of war and announced, ''Some goddess with illusory powers now confronts us. How we should conduct ourselves on this occasion is something for you to decide.'' All his councillors began to talk at once. Mahisha could not make out what they were saying, although he cocked his ear, tilted his head, and did various things to catch the purport of their speech. Finally he shouted, ''Quiet, everyone! Speak one at a time.'' His eyes blazed with anger. It looked as though he would draw his sword and rush at them if they did not stop. He turned to one and asked, ''What have you to say?''

''An adviser should speak the truth and yet not offend, my lord. . . .''

''I leave it to each of you to say what comes to your mind. Don't fear, but don't babble all at once. I will listen to each one of you and then decide to act as I think best.''

Said one, ''Can anyone take seriously the words of a girl who may be out of her mind? Pretension and falsehood are all part of a woman's nature. Can a conqueror of the three worlds possibly think that a girl like this is worth his consideration? Permit me; I will go and put an end to her caprices without further ado.''

Another said, ''You must understand and interpret a woman's talk. We must all understand a woman properly! What are a woman's potent weapons? Eyes and curves.'' And the assembly sniggered politely at this pleasing interpretation. Warming up to his subject, he said, ''And so when she offers battle, you know what it means! Permit me, your majesty, I will go and bundle her up and throw her on your bed.''

Another said, ''It is no joking matter; she is Maya.* Eighteen-armed! Never heard of such a thing. This is no ordinary woman. We must take her seriously.''

Mahisha considered their suggestions and finally told the last speaker, ''You are the one who should approach her. Don't irritate her, keep your army out of sight, and approach her diplomatically. Find out why she made that terrible noise; ask her if she is angry with us and why. Don't be afraid of her and don't frighten her. You must somehow find out what she has on

---

* The goddess of illusions.

her mind and then come and tell me everything. Capture her first and bring her to me.''

Mahisha gave so many instructions, each contradicting the other, that the demon he chose for this errand was not clear in his mind whether he should beg, pray to, or challenge the strange lady.

He came back panting from his mission.

"Have you been running for your life?" asked Mahisha.

"Your Majesty, the tone in which she addressed me and the roar of the lion on which she was seated deafened my ears. I have become deaf, my lord, I can hear no more.''

Mahisha said, "You, my advisers, will have to give very deep thought to the situation. There is no doubt that she has been created by our enemies. We must not rush headlong into a decision without duly considering all its aspects.''

With an air of making a profound discovery, another adviser said, "There is more to this than meets the eye." And another: "A council such as this does too much honour to a vagrant girl by discussing her! Let us ignore her.''

Still another said, "She thinks that by flourishing her eighteen arms you will be frightened. What childishness! We must prove to her that we are not taken in by all this puppet show.''

"Very well," said Mahisha. "Now you go and kill her or bring her to me as a captive. Go." The man who had spoken so bravely a minute before now hesitated. Mahisha said, "All right, take an army with you and also an extra commander. Two such brilliant commanders should be able to accomplish a lot." So a fresh party set forth with many flourishes and war cries.

Only a single soldier returned later, footsore and completely battered. He wailed, "They spared me. . . .''

"Who are 'they'?" asked Mahisha.

"I beg your pardon, my lord. I mean she, she spared me so that I might come and describe the scene. All the others are dead, and there is no trace of them; all were devoured by the lion on which that terrible lady rides." He shivered at the memory of her, and continued, "Vultures circling overhead got not even a scrap; that lion chewed up even the bones, like candy.''

"Where are your commanders?"

"They were crushed by her mace. She would not even let them complete the message from your lordship. Even as one was speaking, she cut short his career. When others advanced towards her, she plucked the string of her bow and twanged it; at the sound of it, half of our army fainted. The other half fled, but a shower of arrows overtook and finished them. When our surviving commander approached her, she struck him down with her mace, and she also reduced to rubble the grand chariot on which our commanders had been riding. And that lion was ever ready to clean up. When our leader fell, flowers rained from heaven and I heard the gods praise her valour."

"We were right in guessing that she has been set up by the miserable gods, who have no courage to face us and are not ashamed to use a woman," said a soothsayer. And Mahisha picked that very soothsayer to go with a very large body of armed men to conquer the woman.

Once again only one messenger came back to report the results. "Each of her eighteen arms carries a weapon, and she wields all of them simultaneously," said this reporter, and Mahisha ordered this man to be tortured and put to death as a harbinger of evil tidings.

Four of his best commanders with their armies were gone without a trace. He sent two more, with the order "You must come back with her, we will teach her a lesson that she will never forget."

One of them approached the Goddess and appealed to her. "I am an old soldier, but your form terrifies me. O Goddess, tell me the truth, what brings you here? Why are you tormenting us in various ways? You have killed our men, who are all innocent. What pleasure do you derive from this?"

"I am the primordial foe of evil," Devi answered. "I am the eternal witness to everything that happens in creation: I am the witness to all that is right and wrong. I see everything in proportion and against its real background. My duty is well defined. I have to protect the innocent, the pure, and also the laws and scripture. That is my vow. Mahisha torments the gods and usurps their functions. I have come to rid the world of him. Tell him to clear out to his legitimate region, in the *patala*, the nether world under my feet, or come and face me. I have said this again and again. I will keep saying it until you understand me fully. I will spare you both if you will go back and tell your master to come forward instead of staying at home and sending you all to be butchered."

When this speech, which she uttered with such imperiousness, was concluded, the generals trembled and spoke among themselves. "What is left for us to do now? Should we fight or ask for peace? How terrible is the life of one who serves! We have no choice but death. Let us at least fight and die." So saying, one of them showered his shafts on her, in what amounted to an act of desperate self-destruction. The goddess arrested his shafts halfway and felled him with her mace.

Seeing the fate of his fellow commander, the other one said, "O Goddess, our king is stubborn and will not listen to your words. He is out to wipe out the godly and the righteous from the world. Helpless beings like us are driven by circumstances to provoke you and seek our own destruction." Thus saying, he attempted to attack the Goddess.

The Goddess braced herself to meet his attack with such fury that the gods assembled in the heavens to witness the fight were overcome with fear. The enemy commander soared into the sky, spread himself out like a cloud, and descended on the Goddess with all his strength; he flung his enormous mace at the head of the Goddess's lion, the lion let out a roar of pain and stood on its hind legs, the Goddess poised herself on its head, and as the other descended to the attack she slashed his head off with her sword.

When Mahisha learned of the latest casualties he became confused. He suddenly cried, "Summon my charioteer," and ordered his chariot, drawn by a thousand donkeys, to be brought to the gates at once. Another chariot, drawn beside it, was filled with a variety of arms and weapons.

He stood before a mirror and examined himself. "No," he said to himself. "She may feel repelled by my buffalo shape. I must please her. She probably likes a human form better." And so he transformed himself into a human being. He dressed himself in silk and velvet, rubbed perfume over his body, and did not leave until he was satisfied with his own person.

As she saw him approach, surrounded by a sea of warriors stretching away to the horizon, the Goddess blew her trumpet, and it arrested the advance of Mahisha. He stood stunned and astonished at the power of the trumpet.

He addressed her. "Existence is a mixed blessing, we have both joy and sorrow. What really mitigates the gall of existence are the associations we enjoy: a mother enjoys the company of her child, brothers love each other, even the lowest kind of human association, namely the passing companionship of wayfarers, has its own value. But the highest and the happiest association is that between man and woman. It is enhanced when the two enjoy the prestige of high birth, ability, achievement, and so forth. The pleasure that such a union affords is measureless.

"You know me as the greatest warrior," he continued. "If we unite, can there be a limit to the happiness we shall experience? I am capable of assuming any shape or form that I choose. I can provide you with the rarest food, drink, ornaments, and pleasures. Be my chief queen and command me; you will find me a slave. I promise, if it be your wish, that I will never trouble the gods again. I will leave them alone. I am enamoured of your beauty. I want to fall at your feet. Don't desert me. Is it not your duty to receive kindly one who comes to you for refuge? If you reject me, I will kill myself. In my life I have never asked of anyone any favour. One who chastised Brahma and the other gods is now grovelling at your feet for the favour of your love."

The Goddess said, "Even now I give you one last chance. I will forgive you if you decide to disappear this very moment and retire to your own world. Otherwise I will have to fight and kill you."

Mahisha said, "Devi, how can I pierce with sharp-edged weapons that wonderful skin of yours, which has the delicacy of flower petal? I who warred with the gods feel ashamed to fight with you. I give you this choice. If my words appeal to you, marry me and settle down to a happy life. Otherwise go away from this battlefield, go back to where you came from. You have become my friend now, and I have not the heart to thrash you, as you well deserve." He renewed his offer to marry the Goddess, and she rejected him with contempt.

He went on, "There is no sense in remaining single; man and woman should live together. Who has misled you into thinking that there is no pleasure in love? All the gods, haven't you noticed, always live with their spouses? Why has the god of love not hit you with his arrows? Perhaps he is also wondering how he could pierce that silken skin of yours! Yes, I am prepared to fight with you, and I will happily receive attacks from you, but employ the arms that are a woman's natural arsenal—eyes and eyebrows, form and charm. We will fight; and whether you conquer or I conquer, the result will be a happy one for both.''

"Lust is blinding you and twisting your tongue. I have heard enough from you," said the Goddess. "Now you will have to make up your mind one way or the other."

"My mind is made up," replied Mahisha. "It is you who will have to decide. You are still wavering. Why do you want to waste your youth in loneliness? When you find a suitable husband, you must immediately decide, casting all other considerations to the winds. Otherwise you will suffer as Mantotari suffered." Hoping rather desperately, he utilized the temporary truce between them to begin a rather ludicrous story to illustrate his point, thinking that he would win the Goddess over by this significant tale. Since she remained silent he felt encouraged to go on with the story, fancying that his speech was making a profound impression on her.

"There was once a very beautiful girl by the name of Mantotari." (Here Mahisha went into great detail as to her parenthood.) "When she was of an age to be married her father arranged to give her in marriage to a prince. Mantotari obstinately refused the alliance, saying that she did not want to marry because she was averse to being lorded over by in-laws. 'I must live as I please. Moreover, if a woman marries and loses her husband she becomes a widow and has to burn herself on the funeral pyre.' For such flimsy reasons she declined to marry at the time. Later in life she regretted her decision to remain single and married someone who proved unfaithful, and she had to bear her fate with chagrin!"

Before he could point out the moral of this tale, the Goddess said, "Will you stop your prattle and take this!" She suddenly began to hit him with her weapons.

Soon a battle was raging. Mahisha swooned when the Devi's mace merely grazed his shoulder. He revived, assumed the form of a lion, and attacked her until he was overcome by her own lion. He assumed the form of an elephant and heaved mountains and trees and sent them flying at her. The Devi's arrows arrested these in flight and pulverized them in mid-air; and then her lion pounced on the elephant's head and gashed its forehead. Mahisha as elephant collapsed for a moment, assumed his original form of a buffalo and, with his horns lowered, blindly charged. The

Goddess saw through every form that he assumed and had a weapon to match each of his wiles.

She held a bowl of wine in one hand, raised it ceremoniously to her lips, and cried, "Now, your end is come." She sent her discus circling and severed the demon's head. His body rolled in the dust.

The gods burst into a prayer, beginning, "Great Mother, through your grace the Trinity carries on the functions of Creation, Protection, and Dissolution. You are all-pervasive, and everything in creation is a part of you. Wild beasts, poisonous trees, and *asuras* are also your creation. Even to them you afford a victory of the moment, and then punish, vanquish, and help them evolve into better things. Saints who realize your subtle, secret presence attain unshakable peace and understanding, through meditation."

At the end of the prayer the Devi, greatly pleased, said, "Think of me when you need me, and I'll be at your side," and vanished.

The storyteller concluded, "Whoever recites this prayer every Friday will be protected from all evil beings, no matter how mighty they may seem at first sight."

VISWAMITRA

OF THE KINGLY race, the mightiest one, said the storyteller, was the ruler of Chedi. He was mighty in every sense of the term: wealthy, powerful, and favoured by the goddess of prosperity. He never left home without adding another kingdom to his empire, after battering down an independent ruler to the status of a vassal. From time to time he went forth thus, and finally he started out on a circumambulation of the earth with his entire army.

During this trip he came upon a hermit's camp. The king looked about the scene stretching away in valleys and uplands, trees towering above, multicoloured blooms everywhere, creepers and shrubs and greenery; the cry of birds and the chant of sacred verse; holy smoke rising and the scent of sandalwood and flowers pervading the air. The king, who had seen and experienced the finest surroundings, asked his minister, "What place is this, combining in it so much physical beauty and the aura of spiritual essences?"

"It's the *ashram* of sage Vasishta."

"I must meet him," said the king. "Let the army stay here. I'll go alone." At the portals of the *ashram*, sage Vasishta himself approached to welcome the king. They exchanged courtesies. The king was pleased with the meeting, and when he rose to go he said, "It has been a privilege for me to meet the greatest sage of all time in his own *ashram*. Now I seek your permission to leave."

Vasishta did not at once say, "Very well." The course of this entire story would have been different if he had done so and let the king go his way. Instead he said, "O king, I must show you the pleasure I have felt at this meeting. How can I except by offering you my hospitality? Be my guest for at least half a day."

"I'll come again to enjoy that honour. But now I must go."

"Pray, what is the reason?"

"My followers are waiting for my return, and we have to resume our march."

"Fetch them also. Let them eat here."

"They are a hundred thousand in my camp," said the king.

"What if they are a hundred thousand?" said Vasishta. "I can lay a feast for ten times that number."

The king's curiosity was aroused. "How? How? How will you manage it?"

"Call them all in and see for yourself."

The king sent for his army. Presently they poured into the sanctuary. No sooner were they all settled in various corners of the estate than the king began to watch with real curiosity how they were going to be fed. He saw no kitchen, no servants, and no sort of activity of preparing food. The host himself remained with the guest, talking. The king, who had never sat on the hard ground, was preparing to relax on a patch of green turf when suddenly there appeared on it a silk-covered divan, and for his men seats and carpets in thousands. Vasishta directed his chief guest to the seat and said, "Pray honour the seat; that is for you. When a mighty king honours this wilderness with his presence, I want to prove that the wilderness itself will have to stand transformed." The king was pleased and took the seat.

Presently all kinds of food in golden bowls were available for everyone. It was not just any food that an ascetic could provide for a hungry mob, but a great variety of it. The king ate his fill, as did his followers, having come there after a hard day's march.

The king suddenly felt worried. What sort of conjuring was this in the wilderness? He became very solemn as he suddenly said, "You must tell me how you have managed it."

"What?" asked Vasishta.

"O great sage, forgive my curiosity. But I must know how you have managed it. With all my palace and a legion of cooks, I could not have hoped to entertain on this scale. Please tell me how it has been possible for you."

The sage, as if sensing trouble, said, "As a guest, if you are pleased, I'm satisfied. Have you or any of your men found anything wanting?''

"No," replied the king. "You have provided my legion with everything. Our men will remember it for a long time, without doubt. Even the cloves and cardamoms that one likes to chew after food were not forgotten; those tender betel leaves are not of this world. O perfect, perfect host, tell me how you managed it, in this solitude and seclusion." Finally, when he was not enlightened on the subject, he said, "All this grand feasting and entertainment will be worth nothing, unless you also explain where they flow from. When one has quenched one's thirst with its crystal-clear water, one also likes to take a look at the whole river.''

"When you have looked at the river, you will trace its origin to some remote mountain peak, where the clouds lower themselves, and then you will want to investigate where the clouds come from, and that's an endless quest.''

"I enjoy an endless quest," said the guest.

Seeing his determination, Vasishta said, "Now, follow me, if you please. Let your men rest there for a while." He took the king along the forest path to another grove, thickly shaded with the leaves of mango, nerium, fig, and a variety of fruit trees, their intertwined branches almost shutting out the daylight; walls of green vine and a lotus-covered blue pool; and green turf everywhere. In the midst of this was a milk-white animal with the head of a lovely woman and the body of a cow. Vasishta went near it fondly and said, "Sabala! Here is our guest, who desires to meet you.''

Sabala, who was half human, said, "I hope, sir, you were pleased.''

The king asked, "Do you say that you supplied the feast?''

Vasishta explained. "On the occasion when the gods and demons churned the ocean of milk to obtain nectar,* I officiated as the high priest, and as my *dakshina* the gods gave me Sabala. She is really the daughter of the divine cow Kamadhenu. I have only to ask, and she provides it, whatever it may be.''

---

* A famous episode in the *Bhagavata:* Mount Meru served as churner, and the mighty serpent Adisesha lent his coil to serve as the churning rope; the gods held one end of the rope and the *asuras* the other.

The sage described the qualities of the cow, and they roused the king's cupidity. And at the end he merely said, "This cow ought to belong to me."

The sage laughed and said, "Come away, let us be going." Sabala watched the trend of their conversation with fear in her eyes.

The king said, "A treasure like this ought to be housed in a king's palace. Let her go with me."

Vasishta explained, "Even in a hermitage, we have to be hospitable. Otherwise you would have gone back starving, with all your men."

"She will be even more useful in a king's palace. O sage, don't you know, need I explain to you, that a king is obliged to practise unwavering hospitality morning and night, dark period of the month and the bright half of the month, dark half of the year and the bright half of the year—all through? Imagine the hundreds of persons that keep coming—kings, ambassadors, emissaries, with their retinues, and learned men and performers of all kinds. When you send Sabala with me, I will see that she is transported in all comfort, in easy stages. Your grand hospitality will be complete only when you give me that cow."

"Hospitality can never be complete; it has to be left incomplete at some stage."

"Why do you care for this cow? I'll give you a hundred thousand head of cattle in exchange."

"You keep them."

"I'll give you gold in a heap that will cover the back of an elephant."

"Remember to whom you are talking."

"Yes—to a sage who holds fast to a gift cow. O sage, don't you follow your own teaching that all these gifts are illusory?" He assumed a mocking tone and also pleaded and cajoled by turns. "I'll give you a golden chariot; ten times more of everything that I have so far promised; only let Sabala go."

Vasishta simply said, "You have succumbed to greed. A tree may yield you shade, fruit, and blooms; in return for this service you should not try to uproot it and carry it off. Acquisitiveness makes you clutch at a thing that pleased you and drives you to fight for it, just as you would also fight for a thing that stirred your ill will. In either case, the world has no respite from people like you, swollen with pride and ego and intoxicated with the strength of arms. It's the way of conquerors and kings. This is how wars start and mankind is troubled."

This homily had only the effect of stiffening the king's attitude. He said, "You are entitled to speak and advise, as you are a well-known sage. I agree with everything you say but still am convinced that Sabala is in the wrong place. She must go with me. I am convinced of it, otherwise would I be speaking at this length? I know my mind. I know what I'm asking for and why."

Vasishta calmly said, "This is a place whose sanctity is maintained by sacrifices and offerings to the gods. It's Sabala who provides us all the offerings for the gods, hundreds of things that we need for the sacrifices; and she is the one who gives us also food for the yogis and acolytes who spend their hours in meditation here, and grand feasts for distinguished wayfarers like you. How are we to carry on here without Sabala?"

"I am offering you a million cows and gold and everything. I'll multiply them ten times—and you can use them for discharging your hospitality and sacrifices. When they are exhausted, you have only to send a messenger and you will have them again. I'll get Sabala to supply your wants from my end, if that's your will."

"So you want me to surrender what is god-given and wait upon your pleasure?"

"You have only to indicate your desire."

"Oh, enough of your boasting and bragging and the vaunting of charity. Be gone now."

The king merely said, "Don't blame me. I have done my best to be reasonable and fair."

While this debate was going on some of the king's bodyguard had gradually edged nearer and were now watching the scene grimly. The ruler beckoned to one of his officers and ordered, "Take ten men and drive this animal along carefully to our capital."

A band of men seized hold of Sabala and dragged her away. The king watched the operations with satisfaction, but murmured again and again, "Gently, gently, don't be rough. . . ." He turned to Vasishta, who stood with folded arms, watching the scene with detachment, and announced, "I'll send back the promised exchanges without loss of time, the minute I reach my palace." Still Vasishta said nothing, but merely looked on.

Sabala turned her head pathetically as she was being dragged along and pleaded under her breath, "O sage, why do you abandon me thus? Have I not served you satisfactorily? Or has there been some lapse on my part?"

"You are a sister to me, I'll not abandon you. Only, I was hoping, hoping. Remember that he is a Kshatriya and possesses the strength of steel weapons and muscles. Have you faith that we can resist him?"

"You possess, O sage, I need not say, the strength of the spirit, which is matchless. I thought we might not have to demonstrate it. But without it this war-minded autocrat will abduct me."

"Very well, act, then," said Vasishta. "But don't create more force than is necessary. I see just ten men pushing you. Resist their insane action with ten and not eleven."

"I understand and obey," said Sabala, her eyes lighting up with relief. Now she bristled, shook her coat, and grunted, and out of her hair emerged ten warriors fully armed, who immediately jumped into the fray and laid low the ten men who had held her.

The king's eyes blazed with anger. He ordered fifty men to come and take Sabala. Sabala created fifty warriors. The king shouted, "Let a hundred men be deployed." There was a fierce fight, and his hundred men were repulsed and destroyed.

Vasishta cried, "King, don't shed any more of the blood of these harmless, innocent men."

"If you are so keen on peace, let go your animal. Why do you cling to it? Let go, if you don't like the sight of blood. Personally, the sight of blood does not disturb me."

"Yes, it's obvious, otherwise you would not be what you are. Now events will follow their own course. You will see wisdom eventually, but, like others of your sort, you prefer to reach it the hard way."

The king paused for a moment and cried suddenly, "Never heard of anyone throwing in a battalion to rope a cow! But if it is necessary, I'll not hesitate to sacrifice all my men here." And he ordered, "Let no one remain idle. All of you as one seize that animal. The time for persuasions is past."

Now the scene became wild. The hundreds and thousands of men threw themselves on Sabala. Vasishta never stirred from his place. One heard only the grunts of Sabala, and out of every pore of her body men emerged, strangely armed and dressed, and each of a different complexion, stature, and type. The air was filled with war cries and the clang of arms. The abode of peace became an abode of strife, groans, blood, and torment.

The warriors from Sabala reduced their numbers as the opposite side dwindled, and finally Sabala stood alone quietly, as if nothing had happened. When the last soldier of the king's army came up, Sabala said, "The fight is over, go home and report," and she withdrew from the battle.

Vasishta asked the king, "Are you satisfied? Go back to your capital now."

The king remained in deep thought and said, "These men were great fighters. My army was the mightiest on earth, and yet there they lie in the dust. I cannot shut my eyes to this fact. I was the mightiest conqueror known, but it is a past story. Please tell me what is your power, and I'll go away. What exactly gives you this strength?"

Vasishta answered, "You are an inquirer and it is my duty to answer you. You must understand that my strength comes from my inner being. Within every one of us there is a spark of godhood. When you are able to rouse it and employ it, you will acquire matchless strength. Sabala is only a visible agent of that strength."

"Do you mean to say that your war-machine is nothing more than that?"

"Yes."

"How does one acquire this power you speak of?"

"By meditation and the practice of austerities."

The king said, "I seem to have been hugging an illusory power all along. I will not rest until I acquire the power that you possess. I promise you that I will return here some day with a new army." He called his son, who had accompanied him, and said, "You must return to the capital and rule the kingdom. I am not interested in pomp and illusory conquests any more. I am renouncing my throne."

He took off his royal robes and gave away his sword and other arms, clad himself in a loincloth, and turned his back on everyone. He went northward, found seclusion by a mountain creek, and sat in rigorous meditation for a thousand years. His concentration of mind was perfect, and Iswara appeared and asked why he was subjecting himself to such rigors.

The king replied, "I want to match my strength with Vasishta's in every respect. I must possess the subtlest knowledge of archery. I must have an inexhaustible army equipped with the subtlest of weapons and missiles, enough to vanquish Vasishta's army. More than all, I demand the right to possess and wield Brahma Astra."*

Iswara granted all his desires. The king mustered a fresh army, trained it, equipped it with the latest weapons and missiles he had acquired, and marched across the country, shouting war cries, to Vasishta's hermitage. The inmates of the *ashram* were in a panic. Vasishta went about without paying any attention to the shouts of the soldiers at the gate. He could hear the king's command, "Attack and wipe out this place; don't spare anyone." The quiet-going hermits became alarmed and cried, "We are undone!"

"Now all of you must go back to your duties. Be deaf to the uproar. No harm can befall us," said Vasishta to his followers.

Fires were started outside, arrows came whizzing in, and the violent men attempted to storm the gate, with the king personally leading them in battle. Vasishta picked up his staff, planted it right in the middle of the approach to the gate, and went back without further ado to his hut. The staff repelled every kind of attack. No soldier could get past it. Every arrow aimed at the hermitage fell back, neutralized. The king employed special missiles which he could stir into activity with incantations of unquestioned power, but they were all neutralized by the simple, single staff planted at the gate without any of the defenders' even watching it.

Finally the king decided to employ the strongest power in his arsenal, the Brahma Astra. When he decided on it the gods were agitated over the security of the sage Vasishta and crowded the skies as anxious onlookers. The king invoked, by appropriate incantations, the powers of Brahma Astra and shot an arrow. The arrow went through the air, emitting flames, but never got past the staff; it fell down, quenched, at the foot of the staff.

---

* The ultimate weapon.

The king stood at the gate and cried, "O sage, I am defeated again. Before I retire I want a word with you."

The sage came out of his hut. "What power have you in that staff?" asked the king.

"We live in two different worlds, O king."

"Don't call me king. Didn't you see me renounce everything?"

"What are you now?" asked the sage.

The king spurned the question. "You know the answer," he said. "I have given up everything to acquire the powers you possess. And the gods have favoured me. I meditated, I performed rigorous sacrifices, I went through austerities, until Iswara appeared before me to ask what I wanted."

"And you asked only for the power to attack me again. You could not seek anything better!" said Vasishta, bursting into laughter. "You are a Kshatriya, born into the class of fighters, and, whatever other achievements you may attempt, you always come back to your original self. Your nature will not permit anything different."

"You talk superciliously because you think you were endowed with all these powers even at birth!"

"Perhaps as a result of my spiritual efforts in previous lives," said Vasishta.

"Wrong, wrong," said the king. "I will prove you wrong. Anyone can become what he lives even in this life. You will see me endowed with the same rank as you and addressed as Brahma Rishi.* I will not rest until you acknowledge me as a Brahma Rishi."

"I will be happy when the time comes for that. This staff which, as you yourself witnessed, repulsed your entire army is called Brahma Danda,† the staff empowered by knowledge, whereas the strength you tried to employ was purely physical, although

---

* A *rishi* is a sage who has attained perfect knowledge and maintains a high spiritual position. A Raja Rishi is a sage of kingly origin and stature, slightly lower in rank than a Brahma Rishi, one who attains his position through sheer spirituality, and who has realized the god within.

† The staff of authority of the god Brahma.

subtly manifested. Even the spiritual incantations you uttered had material aims, and you have seen how they end!''

The king was seized with a sense of inferiority before this man. He looked him up and down. First the man's merest cow vanquished his army; now a second time he was quelled, not even by the cow, but by an inanimate staff endowed with spiritual powers. The king renounced the fruits of his first meditation, went off northward, accompanied by his wife—four sons were born to him in this period—and sat in meditation.

A thousand years passed. The Creator Brahma appeared before him. The king opened his eyes. Brahma said, ''I approve of your effort. Henceforth you shall be called a *rishi*. You shall be called Viswamitra Rishi.''

Viswamitra was pleased, but still, to clear away the last vestige of misgiving, asked, ''Of what class?''

Brahma answered promptly, ''You will be the greatest Raja Rishi, kingly sage, known in the worlds.''

''Raja Rishi! Am I not qualified to be called *Brahma Rishi?* How am I different from Vasishta?''

God Brahma did not deign to answer on this point, but reiterated, ''I'll call you unhesitatingly a Raja Rishi, for you are that,'' and vanished.

Viswamitra remained brooding. How dare anyone, even if he be a god, offer him a title except the highest? He said, ''O Brahma, you are a Creator, I'll be your equal. I'll show you sooner or later that I'm as good as you, at least to prove that the title you give and your rankings are contemptible.'' His *tapas* had endowed him with extraordinary powers. He rose from his long penance, resolved to show the world that he had attained the summit of sagehood.

He got his opportunity presently. A man named Trisanku, a member of the Ikshvahu race of kings, enters the story now, as if to fulfil the ambitions of Viswamitra. This man was seized with an inordinate ambition to reach heaven in his physical frame. He went from place to place, canvassing support for his idea. The first person he approached was Vasishta, whom he commanded, being a king, to perform appropriate sacrifices and rites to enable him to rise to heaven.

Vasishta laughed him out of his request and said, ''What is the reason for this extraordinary ambition of yours?''

Trisanku could not easily explain. Like all such types, he blustered and replied, "It's not your business to ask. I've come to you because you are our family priest and counsellor and your powers are well known. Will you do it or not?"

"No," said Vasishta in a single word and dismissed the man from his presence and the subject from his mind.

Trisanku went out haughtily. He sought Vasishta's sons. These being juniors, Trisanku felt that he could command them more easily. He merely ordered, "Make all preparations for a huge sacrifice and appropriate rituals. Spare no expense or trouble. It must be the only one of its kind."

"What for?" asked Vasishta's sons.

"I want to go to heaven in this body, and I do not want you to waste time. Tell me what you require for the ceremonies."

"Preposterous suggestion!" they cried. "What makes you think that you are entitled to go to heaven?"

"Why not?" said Trisanku, who had brooded on this possibility so long that it seemed to him a perfectly normal aim.

Vasishta's sons said, "We are not prepared to attempt this ridiculous thing."

"How dare you reject my suggestion!" cried Trisanku, greatly upset. "I'm your king, and I command you as the sons of my chief priest. Otherwise . . ." He menaced them.

In his lust for heaven he became aggressive and mendacious, until his priests said, "You are unworthy to be a member of the great Ikshvahu race, unworthy to remain in the kingly caste. May you become a Chandala for the sin of misbehaving towards your own priests."

Thus accursed, Trisanku went his way, worrying how he was going to gain admission to his own palace, now that he had become a Chandala. He no longer thought of heaven; it seemed sufficient for him if they would be willing to let him enter his own palace now.

Viswamitra was just emerging from his austerities, considering how he should demonstrate that he was not inferior to Brahma the Creator himself. "I'll go further than Vasishta. I'll create anything I want. If I don't possess a Brahma Danda, I'll create one of my own and match it with Vasishta's."

In this mood he accosted Trisanku. "You, scion of Ikshvahu!" cried Viswamitra. "Why this gloom? Where are you going? Why do you look downtrodden? You pass people without a word of greeting—why?''

"I feared that I might not be recognized," Trisanku replied and asked, "Am I all right? How do I look?"

"Have you never seen yourself in a mirror?" asked Viswamitra. "What's happened?"

"I'm cursed to be a Chandala, and I thought my appearance was already changed," Trisanku said and explained his predicament.

This was just the sort of situation that Viswamitra seemed to have been waiting for. He exclaimed, "How could Vasishta and his sons refuse to send you to heaven? I'll help you. Your ambition is noble, and you deserve to achieve it. I'll help you."

"And they cursed me to be a Chandala. Do I look like one?"

"Not yet," said Viswamitra. "But you are bound to become one soon. You won't escape it."

Thereupon King Trisanku let out a wail. "Alas, that I should lose the rank of my birth!"

"Don't be a fool," said Viswamitra. "I have sworn to abolish the ranks attained by mere birth. I'll not rest till I'm addressed as Brahma Rishi, although I'm a Kshatriya by birth. You were born a Kshatriya but you are cursed to be a Chandala. One shall attain the caste one seeks, the accident of birth shall not matter. I'll prove it in my case, and I'll also prove it in yours. You shall lack nothing at all. Rejoice that you have now the chance of participating in an experiment to prove that there is no such thing as caste or achievement of birth. I'll help you. Come with me.''

Viswamitra took him to his *ashram* and made preparations for one of the greatest sacrifices and rites ever known, which would open the gate of heaven to Trisanku. Denizens of this world and other worlds watched the effort with concern. Viswamitra sent invitations to all the sages and kings to witness the great sacrifice. Trisanku sat near the sacrificial fire with his eyes shut, muttering incantations taught him by Viswamitra.

After ten days of intense concentration and single-minded performance, Viswamitra was able to neutralize the pull of the earth on Trisanku, who began to levitate, soar skyward, and was soon lost to view. The assembly cried, "Trisanku has after all

attained his ambition to reach heaven; all honour to sage
Viswamitra.''

"Will people now realize that I have done something that
Vasishta failed to perform and call me henceforth Brahma Rishi?"
No sooner had Viswamitra said this than there was a commotion
as people pointed skyward and cried, "Trisanku is coming back!"

So he was. Viswamitra rushed out, and by a magic utter-
ance was able to arrest the fall of this unfortunate man. But
Trisanku had come head down and feet up, and he stayed thus.
Viswamitra said, "Tell me, O Trisanku, what happened."

Suspended head down, Trisanku said, "Please leave me
alone. I'll never aspire to anything hereafter. Let me come back
to earth."

"First explain how and why you are back and not taking
your golden seat in heaven."

"By your grace I reached heaven, shooting through the
space like a rocket—thanks to your great penance. When Your
Grace orders, nature obeys, and the elements become soothing at
your command, and so I felt no discomfort. There was no
discomfort whatever during the passage; only at the destination."

He was talking with his head down and feet up, his listeners
having to twist their necks to follow his words clearly. He
pleaded, "Please let me stand on my feet. I find it hard to carry
on a conversation this way."

But Viswamitra said, "Not until you explain fully what
happened."

The poor traveller to heaven said, "The moment I set foot
in heaven I was thrilled, having attained the ambition of my life.
But Indra, the chief of gods, would not admit me. He just
pushed me out, saying, 'No place here for a Chandala,' and the
very worst I feared happened to me." He quietly sobbed.

Viswamitra stood watching him for a while, even with a
certain amount of severity, and declared, "You are very foolish
and very weak. You have soaring ambitions but not the strength
to hold on to them; no steadfastness. I take all this trouble to
send you up, and you have not the strength to hold your ground.
You let yourself be pushed out head first—not even taking time
to right your direction! Shame on you."

Trisanku became very sad on hearing this; tears welled up
in his eyes and rolled down his forehead. He pleaded patheti-

cally, "Leave me alone, sir. I have learnt my lesson. I'll never aspire to anything more than walking on the fair earth. Forget me."

Viswamitra said firmly, "Don't be spineless and squeamish. You are going back to heaven, as surely as my name is Viswamitra."

The upside-down victim of his championship pleaded and begged to be let off. Viswamitra was unrelenting. "Do you want me to curse you to become an earthworm, burrowing and living under the dust of the fields?" asked Viswamitra grimly.

"No, no, no, have pity on me!" Trisanku cried anxiously. He had had nothing but trouble and curses all the way—as much hardship from those who spurned him, like Vasishta, as from the champion of his cause, Viswamitra. He rued the day he ever came out of his palace chambers. "I do not mean to offend you, O master," Trisanku said. "I only wanted—"

"Be patient," commanded Viswamitra. "A few setbacks are inevitable in great enterprises. Watch me patiently, and I'll see you back in heaven."

The more he heard the word "heaven," the more agitated Trisanku felt. He had lost the taste for heaven, but his champion would not let him retreat. He resigned himself to the situation and asked, "Now what shall I do? How long shall I remain suspended head down like this?"

"Not too long," replied Viswamitra and set about the preparations for a sacrifice to overpower Indra himself and force Trisanku into heaven and keep him there. Sacrificial fires roared and offerings poured into them; Viswamitra sat muttering, his mind fixed inflexibly on the objective in a fierce concentration; the forces of nature and the elements could not but yield before this massive attack from a yogi; and Trisanku shot heavenward again.

Before they could heave a sigh of relief, he was back, head down. "Indra pushed me off again," he cried. "At least let me stand on my feet now." Viswamitra gave him no time to complete his sentence but shot him back into heaven; Indra pushed him down a third time. Trisanku was tossed like a ball between two resolute players.

During one of his visits down, Trisanku asked, "O sage, why will you not let me set myself on my feet at least? Then you can toss me wherever you may choose."

"Not at all necessary," replied Viswamitra. "I want you to reach your place in heaven on your right end, feet foremost, so that you may plant yourself properly and not bang your head there and receive a concussion." The assembly let out a laugh at this possibility.

Trisanku had no choice or initiative. The strength of Viswamitra's concentration and powers lifted him up, but Indra called him a Chandala and pushed him down every time. When this had happened a sufficient number of times, Viswamitra said, "Don't despair. I will teach Indra and all the gods a lesson that they will never forget." He willed and created a special heaven amidst the galaxies and sent Trisanku there. There was no one to bar his entry, since it was a brand-new heaven. "You will live in a universe all your own, with suns and stars and peopled with celestial beings. . . ."

"But I want to be on my feet," persisted Trisanku.

Viswamitra somehow could not get over his notion that being feet up was the most natural position for his ward. So he said, "Learn to take things as they come and feel grateful for help received. The new world I have created for you is all upside down to suit your present position; and when you get there you will find it all right, although in relation to the rest of the universe it may seem topsy-turvy. I want it to be different from Brahma's own creation of the universe. So good-bye," he said, and as Trisanku sped heavenward Viswamitra watched his going with great satisfaction, only murmuring, "I want my universe to be different from Brahma's dull, routine creations. Anyway, what is up and what is down in all that vast directionless space beyond the blue skies?"

The storyteller paused after this and said, "And so the poor Trisanku was lost sight of once and for all. One presumes he's happily settled in a heaven of his own, lacking nothing, enjoying everything. Perhaps, if any modern astronomer or one of those we hear about who circle the heavens were to spot a new universe out beyond the Milky Way, who knows, it might be Trisanku's world, especially if it looks topsy-turvy.

"When there is someone to champion them, causes arise in plenty," said the storyteller. Viswamitra next busied himself with the affairs of a certain king of Ayodhya, called Ambarisha, who had arranged an elaborate sacrifice but found the sacrificial animal missing at the last moment. The date of the sacrifice was approaching and Ambarisha became desperate, as it would cause a serious deficiency in the performance if he did not have the animal ready at hand for the sacrifice. He was advised by the priests that if he found a human substitute the gods would be pleased. He went from place to place in search of a human being willing to be sacrificed.

During his quest he met a poor man living in a forest cottage with his wife and three sons. Ambarisha told him, "I'll give you all the riches you may desire. Give me one of your sons for a higher cause."

The man replied, "You may offer me what you will, I'll not let my oldest son go at any price. He is my favourite."

The mother rushed forward to announce, "The youngest son is my favourite. I can't survive without him and I will not let him go. You cannot have him at any price."

The middle son, named Sunashepa, watched these transactions and suddenly realized, as all midway-men do, that no one was claiming him. He pushed aside everyone and said, "King, take me with you, as I am not claimed by either my father or my mother."

The king was happy to accept him and declared, "You will be rewarded in other worlds for your service to the sacrifice."

Whatever might be Sunashepa's promised future in another world, his prospects in this seemed bleak. He followed the king with the look of a condemned man.

They arrived on the banks of the Pushkara River, where Viswamitra, about to begin a third phase of meditation, was camping. Viswamitra noticed Sunashepa. His nature would not let others alone without questioning, and he asked Sunashepa what was troubling him. Sunashepa narrated his woes, whereupon Viswamitra took up his cause immediately. "I'll save you, don't you worry," he assured him.

He advised Ambarisha to let the boy go. Ambarisha explained why he could not. Viswamitra said, "If the sacrificial animal has been stolen, the ceremony will have to go on without a sacrifice, that's all. How can you victimize this young fellow? I'll not permit it." He pulled the boy to his side.

All the pleadings of the king were in vain. Viswamitra fulminated against sacrifices in general and finally proposed that one of his, Viswamitra's, sons should take Sunashepa's place, which they angrily refused to do. He cursed his sons, for the sin of disobeying a father's command, to become aimless wanderers and eaters of dog's meat; and then secretly imparted to Sunashepa two mantras which he was to utter when they came to cut off his head. He then let the boy go with Ambarisha. Later, when Sunashepa was anointed and tied to the sacrificial post, he uttered the mantra and the sacrificial knife could not touch him.

Viswamitra was essentially a reformer, ever involving himself in other people's affairs. He soon realized that all this activity was a drag on his spiritual growth and so isolated himself completely and resumed his meditations. Indra sent down the divine beauty Menaka to distract the sage. Viswamitra succumbed to her charms at first, but in due course rejected her and her baby, Shakuntala,* and resumed his meditations.

Indra now decided to send down an even greater beauty from his world, called Rambha, in order to disturb Viswamitra's mind. With trepidation she came down to the earth and danced before Viswamitra. Viswamitra awoke from his meditation, watched her, and, instead of following her amorously, cried, "Oh, for what foul purpose you are employing your beauty! May you become a stone image for ten thousand years."

She looked forlorn and cried, "O sage, why do you blame me? I have only obeyed an order."

"I know, that's why I place a time limit on my curse. Otherwise, you'd have been cursed to remain a stone forever. Let this be a lesson to everyone, especially Indra."

When he saw Rambha petrified into a statue, Viswamitra felt sorry for himself. The outside world and its forces seemed to press upon him constantly and provoke him to acts of challenge or anger, both of which he expressed unreservedly, and offset whatever spiritual merit he had acquired by his rigorous *tapas*. His spiritual attainments seemed to balance off mathematically his material aims; first he lost everything to Vasishta; he expended superhuman energies in achieving a heaven for Trisanku; he saved Sunashepa, but only after cursing his own sons. Now he had finally reduced a beautiful celestial girl to a statue. Spiritual power was a thing to be cherished and guarded, it

---

* This episode is elaborated on pages 168–70 in the story of Shakuntala.

flourished and grew stronger when it was conserved; Vasishta owed his eminence perhaps to his capacity to mind his own business and remain unperturbed even when there was provocation.

Viswamitra realized this about himself, that he was a typical warrior attempting to turn sage; if he wanted to attain the status of a complete sage he must rid himself of *krodha*, the instinct to challenge. No wonder Brahma would not go beyond calling him a Raja Rishi, especially as, when he had retired to perform *tapas*, he was followed by his wife, who gave birth to four children during that period. "What have I renounced to attain sainthood? Nothing. I have always lusted for conquests on other planes, although I am supposed to have renounced a worldly life." He realized that he must go away and begin a new attempt, this time without distraction: no one should follow him, no one should cross his path.

He sought a new seclusion, went northward to the Himalayas, and sat in meditation. The fire of his concentration seemed to burn and reduce all creation to ashes. The gods appealed to Brahma to stop Viswamitra's austerities. Viswamitra had spent a thousand years in rigour and self-forgetfulness. He had renounced all speech (remembering that every word that he had uttered was either a curse or a challenge); he conquered his temper completely and practised utter silence; at a later stage he even reduced his breathing to a minimum wisp of air; he lived on water, sat motionless, with his mind unwaveringly fixed on his aim of attaining the rank of a Brahma Rishi.

For a thousand years he remained foodless, and the time came for him to end his fast. He was on the point of breaking his fast after prayers and ablutions when a mendicant appeared at his door and cried, "I am fainting with hunger," and Viswamitra, without a second thought, surrendered all the food that he had, saying, "Help yourself to all that I have. I am sorry I am unable to provide you with anything better." For the first time in all his existence he forgot his ego and its needs totally.

The mendicant, who was Brahma in that form, at once revealed himself and said, "Viswamitra, your lifelong attempts have borne fruit. From this moment you will be known in all the worlds as a Brahma Rishi, worthy of officiating at sacrifices, guiding people, and imparting all the sacred and esoteric terms to whomsoever you wish."

Viswamitra felt happy for the first time in his life. But he said, "Will Vasishta come and address me as a Brahma Rishi?"

They brought Vasishta to where he was, and Vasishta embraced him and declared, "You are a true sage, a Brahma Rishi, I acknowledge you so without any hesitation."

Viswamitra said, "If you had not pressed on me your hospitality on that memorable day, with the help of Sabala, I would probably have lived and died and been forgotten as just another king. I am grateful to you for your help in starting me off in a totally different direction."

MANMATA

BRAHMA THE CREATOR surveyed his output with satisfaction. The universe with its fauna and flora, all creatures from a gnat to an angel, and all the stars and the suns—everything was his handiwork. After all this achievement, he desired to create something new and with a difference. In such a mood he brought into existence a unique damsel and named her Sandhya. ("The indefinable hour between sunset and darkness, and between the dark night and dawn, full of whispers and suggestions, of outlines melting or emerging, is also known as Sandhya," explained the storyteller.)

As soon as she could speak, the damsel asked, "Why have you created me?"

He replied, "Just to enrich this universe."

"But I'm lonely," she said.

"You shall not be lonely," he said and created a brother for her. A youth of great beauty of face and form, he was equipped with a bow of sugar cane, bowstring of murmuring bees, and five shafts made of five rare fragrant flowers. His face was like a bright moon, his nose was aquiline, his shoulders high, his limbs and features as if sculptured. His neck had the sweep and slenderness of a conch shell, and he was broad-chested, majestic. He was clad in blue, with *kesari* flowers in his hair, and he carried a flag with the sign of a fish on it. He attracted both men and women. Everyone gasped at the sight of him.

"Why have I been created?" the youth asked in his turn.

Brahma answered, "You are the god of love. You are potent. Since you go straight into the minds of people, you will be called Manmata; you will also be known as Kama, because your shafts will rouse passion in the hearts of men and women, which is vital for the sustenance of the world.''

The boy brooded and asked, ''How am I to know that I am all that you say? When can I test my powers?''

''Now,'' said Brahma incautiously.

There was a big assembly, including Brahma's eminent sons, the Seven Sages; Daksha, the progenitor of gods; Prajapati, lord of the universe; and other immortals. The youth raised his bow, and aimed a shaft first at Brahma. Afterwards he sent his arrows into the others in the assembly. All hearts began to palpitate with passion for the single object near at hand, which was Sandhya herself. The entire assembly fell in love with her, although she was daughter to one and sister to the rest. They grew suddenly aware of the intoxication of her form and vied with one another in making passionate approaches to her—they became blind to everything else, every other consideration, limitation, and propriety.

At this moment Yama Dharma, the god of death and the grand custodian of the scales of justice, became aware of what was going on and prayed to the Infinite, Changeless, and Ultimate God Iswara (from whom all others emanate) to intervene and stop the improper activities. In response to this, Iswara descended into the world of Brahma, arraigned him and his sons, and put an end to their incestuous proposals. But in spite of this a certain amount of mischief had been done; Brahma's sweat at the moment of his most passionate attention to Sandhya fell on the ground before her, and out of it was born numerous progeny; and out of the vital fluid of Daksha flowing down was born Rati, the beauty of beauties.

After Iswara left, Brahma felt angry at the memory of the insult he had suffered in the presence of his children and cried, ''O Manmata, you are responsible for the humiliation I have suffered. You shall suffer at the hands of the same Iswara. May you be burnt up by him.''

Manmata pleaded, ''How unfair you are! You created me; you endowed me with extraordinary powers, and you told me to try them. It was at your instance that I put arrow to bow. Now how can you blame me for what has happened?'' Brahma saw the logic of his protestation and slightly modified his curse.

Daksha offered Rati in marriage to Manmata. Manmata,

whose shafts proved deadly to others, succumbed readily to the charms of Rati, whose eyebrows were more perfectly arched than Manmata's brow; whose breasts were lotus-bud-like, pointed, with nipples dark as honey bees, and so hard that a teardrop falling on them would rebound in a spray; and the line of downy hair between whose breasts made Manmata wonder if by chance his bowstring had been transposed there. Her thighs smooth as banana stalks tapered down to her delicate feet, pink-tinted at heel and toe. Her hands were like sprouts of laburnum, and her tresses were like the monsoon clouds. Manmata was overwhelmed with love for Rati and married her.

Brahma, still smarting under the reprimand of Iswara, told Manmata, "You and Rati will go, with all the weapons at your command, and attack Iswara so that he may be brought to the same predicament in which he found us."

"But there must be an object for his love," said Manmata.

"You are not to worry about that," said Brahma lightly. "I will provide you with a valuable ally." He heaved a sigh and created Vasanta (Spring), who accompanied Manmata, carrying with him all his apparatus of enchantment—the song of summer birds, green shoots, sap rising in their core, birds and blossoms, and evening breeze and a magic hour, all of which induce a mood of love.

With these preparations, Manmata went to try his strength on Iswara and returned to report, "I have never been so much ignored in my whole existence. I followed Iswara everywhere—to Kailas, Meru, and all over the Himalaya mountains, but he showed no awareness of my presence. Vasanta helped me by blowing a sweet southern breeze, the sort of thing that generally intoxicates the mind, but it had no effect on Iswara; I spent all my five arrows, but they fell ineffectually. I created a couple of *chakravaka* birds, which engaged in love-play in his presence, but he looked at them coldly; I created bigger creatures, such as a peacock coupling with its hen, but he might have been looking at a lump of clay for all it mattered. I went further, created love symbols even out of other objects, huge trees entwined by creepers, and so forth. I implored Vasanta to be more effective, and he filled the scene with the scent of *champak, punnaga, patala, mallika* and *talé* flowers, their mingled fragrance overpowering all discretion. I made virgin lotus buds unfold their petals, but Iswara was completely indifferent." Manmata looked doleful and defeated. "I could not stand it, I had to flee from his burning presence," he concluded.

Brahma felt completely frustrated. He heaved a big sigh, and out of it were born strange grotesque creatures, whom he sent into Iswara's presence to execute provocative dances and gestures; and he told Manmata to go a second time. Accompanied by Rati and Vasanta, Manmata sallied forth obediently, but came back with the same story of defeat.

"We'll deviate for a moment from Manmata," said the storyteller, "and watch the entry of a totally new personality, which brings on a set of new responsibilities for Manmata."

At about this time was born to one Vajranga (meaning "Limbs of Diamond") a son named Taraka, at whose birth all the omens spelt ill for the world; jackals howled, donkeys brayed, the skies darkened, and strange unholy noises filled the air.

When he grew up, Taraka performed penance for one thousand years in order to attain strength and invincibility. He underwent remarkable mortifications. For one hundred years he stood on one toe and prayed with upraised arms; he lived on water for a hundred years, and for a hundred years he poised himself on a bare rock and prayed. From his head emanated a strange glare which threatened to reduce the universe to ashes.

All the *devas* and their chief, Indra, were terrified; they thought that their end had come and approached Brahma to stop this frightening experiment. Brahma intervened, but Taraka refused to budge or stop his tests. Brahma appeased him by offering him boons; he accepted the compromise, agreeing to stop his performance on condition that he was granted invincibility under all circumstances.

When Brahma grumbled that this sort of boon led to a lot of trouble and must have a limitation, Taraka said, "Very well, I will accept this limitation: no one in any of the worlds should be able to kill me except one born to Iswara." And he smiled, because Manmata's failure with Iswara was common knowledge in all the worlds.

Brahma understood that this might be a trap and hesitated, but Taraka was adamant. "I have said my say. Grant it or please leave me to continue my penance."

Brahma took a few moments to make up his mind. He

remembered that Indra and his followers were anxiously waiting for his return with news. So he said, "I grant it."

With his strength and power assured, Taraka gave up his austerity and became the ruler of Sonitapura. He tyrannized over all the worlds. He oppressed the weak and the strong alike, assaulted women, grabbed whatever he wanted. He snatched away Indra's great elephant Irawata; from the *rishis* he took Kamadhenu, the cow that yielded whatever one desired, mother of Sabala. The sun god parted with his chariot horse and was so afraid of incurring Taraka's displeasure that he tempered his heat and light; the god of wind himself was so nervous that he seldom showed his presence except in the gentlest of wafts.

Vishnu, who was asked by the other gods for his help, and who always acted as a redeemer, sent his famous discus flying across the heavenly spaces. Generally it chopped off everything in its way, but now it flopped upon Taraka's chest harmlessly; he stuck it on his robe as a medallion.

Brahma was again approached, but he said, "I cannot destroy the person to whom I have promised indestructibility. If someone plants a poison tree, it is up to others to uproot it; the planter himself cannot do it."

Vishnu and Brahma were helpless. Out of the Trinity only Shiva was left. The gods held an agonizing council among themselves and decided to appeal to Shiva. Being the embodiment of Iswara, he could help by begetting a son, who alone could destroy Taraka. He could not have a son unless he gave up the rigor of his penance.

Into the story now comes another person, Parvati, the daughter of Himavan, the lord of the Himalayas. The wife of Himavan had been a devotee of Shakti, the Mother Goddess. When her baby was born all the signs indicated the coming of a saviour. At a moment when they were alone, the infant whispered to her mother, "I am the real Shakti, the Goddess to whom you have prayed all your life. You are indeed blessed," and revealed herself in all her glory, but resumed her infant form instantly.

The child grew up normally. When she attained girlhood, she accompanied her father on his visits to Kailas, where Shiva was meditating. Shiva advised Himavan, "Don't bring any woman into these precincts. I wish to have no distractions," but the girl was fascinated by this austere being and insisted on accompanying her father whenever he visited Kailas. She reached the stage of wanting to stay behind in order to serve Shiva as a disciple-attendant. She brought him flowers for worship, washed his feet, and kept watch so that he was not disturbed.

The gods realized, after a desperate search for a conqueror of Taraka, that Parvati could be their best ally, if only Shiva would take an interest in her as a woman. But they wailed at the memory of his indifference. They turned to Manmata and said, "You can be our saviour, O god of love. Sharpen your weapons and attack this blind, austere man. Make him take an interest in the girl, and the rest will be easy."

Manmata looked desperate. "Not again! Ask me to soften the heart of a *rakshasa* with the shafts of love, or to overwhelm the gods; but leave me out if it is Shiva, who is Iswara, before whom I am powerless and feel like a speck of dust. I can do nothing with him."

All the gods appealed to him jointly. "You are the god of love, you may have failed once or twice, for various reasons, but is there any creature who is unaffected by your shafts? What is your existence worth unless you help us? Last time you may have failed, but you will succeed now. Parvati is always there, attending to his wants. She has youth and beauty. It is up to you to make Shiva notice her qualities." They added, "You must help the gods to survive; otherwise Taraka will soon exterminate us."

So Manmata went to Kailas with all his armoury polished and sharpened. He saw Shiva sitting stock-still and meditating, and hid himself behind the shrubs. Parvati was, as usual, in attendance. Manmata waited for the right moment, first setting Vasanta to blow a cool breeze and bring into operation all his enchantments. Shiva noticed the air around him and wondered for a moment at the out-of-season spring manifestations. Manmata bent his sugar-cane bow and sent off his first shaft, timing it for the precise moment when Parvati should come close to his presence with a tray of flowers in hand.

Normally Shiva never noticed anything more than the flowers when they were brought. Now, opening his eyes slightly, he noticed the fingers holding the tray, the redness of their tips. "Are these fingers, or the bloom of . . . ," he reflected. He checked his thoughts, shut his eyes again, and resumed his meditation.

Manmata bided his time. He commanded Vasanta to create the plaintive note of the cuckoo calling its mate. At this Shiva opened his eyes and saw Parvati busily sweeping away the dry leaves shed by the trees; and Manmata sent his second shaft. Shiva kept his eyes open a little longer, and in that time wondered, "Are those really lips or red cherries?" He checked his mind again.

One by one the shafts went home. Shiva found himself opening his eyes at the slightest rustle and watching Parvati, who had also been hit by the shafts. She did not perform her duties with the usual self-forgetfulness. She seemed to tarry a little longer in the line of her master's vision. Her hips swayed and her movements became studied and seductive.

Shiva now became rather reflective on the subject of this person. "Are those eyes or blue lotus? Does that chant emanate from a human being or from a *koel* bird? Is this the gait of a human being or of a spotted deer? How all aspects of beauty in the whole universe seem to be concentrated and contained in one person. Such a delight to the sight! What would she not be in an embrace?" He found it difficult to turn his mind back to its normal action of meditation.

He looked more keenly at Parvati and realized that she was the same girl she had been yesterday, although he was making fresh discoveries about her; he wondered what this might be due to. He subjected his present stirrings to a keen examination and realized that some extraneous influence was at work. He saw the mischief-maker behind a bush.

The love god was aiming his fifth shaft and found to his dismay that it fell off ineffectually because the victim had become aware of its coming.

Shiva's anger was roused at the disturbance planned by the love god. When Manmata peeped again, to decide whether he should begin the series all over, Shiva opened the third eye on his forehead. A glance from this eye reduced all objects to their true substance as if assayed in fire. With the third eye, once upon a time, Shiva had reduced to ashes a whole city of *asuras* called Tripura. It struck Manmata now like a flame; he shrivelled up and was reduced to a handful of ashes immediately. Shiva resumed his meditation, having disposed of the distraction, and later moved away from Kailas itself, defeating Parvati's plans.

She went back to her father and lamented, "I have failed, Shiva is gone."

At this time the sage Narada,* the great entangler and disentangler of the affairs of several worlds, arrived at Himavan's palace and advised Parvati, "If you tried to overcome Shiva with your youth and physical beauty, you would not succeed, since such things evaporate when his third eye is opened. If you want to win Shiva, you will have to depend on your own inner resources rather than on physical charms and the aid of creatures like Vasanta and Manmata. Go back to your mountain solitude and pray." The sage also taught her a mantra of great potency, *Om Namasivaya,* and advised her to keep her mind fixed on it, to the exclusion of every other thought. Parvati went away to the mountain and undertook a great penance.

Meanwhile Rati, Manmata's wife, approached Shiva and cried, "You have reduced me to widowhood, please save me."

Shiva said, "I grieve for you, but I can do nothing now. Your husband risked himself. I cannot help you. He is not lost, he is bodiless, that is all; his grossness has been burnt up, but he lives in essence. I grant that his activities may continue, though unseen, and I also grant that he may stay about my presence, along with my other unseen, invisible attendants."

"Oh, how long, how long? How long shall I remain the wife of an unseen husband?" Rati cried.

"You will both be reborn ultimately in *Dwaparayuga,*† and become husband and wife again." Rati had to content herself with this promise.

Brahma and others intervened and explained, "O great god, what have you done? You have destroyed the god of love; how are the functions of the universe to go on? After all, he did not come to make mischief, but to help us."

Shiva explained, "He is not destroyed but exists in a sublimated state."

Parvati's penance began to take effect. On the mountaintop

---

* One of the greatest of sages, who moved with ease in all the worlds, loved and respected by all the gods and men, owing to his eminent intellect and understanding.

† See p. xiii n.

she had a visitor. Shiva assumed the form of an ascetic celibate, appeared before her, and asked, "What are you praying for?"

"To attain the hand and heart of Shiva, nothing else. I will not waver from my purpose, whatever may happen."

The youth laughed at her and said, "What a simpleton you are! Why do you want Shiva, that rough, rugged, unresponsive fellow, who did not hesitate to scorch the poor god of love? A man of unnecessary fury and fire, who has smeared his body with the ashes, whose retreat is the graveyard, who has clothed himself with the hide of a tiger, and whose coronet and armlet are live snakes! Nothing is elegant about him, forget him." When Parvati did not appreciate his advice, the young man explained, "He has also proved to be a reckless and inconsiderate husband. Don't you know that once upon a time he was ignored at his father-in-law's banquet because of his crudities?"*

"Stop it, please," cried Parvati. "It is sinful to speak ill of a great soul, equally sinful to let such evil words fall on one's ears. Leave me now." The young man went away.

Presently Shiva appeared before Parvati in all his grandeur, and accepted her as his wife. At their most felicitous moment once again came Rati, wanting to make a last effort to retain her husband. She appeared before the sporting couple and said, "You are so happy now in the felicity of love, whereas the god who began it . . ." She wept and untied the end of her sari and produced a handful of ash. "You have reduced my husband to this!" She lovingly held up the ashes of Manmata.

Shiva was in his happiest mood and said, "Very well. You shall see your husband immediately in his original form, but remember that he will remain invisible to others. You alone will see him. Now go and be happy with him. He will resume his

---

* Parvati, in an earlier incarnation, as Sati, was married to Shiva. Her father held a grand sacrifice and feast, inviting all the gods from several worlds; the sky was crowded with the gods in their various vehicles, proceeding to the feast as honoured invitees—all except Shiva and his wife, who were kept out deliberately. All the same, persuaded by Sati, Shiva went to the feast and was insulted by his wife's father. Unable to bear the humiliation, Sati jumped into the fire and destroyed herself.

original form for all others to see only in *Dwaparayuga*." And the god of love revived from his ashes and joined his wife, Rati.

Out of the marriage of Shiva with Parvati was born the six-faced god Subramanya, the rider of a peacock. His birth foredoomed the career of Taraka. When still small, he led his forces against Taraka and destroyed him, in accordance with Taraka's own condition that he should be destroyed by no less a being than one born to Shiva.

THREE

RAVANA

VALMIKI

DRAUPADI

God himself participates in the action of these stories. He incarnates himself as much to destroy the demon Ravana as to inspire Valmiki, the composer of the *Ramayana,* and to help the heroine Draupadi fulfil her lifelong mission of annihilating her husbands' rivals and tormentors.

RAVANA

"RAVANA" MEANS "SCREAM," and this *rakshasa* earned the name by screaming. The name came to him when he attempted to move Mount Kailas, where Shiva was consorting with his wife; Shiva answered this masterly impudence by steadying the swaying mountain, pressing it down with his toe so that Ravana was caught under it and shouted for his life, recognizing after all a superior force in Shiva. Ravana's advisers suggested that he should pray for relief, and Ravana prayed intensely to a tune called *Sama* (which is the origin of all musical sound). Shiva, greatly pleased, appeared before him to confer a boon and named him at that moment "Ravana."

To understand why Ravana thought of dislodging the Kailas mountain from its foundations, we must go a little further back in his life story. His original name was not Ravana but Dasagreeva, meaning "ten heads." At birth he had ten heads and twenty arms. When he was born wolves howled and shrieking noises filled the air, portents of evil. His mother, Kaikasi, knew when he was still in her womb that he would be a demon. She was the daughter of a demon chief called Sumali, and had enticed a saintly man of great beauty, radiance, and spiritual powers while he was at meditation. The saint warned her, "This is an unholy hour of dusk for union, and the issue coming from this union is bound to be monstrous." She begged for some consideration, and he said, "If several are born, at least one shall be virtuous." Out of this parentage came forth first Dasagreeva, later known as Ravana; then Kumbhakarna; a daughter, Soorpanakha; and lastly Vibhishana. At the birth of each one of them except the last, wolves howled and the skies darkened.

Kubera, the distinguished ruler and a son of the saint by a

previous wife, was a stepbrother. Once, when he came to see his father, Kaikasi, the mother of the monsters, said to Ravana and the rest, "Ah, here comes your brother, salute him," half in jealousy and half in admiration. And the stepbrothers went up to him reverently. Thereafter, as they grew up, they constantly heard praise of this brother and demanded, "How is it that he has acquired so much distinction?"

"Because of his *tapas*," said their father.

At once the brothers went into seclusion on a river bank, in order that they might also acquire strength and merit through proper penance. Each sat in *tapas* for thousands of years. Ravana nipped off one of his ten heads to mark every thousand years of penance. When he had thus sacrificed nine heads and was left with only one, Brahma the Creator appeared and said, "I admire your tenacious penance, what's your aim and desire?"

"I want immortality."

"Impossible," said Brahma. "Whoever is born must die some day—that's the law of the world."

"Grant me, then, the boon of indestructibility—that no god, celestial being, element, or any power on earth or in the heavens shall ever overcome me."

"Granted," said Brahma. "No power in any world shall defeat you. What of humans?"

"Worms!" declared Ravana. "These pitiful, contemptible creatures; I don't have to perform a *tapas* for protection from them."

"So be it," said Brahma.

"And every time one of my heads is severed, it must return to my shoulders."

"So be it," said Brahma.

Kumbhakarna was about to phrase his demand when Brahma got help from his spouse, Saraswati, the goddess of learning and self-expression; she affected the demon's tongue so that, whatever he might have intended to ask for, he only succeeded in saying, "I want to sleep—uninterruptedly." This was granted immediately, so that instead of becoming a public menace Kumbhakarna slept for long stretches of time and humanity did not have to blame Brahma for creating yet another danger for it. When Brahma asked Vibhishana to name his desire, he said, "May I have the strength never to swerve from righteousness even under the most trying circumstances"—a strange man in this family.

Now, strengthened by fruitful penance, the brothers returned to the world of action, wanting to test their powers, and the indestructibility promised to Ravana. Ravana's grandfather visited him and advised, "Why don't you attack Lanka and take it back? After all, it's our country, unfairly handed to Kubera."

"Kubera is my elder brother, I'll not act against him," said Ravana.

But Mareecha, his uncle, argued with him, as did his grandfather. They explained, "You are a warrior—the exercise of valour is your proper prerogative. What are your gifts worth if you are not going to use them? After all, Kubera is only a half-brother; a half-brother is no brother at all. Even if he were a brother, what of it? If he is so close to you, let him give way to you!"

As they pursued this line of argument, Ravana saw the light. In the pursuit of fame and conquest, considerations of right and wrong did not arise. Ravana mustered an army to march on Lanka. Kubera received an ultimatum, and he submitted to avoid bloodshed. He met Ravana at the border and handed over the city to him, and took himself off to Alakapuri, in the Himalayan region, placing himself out of his brother's reach, many thousands of miles away, at the northern extremity. But all this great space between did not prevent news of his brother's activities from reaching him.

After establishing himself securely, Ravana never allowed anyone of possibly equal status to survive around him. He delighted in tormenting other kings. It was not only physical or material qualities in others that roused his ire; he disliked even those who strove to attain spiritual qualities or pursued learning or religion. It was safest not to come under his notice. No category of creature could hope to escape his attention. He tormented those whom he did not exterminate.

Kubera sent an emissary to Ravana's court, advising him to leave everyone alone. Ravana's immediate reaction was to reach for his sword and chop off the emissary's head. His courtiers in the assembly enjoyed it as a joke. But this did not lessen Kubera's zest to improve his brother and wean him from evil. He continued to send his messages of advice.

The only normal thing that Ravana did at this time was to

marry. When he was out in the forests one day, hunting, he met a girl and her aged father trudging along the forest path, and stopped to ask, "Who are you? Why are you here?"

The man replied, "My name is Maya. I am an architect. This is my daughter Mandodari. Her mother was a celestial creature. She lived with me until this child was born, then she deserted me and went back to her own world. Since then I have been the unhappiest creature on earth. I've brought up this child. You know the anxiety of a man who has a daughter to marry. Help me to find a bridegroom for this child."

Ravana performed the single commendable act of his life by saying, "I will marry this girl." It turned out to be the happiest marriage known. For although Ravana's nature would not let him leave women alone, he proved a good husband, and Mandodari, known for her beauty, also came to be classed amongst the five perfect women in God's creation.

Ravana suddenly realized that his brother was acting as an irritant and decided to put an end to this intolerable situation. He undertook an expedition to the far-off Himalayas. No country was too far away for him, when he set his mind to attack it. He marched to Alakapuri, sacked it, and vanquished his brother, whose only fault was that he had presumed to advise him. Finally he seized his prized possession, Pushpak—a flying chariot which could take one along the skies wherever one liked and also grant all wishes.

While flying back to his capital in Lanka, or Ceylon, Ravana found a mountain peak obstructing his passage. He felt irritated, got out of his chariot, muttering, "How dare this miserable mountain get in my way!" and, putting his shoulder to the base of the mountain, attempted to lift it off. The mountain shook. Shiva's spouse Parvati was frightened. All the god's attendants feared that a cataclysm was uprooting them.

Shiva's personal guard and aide, Nandi, went down to see what the matter was, saw Ravana, and ordered him to go away. Ravana paused, wiping the perspiration from his brow, looked at his adviser, and laughed contemptuously.

"Why do you laugh?" asked Nandi, and Ravana answered, "You monkey, how dare you advise me?"

Nandi was put out—he resented being called a monkey. He was deformed, dwarfish, brown-and-black coloured, with the head of a bull, anything, but not a monkey. And so he cursed

Ravana. "Your end will come through a monkey, the thought of which titillates you now. A monkey will give you food for thought."

Proceeding from Kailas, Ravana attacked every kingdom that he noticed in his flight. He would poise himself on the border and send an ultimatum to the ruler to yield. If he resisted, he destroyed him; if he yielded, he mutilated and enslaved him. He added several kings to his band of slaves. He also ravished their women. In one of his wanderings he encountered in the zone of Himalayan foothills a beauty named Vedavati, daughter of a sage. Ravana made advances to her. She recoiled from his touch and explained, "I can marry no mortal. I am under a vow to marry only God, the great and only god Vishnu. I'm betrothed to him."

Ravana sneered at this explanation. "You foolish one, don't you know that I'm superior to your god Vishnu?" And he seized her by the hair and dragged her into his arms.

She freed herself by cutting off her hair and jumped into a sacrificial fire that her father had lit, saying, "Only fire can cleanse me of the pollution of your touch." Before giving up her life she cursed him. "I'll be the sole cause of your destruction in my next birth."

Ravana had acquired in his career three cardinal curses, which caused his downfall at the end. Nandi had given him an inkling of the agent of destruction, Hanuman, the monkey-faced god; Vedavati was reborn as Sita, the wife of Rama, an incarnation of Vishnu, in order to destroy Ravana; and Rama's coming itself was foreseen by one Aranyaka, the king of Ayodhya, who was attacked and tormented by Ravana on one of his excursions and who cursed Ravana that he would be destroyed by a member of his own, Ikshvahu, clan. Not satisfied with his conquests on earth, Ravana lusted for other victories. When sage Narada, the traveller in all the worlds, arrived and suggested, "Why don't you attack Yama in his own world? He considers himself invincible," the idea appealed to Ravana, and Narada felt that here was a possible way in which this mighty demon might be put an end to.

Ravana made an expedition to the world of Yama, the god of death, was repulsed by him, and was about to be struck with his staff, called Yama Danda, the very sight of which is said to spell doom for the beholder. But at this moment Brahma reminded Yama that he had conferred the boon of indestructibility on Ravana, and Yama, out of consideration for this promise, simply vanished from the spot, leaving Ravana to imagine that he had vanquished him.

Ravana's next expedition was to Kishkindha, in order to subdue its ruler, Vali, a monkey chieftain of enormous strength. His followers advised Ravana to desist from this expedition. He brushed them aside, but when he arrived at Kishkindha he found Vali gone. Vali's wife and brother told him that Vali had gone out to the shores of the four oceans in order to perform his evening prayer, and that Ravana was welcome to wait for his return. Ravana did not care to wait, but went after Vali.

He found him praying on the southern shore, facing the sea. Ravana fell on him from behind. Vali just picked him up, tucked him under his arm, and went through his prayers without even turning to notice the disturbance. After his prayer he moved around the three other shores without setting Ravana down. It was only after his prayers, when he had returned to his palace at Kishkindha, that he released Ravana from under his arm and asked, "Now what? What do you want?"

Ravana, as ever, respected superior strength. He broke into praise of Vali, called him the greatest being that he had ever seen in his life. He begged him to honour him with eternal friendship and offered him a share of all his spoils in territory, cattle, slaves, wealth, and women, and sealed the pact before fire.

After that Ravana settled down to a routine life, ruling, tyrannizing, enjoying the pleasures of life, a man of tremendous dynamism and accomplishments, achieving success in all that he attempted. This life continued peacefully until he began to hear of a young man called Rama, son of Dasarata, the ruler of Ayodhya. Constant reports reached him of the greatness of this young man: his uprightness, personality, skill at archery, strength, learning, humility, godliness, fearlessness. Above all, he had qualified himself to marry the daughter of King Janaka by lifting, bending, and stringing an ancient bow, while other contestants failed even to move it.

The whole world seemed to be engaged in singing his praise. "He is after all a human being—miserable human being, why are people going mad about him?" thought Ravana. He shut his ears whenever he heard the name "Rama" mentioned. "Does this miserable human being hope to rule the world as I do?" he often asked. The situation was intolerable. He racked his brains to find ways and means of wiping out this rival on earth. He consulted one of his henchmen called Akampana, the "Unshakable," who advised, "This man is now in Dandaka forest with his wife and brother, living the life of an exile. All that you have to do is to abduct his wife and take her away to your palace, and he will die of a broken heart. There is no other way of attacking him as he is practically invincible. Moreover, Sita is worth adding to your collection."

Ravana thought this a sound procedure, sought his uncle Mareecha, and asked for his help. Mareecha said, "Don't go near Rama or his wife. He'll finish you. Don't be foolish." Mareecha having argued him out of it, Ravana went back to his palace to think over the matter himself.

While he was resting thus, his sister Soorpanakha burst into his chamber with blood on her face. She wailed, "What men you are! What brother worth the name would be resting and lounging while his sister is gashed and hacked? Get up and act!"

Ravana was fond of this sister and sprang to his feet, crying, "What's this blood? Who has molested you?"

"Rama," she cried. "I was in Dandaka when Rama and his brother attacked me. Rama told his brother, 'Cut her up, snap off her nose,' and that brother chopped off my nose and ears and gashed my face in a dozen places." She lamented and cried and finally said, "Unless you go and avenge this, you are not my brother, you are not a warrior, and all your achievements will count for nothing."

Akampana once again advised Ravana to abduct Sita. Ravana sought his uncle Mareecha again and commanded him, "You shall help me in this task. No argument about it."

Mareecha once again expatiated on the greatness of Rama and ended up by saying, "I have no doubt that Rama will kill me if I go there."

Ravana said, "If you don't go I will kill you, make up your mind." Rather a strange order from a nephew.

Mareecha said, "If I've no chance of living, I'll die by Rama's hand; he is at least an enemy. Let me be killed by him rather than by a nephew. I have watched him in action while he guarded the sages of Dandaka, whose sacrifices we once attempted to disrupt."

Ravana let out an imprecation at the mention of Rama's

valour, but felt happy to have made a start on the whole business of abduction. They evolved their plan of action.

Mareecha, fully aware that he was going to his doom, assumed the form of a golden deer and strutted up and down in front of the hermitage where Rama was staying with his brother Lakshmana and his wife Sita. Sita was fascinated by the deer and said, "Catch that beautiful animal for me."

Rama said, "Leave it alone, content yourself by looking at it."

"I want to have it," insisted Sita.

"It's good to watch, but it may be anything; don't be misled by appearances."

Fates were at work, and Sita, normally docile and self-effacing, became unusually demanding and insistent; the golden deer seemed to have stirred up a lot of hidden obstinacy in her. Rama argued with her, but she was firm in her demand.

Rama said, "It may be an evil spirit in this form. I have known such."

But Sita countered him by saying, "Why do you say such things of a beautiful creature?"

Rama hesitated for a moment. Here was this tender being following him into exile ungrudgingly, accepting her lot without a word, wearing the bark of trees for clothes, eating roots and leaves, living in the open, and lying on hard ground at night, although she had been brought up in her father's palace in every kind of luxury. Rama said, "All right, wait here. If it's real I will bring it alive; if it's an evil illusion, I'll kill it and bring the hide for you. Don't let anyone approach you here." He asked his brother to stand guard at the gate and followed the deer.

At his approach the deer receded a few yards. It drew him after it. In the heat of the chase Rama hardly noticed how far he had gone. Then, suddenly understanding the true nature of the creature, he shot an arrow, wounding it mortally. Before dying, the deer assumed the voice of Rama and let out a wail, "O Sita, O Lakshmana, I'm dying, come at once!"

This was heard over the babble of birds and other forest noises by Sita, who became hysterical and said to Lakshmana, "Go at once to your brother's assistance. He is in great danger."

"He is not," said Lakshmana. "No danger can come to him."

"How can you stand there and talk? Didn't you hear his cry?"

"His command to me is not to leave your side. I must obey him."

Once again the voice called for help. Sita became desperate and cried, "Will you go or not?" When Lakshmana still refused to leave her unprotected, she spoke harshly. She insinuated that he wanted to see his brother dead so that he might possess her. This hurt Lakshmana deeply, and he left, after saying, "God alone should save you."

This was the moment Ravana had been waiting for. His strategy had worked perfectly. He emerged from his hiding, stood at the door, and cried, "Alms for a mendicant."

Sita opened the door. There stood a perfect mendicant, with sacred marks on his forehead, rosary around his throat, wearing ochre robes, and holding a wooden bowl in his hand. She said, "Mendicant, please wait there."

The mendicant answered, "This is indeed wonderful courtesy, to ask me to wait at the gate! Tell me to go away, and I'll go."

"Don't be offended, sir," Sita said. "My lord will be back soon."

The mendicant laughed contemptuously. "Hunger cannot wait for the return of men."

There were certain codes of hospitality that had to be respected. Sita unrolled a mat of woven grass for the guest, set some fruit before him, and withdrew into an inner part of their hut.

He called her and, when she came out, seized her arm and revealed himself. He explained, "Come with me. I'm the most invincible being in all the seven worlds. Brahma has granted me immortality. I'll give you a palace to live in and every comfort and luxury. You don't have to allow your beautiful self to languish here. Come with me. I'll make you my queen. Your order will be a command for every soul in Lanka. . . ."

"Rama will kill you, begone before he arrives."

"I am greater than Rama."

She screamed and called for help, tried to wrench herself free, but Ravana just applied his favourite stranglehold whenever he wanted to take a woman. He seized her by the hair, lifted her like a child, and sped away in the Pushpak Vimana to Lanka.

When Rama returned to the *ashram* and found it empty, he lamented and cried, but did not fall dead as Ravana and his advisers had anticipated. He set himself the hard task of searching for his wife and recovering her, and followed her trail with the help of various forest creatures.

Ravana's capital, Lanka, was a city of palaces, museums, and gardens, encircled and decorated with all the booty of his various campaigns. The people moving in the streets reflected their ruler's prosperity in their dress, ornaments, and general deportment. The air was charged with music, the chanting of hymns and songs glorifying Ravana. Ravana's palace itself was a jewel set in the midst of all this, heavily guarded by armed *rakshasas*. The halls were packed with souvenirs and relics of Ravana's various expeditions, and his own inner apartments were filled with gold and gems.

In his chamber hundreds of beautiful women lay about languorously. He was a gigantic person of enormous capacity and versatility in love, able to assume any form or shape and to please all these women, including his chief wife, Mandodari, who occupied a golden cot of her own in the midst of this crowd of fair women garnered from all corners of the world. The women sang and played for him continually. He had halls for drink, separate halls for food, music, and pleasure.

Ravana woke up at dawn, to the chanting of hymns and the recital of scriptures. He elaborately groomed and decorated himself. Followed by an imposing retinue of men and women, he went forth to visit Sita, whom he held captive in a secluded wood named Asoka Vana, a place of waterfalls, garden walks, orchards, and grottoes, surrounded by ramparts. Sita sat in dejection under a *simsupa* tree. Ravana's aim was to break her spirit and make her yield, through loneliness, solitary confinement, or—worse—the terrifying company of fierce *rakshasa* women, dwarfs, and freaks. Sita was in mourning. She had removed her jewels and stuck them in the branches of the tree; her hair was wild and unkempt, her face mud-stained, and she was clad in a sari of yellow colour.

Ravana entered her precincts, but in spite of all the care he had taken to make himself attractive, he could never get her to look up at him, nor did she take note of the retinue that followed him: She seemed oblivious of her surroundings. Ravana stood before her to attract her attention and, failing, addressed her somewhat aggressively. "Woman, this obstinacy will do you no good. Be my friend. As a *rakshasa*, it is within my right to abduct anyone's wife and force her to yield to my wishes. It'll not be difficult for me to take your love by force."

Sita raised her hands and covered her ears, unable to bear the word "love" from anyone except Rama. She averted her face, and Ravana felt infuriated. He said, "I'll have greater pleasure if you yield to me voluntarily. I'll wait for it. Look at me, I'm the greatest being in all the worlds today. The gods tremble at the mention of my name. My wealth and strength are unparalleled. My prayers, meditations, and learning are unmatched. By my special strength I can summon the great gods like Brahma and Shiva when I want them. Don't be a fool. Don't waste your beauty in seclusion and sorrow. I'll make you my chief queen. You will enjoy all my wealth and authority. You may give gifts to whomsoever you desire. Be my queen and let us go round the world happily; come, decide. You have tried to make yourself bad-looking, but still your beauty remains unimpaired. I long for your touch. I'm maddened by your beauty. I have no other thought."

Sita plucked from the ground an insignificant blade of grass, threw it before her and addressed it, shunning to talk to Ravana directly, and to show that she viewed him as no better than that straw. "You are seeking your own doom," she said. "Is there none in all this crowd around you who can give you good advice? You and your capital will perish. Rama's anger is like the great fire. You won't be able to withstand it, for all your boasting and bragging. You are trying his patience. Ravana, don't seek your own destruction. Were you not ashamed to steal me from my husband when he was away? Would you have dared to approach us, if he had been there? You sneaked in when—"

"Stop that," cried Ravana, his eyes rolling in anger. He resented being criticized in the presence of his followers. "Don't speak of that man again, a worthless fellow who instead of ruling his kingdom has preferred to wander in the forests like a tramp, wearing the bark of trees instead of finery. How dare you mention him to me? You are foolish and lack discrimination. How could you think of him as a husband? Forget him."

"Don't you remember how he destroyed single-handed your kinsmen, who attempted to disturb the peace of the sages in the forest? You will share their fate presently. It is not too late for you to mend your ways. He'll forgive you. Let me go back to him.''

Ravana ground his teeth and leaped up and down in rage, until one of his wives embraced him before all and said, ''O love, why do you care for this simpleton, when you have all of us to worship you as our lord? Ignore her and treat her like dirt and she will come round. Come, let's go and enjoy ourselves, O resplendent one.'' She held him in her arms and tried to lead him away. He was appeased and emitted a sound almost like laughter.

Before going away, however, he uttered a stern warning. ''You have already wasted ten months; only two more are left for you to make up your mind. If you do not yield by then, I'll ask my cooks to take you and prepare a meal for me of your flesh and bring me your blood to drink.'' He also ordered the guards around to frighten her.

After he was gone some of the women went on praising the glory of Ravana and upbraiding Sita's foolishness in trying his patience; the other women, the fierce grotesque ones, approached her and spoke among themselves. One said, ''I'd like to feast on her liver, she looks so tender, I'd like to bite her off and chew her up raw. I'm pregnant and a longing is coming over me to taste human flesh.''

Another said, ''Let's kill her and feast on her—send for strong liquors and strong condiments to go with the delicacy, to make our dinner perfect.''

''If we kill her and swallow her without further ado, our lord'll be happy again, because he will forget her when she is no longer there.''

All this nightmarish talk affected Sita in the end, and she broke down and sobbed. ''Rama, Rama, have you deserted me?'' She brooded for a while and decided to end her life. With this resolution she arose; she wound her long tresses about her throat with a view to strangling herself.

All this was being watched by Rama's emissary Hanuman, sitting in the top of the tree. Hanuman, son of the god of wind, endowed with enormous strength and also the gift of assuming any stature or form he desired, had surrendered himself totally to the service of Rama. (It is said that even today he is inconspicuously present wherever the name of Rama is mentioned.) He had been given the task of tracing the whereabouts of Sita; he

followed various trails and clues and had arrived in Lanka by
assuming an enormous stature and striding across the ocean that
separated India from Lanka. After stepping on the soil of Lanka
he shrank himself to the size of a little monkey, which enabled
him to move inconspicuously all over the capital while searching
for Sita. Finally he arrived at Asoka Vana and sat amidst the
branches of the *simsupa* under which Sita languished. He watched
Ravana's arrival and departure and the torment that Sita was
subjected to, and, when Sita had lost all hope, he made his
presence known; events took a different turn from that moment.

Ravana, revelling in the thought of his invincibility and
invulnerability, received the first shock to his complacence one
morning when the fierce guardians of Sita came in a panic to
announce, "An enormous monkey has appeared on the walls of
Asoka Vana, menacing us. This monkey has uprooted every tree
there, destroyed our parks. The place is ruined; even the hillocks
have been smashed up and levelled, the tanks and ponds have
been splashed dry of water, and not a creeper, flower, or tree is
left. Lord, we have no words to describe the devastation."

"How did it happen?"

"The monkey accomplished it all single-handed. He seems
to possess the energy of a cyclone. The only thing he has left
intact is the *simsupa* tree; not a leaf on it has been touched. We
noticed that our prisoner conversed with that frightful monkey;
but she won't tell us what goes on between them or who he is or
where he has come from."

Ravana despatched a band of warriors to destroy the monkey, but none returned. The city echoed with the battle cries of
the monkey as he roared and hurled boulders and rocks and iron
bolts plucked out of buildings at his pursuers. When he struck
the earth with the crashing pillar of a temple he had brought
down, sparks flew up and scorched his pursuers. He perched
himself on the portals of the city's temple and cried, "Your end
is come," and the city reverberated with his roaring challenges.

Ravana became concerned when none of his warriors returned from their encounter with the monkey. Finally he sent his
son Indrajit, the greatest warrior of the times. Every dart aimed
at this creature seemed to glance off and fall ineffectually, while
he puffed himself up to the dimensions of a cloud over the
capital. Indrajit, as a last desperate act, selected his Brahma

Astra, the mightiest weapon known. At the touch of it Hanuman lay limp.

The Brahma Astra was deadly, but Hanuman enjoyed a favor from Brahma himself that if ever he was attacked by it, its effect should last only one *muhoortha,* or four-fifths of an hour. Hanuman welcomed this brief interlude, as he wanted an opportunity to see the *rakshasas* at their worst and also meet their chief, Ravana.

The *rakshasas* were happy when they found him lying helpless but, fearing that he might spring on them suddenly, they brought hempen ropes and fibres and bound him and carried him into the presence of their king, Ravana. Hanuman was impressed with the grandeur and personality of Ravana.

Ravana, when he saw this monkey placed before him, had a momentary flash of memory of the curse Nandi had uttered at Kailas: "Your end will come through a monkey," and reflected as to whether this was going to be the fulfilment of the curse. But this flash passed, and he not only rationalized it the next minute as an unworthy fear, but forgot it in an instant. He addressed the captive through one of his attendants, as it would have been beneath his dignity to talk to him directly. "Who are you? Which of my enemies has sent you in this form? Kubera? Indra? Speak the truth."

The interpreter added, "Hide nothing and you will be forgiven by our gracious king. Speak the whole truth."

Hanuman answered, "Looking at you, Ravana, I pity you. I am sent neither by Indra nor by Kubera; they are not your only enemies. You are your worst enemy. You have brought me here."

Ravana was beside himself with rage at this levity. But he did not want to dispose of the monkey before eliciting some information.

To further questions Hanuman answered, "I pity you, I said, because you have earned the wrath of Rama. Even now it is not too late for you to repent and beg his forgiveness. Do it and save yourself. Even now you may begin a new chapter of your existence. I feel anxious for your welfare. You are so valorous, so mighty-looking, so well endowed. But how unwise!"

Ravana would not let him speak further. He hated to be advised. He immediately ordered his men to kill the monkey.

At this point his brother Vibhishana intervened. "It is not proper to kill a messenger."

Ravana hated advice as to how emissaries were to be treated, but he respected his brother and cried, "What else should one do with a mischievous, destructive monster such as this?"

Vibhishana answered, "He is but an agent, and we cannot kill him. Moreover, if he is spared he will return home and fetch your real enemies to this soil and then you will know everything."

This struck Ravana as a sensible thing to do. He smiled. "So be it. All the same, we must punish this devil for his misdeeds. He has laid waste my most cherished garden built for my women, and razed to the ground our temple."

"Whatever may be his misdeed, he cannot be killed, according to the laws of kings and their messengers. We may maim, mutilate, and torture a messenger, but we may not kill him."

Ravana felt pleased to find this loophole and said, "We will show him what we can do. A monkey's treasured possession is his tail; set fire to it and drag him along the streets of this city so that our people may rejoice."

The attendants at once got busy. They took hold of the end of the monkey's tail and padded it with huge quantities of rags. They poured oil over the rags covering his tail and set it on fire. They then dragged Hanuman through every street, lane, and byway, in order to exhibit their triumph. Hanuman welcomed this, as it helped him to study the plan of the city.

As the fire at the tail raged, men, women, and children lined the way and jeered at the monkey. When this news reached Sita, she prayed to the god of fire not to harm Hanuman. In answer to her prayer, the fire did not scorch Hanuman, although it blazed and roared. Suddenly Hanuman shrank himself to the size of a little monkey, so that the ropes around his body slipped down. He got out of the bonds, jumped on the top of a tall building, assumed again his huge shape, and applied the fire at his tail to the building; then he jumped from building top to building top, covering the entire city thus, and soon set it completely in flames. The god of wind, who was Hanuman's father, helped the flames to blaze and spread. When Hanuman was satisfied that he had performed his task well, he rested for a moment on the summit of a hill and watched the burning city and then went and plunged his tail in the ocean in order to put out the fire, at which the waters of the sea hissed and rose to the height of a mountain.

The time was come for Ravana to take serious note of the developments. He invoked a council of war. He assembled his ministers, chiefs of the army, and his brothers, who were devoted to him, at the council hall and began, "Strange things have happened in this city of Lanka. A monkey has devastated our lovely capital. It is an evil spirit, not a mere monkey. Our enemies are active. To this day no one has entered this island city without our permission. How this monkey managed to enter the city, what the guardian spirits of the city were doing, are matters for investigation."

Ravana made a long oration, by which he hoped to gain the support of his councillors without betraying his anxiety. After a lot of preamble, while his councillors muttered words of praise and approval, he came to the point. "Apparently our city needs guarding, and we must consider how well we may exercise our defences. Let us not forget that this human creature Rama is diabolic and strong. He will surely make an attempt to cross the seas and come here. . . ."

"Let him, we will smash him, it will do him good to try his luck that way," said his commander-in-chief. "Your Majesty may leave it to us."

Another said, "I'll fly across the sea and wipe out Rama and his army single-handed."

Another said, "Permit me and a few of our *rakshasas* to assume human form. We will fly across the seas and merge in their camp. . . ." He gave a long, involved strategy.

One of the warriors flourished his iron club in the air and said, "This weapon has never been washed, as the blood and flesh of my foes dry on it. Let me go this instant and get a new coat of paint on it, that is the blood of Rama, Lakshmana, and this wretched monkey. I will destroy all the monkeys in this world. There should be no trace of that species when I am done with my job."

Capping all this was one *rakshasa* who said, "No one should come with me when I go out to meet this party. I want to suck their blood and feast on their flesh all by myself. . . ." He smacked his lips.

After all these demonstrations of aggressiveness and loyalty, they stood up, raised their arms, and roared aloud, invoking maledictions on their enemy. It was reassuring for Ravana.

In order to offset all this enthusiasm, Vibhishana rose to his feet and waved to the assembly to sit down and hear him. "My dear brother and king, at the beginning you asked us councillors to speak plainly, without varnishing truth. So I will speak now. O brother, it is good to talk of a fight, but that should come last, after we have tried all other means. We must first get an idea of the strength of our enemy before venturing on an expedition. Hanuman, single-handed, has demonstrated what he can do. With an army of similar creatures and Rama's strength added, our kingdom may be wiped out in the twinkling of an eye. But before we consider all this let us examine the primary cause of all the troubles. What is the provocation for them? It is your wrongful act. What justification had you for abducting Rama's wife and subjecting her to such suffering? First restore her and set right your own mistake." Thus he spoke beseechingly, respectfully, with his hands folded and with a deep bow.

There was a roar of protest when he suggested the restoration of Sita. "Oh, no," said the warriors, to please Ravana, "our chief is strong enough to do what he pleases. We will fight, we will fight."

Ravana remained in thought for a moment and said, "Let us meet again tomorrow and consider our plan of action."

At dawn of the next day Vibhishana, who was resolved to save his brother if he could, sought a private audience with Ravana. Vibhishana said, "I do not want to flatter you. Save yourself while there is still time. A war seems unnecessary; if you restore Sita to Rama, there will be an end of this episode. Rama is not vindictive and he will forgive you. Moreover, have you not noticed the portents ever since Sita set foot on our soil? Our sacrifices are rejected by the god of fire, and you never see a flame rise even when you pour a great quantity of ghee; snakes and vermin are everywhere, particularly in places of worship. The gods have deserted us completely. Elephants, horses, and camels are seized with strange maladies. Foxes howl within the city, crows and vultures screech and circle overhead at all times. Let us read the signs correctly and learn our lesson. Send Sita away."

"No talk of giving up Sita. She will yield to me sooner or later. I have brought her here because I want her, that is all there is to it. You are exaggerating everything. You are panicky and frightened. Our enemy is not all that you say. I can smash him. Leave me now." Vibhishana left him and immediately crossed over to Rama's camp.

To reinforce his ego, which seemed to be wobbling, Ravana dressed himself imposingly, perfumed himself, wore resplendent ornaments and armour, drove in a gold chariot through the streets, followed by warriors in battle dress, to the accompaniment of trumpets and drums; people lined the streets in vast numbers and cheered him, and that strengthened his feeling of invincibility and grandeur. A vast army of demons stood guard at the assembly hall, which was decorated. Priests chanted holy verse. The air was thick with the perfume of incense and flowers. Ravana kept thinking, "I have no equals in this or any world." There was a respectful silence.

Ravana addressed the assembly. "We have no place for cowards. We need have no fear of anyone in this world or any world. You are wonderful warriors assembled here, and you have always counselled me properly in all my affairs, and nothing has gone wrong. No doubt a swollen monkey has come and disturbed us. Such unexpected intrusions are common in this world. We should not let that depress us unduly. That monkey has come because Sita is here. Have I not the right to acquire and keep any woman I want? Who can say I have not? Do you fear that this world is going to be destroyed because of this woman? Whoever thinks so is our worst enemy. She will yield to me sooner or later. She is rather eccentric and I do not wish to handle her roughly. She has only asked for time to decide, and I have granted it. Perhaps she has a foolish notion that her husband will come to her rescue!" Ravana let out a laugh at the thought of this, and the assembly joined politely. "There can be no question of restoring her to her people and asking their pardon. That is unthinkable and an atrocious proposal. We have never known defeat, and I now seek your counsel." He paused and felt stimulated when the hall was filled with murmurs of approval.

Kumbhakarna, the sleeper, was awake today and said, "Great king, you were mistaken in seizing this woman when her men were out. If you had encountered them and slain them, this same Sita would have admired you as a warrior and followed you of her own accord. Women adore valorous men. But you made a mistake. If you had consulted me I would have advised you properly. You have earned the enmity of Rama without consulting us beforehand, and now you seek our advice when it is too late to do anything about it. However, I do not wish to waste our time in thinking of the past. Although I do not approve of your procedure in this matter, I am with you. I give you my support, you are my great brother. We will wipe out Rama and all his followers. Do not let Sita go. She is yours. Keep her. Now put away your cares, and leave everything to us.''

With all this brave assurance, a time came when Ravana heard the news that Rama's army had landed on their soil. Various reports were given as to how the sea, considered impassable till then, had been crossed. Rama had stood on the southernmost point of the ocean, in India, and after fasting and praying for three days ordered the ocean to cleave and make way for his army. The sea god did not respond to this prayer, and after due warning Rama shot his shafts into the sea; the waters churned and heaved and all aquatic life perished, and it looked as if the ocean was to become a desert. The sea god appeared before Rama in all humility and explained, ''I am subject to the laws of nature as the other four elements are, and I cannot swerve from them, as you, my lord, know; but what I can do is to grant facilities for your army of monkeys to build a causeway. I will give them every help; please order them to go fetch boulders and rocks and wood. I will receive everything and turn it to good account.'' Thus a causeway came into being and, having crossed it, Rama's armies stood on the soil of Lanka.

Ravana deployed the pick of his divisions to guard the approaches to the capital and appointed his trusted generals and kinsmen in special charge of key places. Gradually, however, his world began to shrink. As the fight developed he lost his associates one by one. No one who went out returned.

He tried various devious measures in desperation. He sent spies in the garb of Rama's monkey army across to deflect and corrupt some of Rama's staunchest supporters, such as Sugreeva,* on whom rested the entire burden of this war. He employed sorcerers to disturb the mind of Sita, hoping that if she yielded, Rama would ultimately lose heart. He ordered a sorcerer to

---

* Sugreeva was crowned by Rama as the head of the monkey kingdom, after the death of Vali.

create a decapitated head resembling Rama's and placed it before Sita as evidence of Rama's defeat. Sita, although shaken at first, very soon recovered her composure and remained unaffected by the spectacle.

At length a messenger from Rama arrived, saying, "Rama bids me warn you that your doom is at hand. Even now it is not too late for you to restore Sita and beg Rama's forgiveness. You have troubled the world too long. You are not fit to continue as king. At our camp your brother, Vibhishana, has already been crowned king of this land, and the world knows all people will be happy under him."

Ravana ordered the messenger to be killed instantly. But it was more easily said than done, the messenger being Angada, the son of mighty Vali. When two *rakshasas* came to seize him, he tucked one of them under each arm, rose into the sky, and flung the *rakshasas* down. In addition he kicked and broke off the tower of Ravana's palace, and left. Ravana viewed the broken tower with dismay.

Rama awaited the return of Angada, and, on hearing his report, decided that there was no further cause to hope for a change of heart in Ravana and immediately ordered the assault on Lanka.

As the fury of the battle grew, both sides lost sight of the distinction between night and day. The air was filled with the cries of fighters, their challenges, cheers, and imprecations; buildings and trees were torn up and, as one of his spies reported to Ravana, the monkeys were like a sea overrunning Lanka. The end did not seem to be in sight.

At one stage of the battle Rama and Lakshmana were attacked by Indrajit, and the serpent darts employed by him made them swoon on the battlefield. Indrajit went back to his father to proclaim that it was all over with Rama and Lakshmana and soon, without a leader, the monkeys would be annihilated.

Ravana rejoiced to hear it and cried, "Did not I say so? All you fools believed that I should surrender." He added, "Go and tell Sita that Rama and his brother are no more. Take her high up in Pushpak Vimana and show her their bodies on the battlefield."

His words were obeyed instantly. Sita, happy to have a chance to glimpse a long-lost face, accepted the chance, went high up, and saw her husband lying dead in the field below. She broke down. "How I wish I had been left alone and not brought up to see this spectacle. Ah, me . . . Help me to put an end to my life."

Trijata, one of the wives of Ravana, whispered to her, "Don't lose heart, they are not dead," and she explained why they were in a faint.

In due course the effect of the serpent darts was neutralized when Garuda, the mighty eagle, the born enemy of all serpents, appeared on the scene; the venomous darts enveloping Rama and Lakshmana scattered at the approach of Garuda, and the brothers were on their feet again.

From his palace retreat Ravana was surprised to hear again the cheers of the enemy hordes outside the ramparts; the siege was on again. Ravana still had about him his commander-in-chief, his son Indrajit, and five or six others on whom he felt he could rely at the last instance. He sent them up one by one. He felt shattered when news came of the death of his commander-in-chief.

"No time to sit back. I will myself go and destroy this Rama and his horde of monkeys," he said, and got into his chariot and entered the field.

At this encounter Lakshmana fell down in a faint, and Hanuman hoisted Rama on his shoulders and charged in the direction of Ravana. The main combatants were face to face for the first time. At the end of this engagement Ravana was sorely wounded, his crown was shattered, and his chariot was broken. Helplessly, bare-handed, he stood before Rama, and Rama said, "You may go now and come back tomorrow with fresh weapons." For the first time in his existence of many thousand years, Ravana faced the humiliation of accepting a concession, and he returned crestfallen to his palace.

He ordered that Kumbhakarna should be awakened. He could depend upon him, and only on him now. It was a mighty task to wake up Kumbhakarna. A small army had to be engaged. They sounded trumpets and drums at his ears and were ready with enormous quantities of food and drink for him, for when Kumbhakarna awoke from sleep his hunger was phenomenal and he made a meal of whomever he could grab at his bedside. They cudgelled, belaboured, pushed, pulled, and shook him, with the help of elephants; at last he opened his eyes and swept his arms about and crushed quite a number among those who had stirred him up. When he had eaten and drunk, he was approached by

Ravana's chief minister and told, "My lord, the battle is going badly for us."

"Which battle?" he asked, not yet fully awake.

And they had to refresh his memory. "Your brother Ravana has fought and has been worsted; our enemies are breaking in; our fort walls are crumbling. . . ."

Kumbhakarna was roused. "Why did not anyone tell me all this before? Well, it is not too late; I will deal with that Rama. His end is come." Thus saying, he strode into Ravana's chamber and said, "Don't worry about anything any more. I will take care of everything."

Ravana spoke with anxiety and defeat in his voice. Kumbhakarna, who had never seen him in this state, said, "You have gone on without heeding anyone's words and brought yourself to this pass. You should have fought Rama and acquired Sita. You were led away by your mere lust and never cared for anyone's words. . . . Hm. This is no time to speak of dead events. I will not forsake you as others have done. I'll bring Rama's head on a platter."

Kumbhakarna's entry into the battle created havoc. He destroyed and swallowed hundreds and thousands of the monkey warriors and came very near finishing off the great Sugreeva himself. Rama himself had to take a hand at destroying this demon; he sent the sharpest of his arrows, which cut Kumbhakarna limb from limb, but he fought fiercely with only inches of his body remaining intact. Finally Rama severed his head with an arrow. That was the end of Kumbhakarna.

When he heard of it, Ravana lamented, "My right hand is cut off."

One of his sons reminded him, "Why should you despair? You have Brahma's gift of invincibility. You should not grieve."

Indrajit told him, "What have you to fear when I am alive?"

Indrajit had the power to remain invisible and fight, and accounted for much destruction in the invader's camp. He also created a figure resembling Sita, carried her in his chariot, took her before Rama's army, and killed her within their sight.

This completely demoralized the monkeys, who suspended their fight, crying, "Why should we fight when our goddess Sita is thus gone?" They were in a rout until Vibhishana came to their rescue and rallied them again.

* * *

Indrajit fell by Lakshmana's hand in the end. When he heard of his son's death, Ravana shed bitter tears and swore, "This is the time to kill that woman Sita, the cause of all this misery."

A few encouraged his idea, but one of his counsellors advised, "Don't defeat your own purpose and integrity by killing a woman. Let your anger scorch Rama and his brother. Gather all your armies and go and finish off Rama and Lakshmana, you know you can, and then take Sita. Put on your blessed armour and go forth."

At last Ravana faced Rama practically alone. Rama's darts struck but did not harm him. The god Indra sent his own chariot for Rama's use in the battle at this moment. As he mounted the chariot, the charioteer whispered to Rama, "Do not delay, bring forth your Brahma Astra."

Rama invoked the spell and sent off this missile as a last resort. Several other weapons, employed before, severed Ravana's heads, but the heads appeared again on his shoulders each time. Brahma Astra went forth, emitting flames, and embedded itself in the heart of Ravana, where he was vulnerable. He had asked only for invincibility from gods and others; Rama, being a god in a completely human form, was able to kill him. Ravana had asked for indestructibility of his ten heads, but he was vulnerable at heart.

That was the end of the demon, the greatest tormentor of men and gods, whose end came exactly as prophesied, through the three cardinal curses that he had incurred in his early career— the instruments of his destruction being a monkey, a woman, and a member of the Ikshvahu clan.

VALMIKI

The time has come to tell the story of the greatest storyteller of all times, that is, of Valmiki, the Adi Kavi. You may know what Adi Kavi means: the foremost poet, or the fountainhead of poetry. Valmiki composed the *Ramayana* in twenty-four thousand stanzas, and most of it, in one form or another, is known to every man, woman, and child in our country. Rama, the hero of the epic *Ramayana*, was Valmiki's creation, although the word "create" is not quite apt if one considers the process by which the *Ramayana* came into existence. Rama was not a "character" created by a "storyteller" and presented in a "work." The "work," in the first place, was not "written"; it arose within the writer. The "character" was not conceived but revealed himself in a vision.

The time scheme of the epic is somewhat puzzling to us who are habituated to a mere horizontal sequence of events. Valmiki composed as if he had a past tale to tell, and yet it was broadcast to the world by Kusa and Lava, the sons of Rama, who heard it directly from the author. One has to set aside all one's habitual notions of movement and get used to a narrative going backwards and forwards and sideways. When we take into consideration the fact that a king ruled for sixty thousand or more years, enjoying an appropriate longevity, it seems quite feasible that the character whose past or middle period is being written about continues to live and turns up to have a word with the historian.

This happened to Valmiki. Once Rama asked

Valmiki, during a meeting of the immortals, in another
world, "How did you learn all about me, even before I
was born?"—unsettling again all one's time sense. What
one had all along thought of as retrospective on the part
of the poet seems actually to have been a prophecy as
well as a piece of contemporary chronicling. However,
an average story-listener accepts these situations without a second thought, never questioning "When?" or
"How?" "Before or after?" To an ordinary Indian
story-listener it seems perfectly natural that events could
spread over before, after, and just now.

Rama was an incarnation of Vishnu, but in human
form he became oblivious of his godliness and was
subject to all the torments and mystifications of the
human mind; and so he had a genuine wonder at a
biographer who could write his full life ahead of his
time and also attempt to solve his personal problems in
the concluding stages of the story.

Valmiki answered Rama by narrating his own life:

ONCE THERE WAS a scholar named Sankha, who, having completed his studies at a far-off place, was returning home along the
banks of Godavari, in deep thought, when he was startled out of his
wits by a shout at his ears; a highwayman suddenly blocked his
path, flourishing some dreadful weapons of his trade. Sankha
babbled, "Who are you?"

"My father's son," replied the robber with a ghastly leer.

"What do you want?"

"Everything you have, except your life, if you'd like to
keep it."

The Brahmin said, "I'm a poor scholar, not a man of
wealth. Otherwise why should I be walking back to my city? I
would be riding a chariot."

"As if I could not overtake a chariot!" said the robber
aggressively. "Let me see what is detachable about you, apart
from the hair and nails. Hi! Hi!" He laughed in a ghastly manner. The detachable articles on the scholar's person were a
goldlike ring on his little finger, picked up at a fair, and a copper
talisman attached to his sacred thread. "O Brahmin, keep your
sacred thread and give me that talisman."

Sankha was very reluctant to give away the talisman. "Oh!"

he wailed. "A wonderful *sadhu* gave this to me two years ago, to protect me from disease and devils. . . ."

"I'm not a devil or a disease, and so it won't protect you from me. Give it here. No argument," the thief cried arbitrarily. The Brahmin handed it over. "What is your cash balance? How cunningly fellows like you tuck away your treasure!" the robber said, running his fingers along the folds at the waist of the Brahmin's dhoti. He found a couple of coins and appropriated them with a sneer. Then he snatched away a piece of cloth covering the upper portion of Sankha's body, leaving him in his dhoti. "Take off those sandals," he commanded finally, looking at his feet. "You do not deserve such luxuries, a fellow treasuring just two brass coins!" The Brahmin slipped off the leather sandals, which were thick with layers of patch and which had protected him from the hot sands of the river.

Having stripped the Brahmin of all his possessions, the robber said, "Now go your way." Grateful to be spared his life, the Brahmin trotted off on the sands, anxious to be gone out of the range of the highwayman.

The sands of Godavari were hot, and the Brahmin felt as if he had been asked to walk on a frying pan. He kept leaping up and forward, unable to keep his feet down. His progress was negligible, and his tormentor watched him, at first with amusement, as he kept hopping away. Presently the Brahmin, casting all propriety to the winds, took off his loincloth, tossed it ahead, and hopped onto it, unable to bear the blistering heat of the sand under his bare feet. This was too much even for the robber, who watched from a distance. The grin gradually faded from his face and he cried, "Hey, come here!"

The Brahmm accelerated his pace forward.

"I will give you something," said the robber.

But the Brahmin replied, "I do not want it."

At this the robber shouted, "Stop!" and ran after the Brahmin, who thought his end had come. When he caught up with the Brahmin, the robber kicked off the sandals he had stolen and said, "Take them back; I don't want them. You don't understand a good turn when it is offered."

The Brahmin gratefully accepted back his footwear. "Now I can reach my village before the evening. You have a compassionate heart, although you like to grunt and behave like a tusked boar. Your compassion is due to a vestige of merit left from your previous incarnation.''

"How do you know?" asked the robber, interested.

The Brahmin said, "I know what you were in your previous life. I'll tell you all about it, if you are interested. But first find me some shade to rest in."

The robber led him to a little grove of wood-apple trees where the river wound in and out pleasantly. He climbed a tree and shook the branches until some hard fruit dropped to the ground. He banged the shells on a piece of granite and presented the rind for the Brahmin to eat.

The Brahmin plunged in the river to cool his body, rested in the shade, ate the fruit, and felt better. The robber watched him with solicitude and asked, "How is it, good?"

The Brahmin muttered an assent and said, "You were not a ruffian in your previous life, but a man of learning. You had mastered the *Vedas,* and could recite and give an exposition of them. You were a master of grammar, prosody, and the scriptures. People looked to you for guidance and enlightenment and brought rewards in the form of grain and gifts to your very door. Your wife was a good and practical woman. A home, a loving wife, honour and riches from your fellow beings—what more could one desire? Normally, nothing.

"But your nature craved for something more—that is, the company of a public woman, whom you met one day on the temple steps, where a crowd was passing; your fate ordained that you should pick up a little flower garland that she let fall on the stone steps. Others ignored it, knowing it to be a common trick to attract notice. But you picked it up, and that was the beginning and end of your life of nobility. You began to spend all your time in her house. You neglected your wife, but the good lady became resigned to it. You treated her gracelessly. Sometimes you made her cook the food and serve you both, and attend on that woman just like a servant. It went on until you became a sick man and also a bankrupt. You exchanged your wealth for all the disease that a woman of her type could give you, and when this transaction was complete she had no further use for your company; she threw you out and shut the door in your face.

"You went back home as an ailing bankrupt. People, naturally, took no notice of you. But it made no difference to your wife. She nursed you, found the money for your food and medicines, and fasted and prayed constantly for your welfare. One day she found a great physician, who carried in his bag the rarest herbs from all the mountains. The paste of certain astringent herbs applied to the inflammations of your body made you groan and squirm; when your wife brought a dose of some medicine to your lips, you bit off her little finger in rage. You died with her finger choking your windpipe, thinking not of her but of the prostitute.

"Still your wife laid herself on the funeral pyre and cremated herself along with your body, and in your next birth you are what you are for your sinful, selfish existence; but the first phase of your life, when you were enlightened, has left in you a vestige of compassion; and that is why you could not bear to watch my feet blister on the sand. . . ."

"What next?" asked the robber softly.

"You will be born a hunter, who will receive the grace of the Seven Sages and become the composer of one of the world's masterpieces," prophesied the Brahmin and went his way.

Valmiki's next birth—he said, continuing his autobiography— was from the womb of a *naga kannika*, a beauty from the nether world of serpents, who had enticed a sage in the forests and gone back to her world after giving birth to a baby, leaving it to be tended by a hunter in the forests. The child grew up, became a full-fledged hunter, always armed with bow and arrows and seeking a wide variety of targets. In course of time he married and had children. He came to have a large family to support. This meant that he had to slaughter more creatures each day to feed his dependents. Animals and birds became familiar with the footfalls of this terrible slayer and fled at his approach.

Gradually it became difficult for him to secure the necessary amount of food for his dependents at home, and naturally he turned to other ways; he held up wayfarers in the forest paths, in keeping with the habits of his previous incarnation, and snatched from them whatever he could find on them—food, money, clothes, and ornaments. He waited for his prey in the shadows of the forest and attacked them ruthlessly. He became notorious, and people remarked, "Oh, there is that bandit, we must be careful."

He killed everything he could lay hands on, chased and attacked whoever passed in the valley, the forest, or the mountain. He was wild, reckless, cruel, and inconsiderate. In this condition he waylaid seven persons who were coming along the forest path one day. He jumped down from the branch of a tree and blocked the path of the Seven Sages, celestial beings who were visiting the earth. The robber flourished a knife and bow and arrows and cried, "Your life or . . ."

The Seven looked at him indifferently, and one of them asked, "You flourish so many weapons and put on all this act just to get—what?"

"All that you have. There may be seven of you, but I'm equal to you, and so do not let your numbers make you fool-hardy. I can string you all together like a brace of birds."

"Why all this unpleasant talk?" asked his victims.

"You are trying to resist me!" he declared.

"No," they cried. "We want to give you all that we have and more."

This was a new experience for the hunter, and he asked, "Why?"

"Not easily explained, but we want to help you."

The hunter became suspicious at this unaccustomed word and asked, "Why?"

"You are asking why again!" the victims said. "Because you deserve our help, that is all."

"In what way will you help?" he asked, growing curious. They just smiled at his question, at which he became suspicious again and declared, "If you are trying to lead me away with clever words, you are mistaken. First hand over—"

"As you see, we are bare-handed men, possessing only the clothes that we wear. What do you expect us to give you?"

"I will search your persons," he said aggressively. "I generally punish those who come empty-handed. The world has no place for such worthless men." He said with a leer, studying their faces closely, "You are seven and may be hiding something among yourselves. Immediately deliver it, will you?"

"Yes," they said, much to his surprise. Their tactics were novel and bewildering, but he tried to cover his confusion with bravado, and he did everything short of attacking them; somehow he felt checked at that point, but he kept worrying them in various ways until they said, "It is absolutely imperative that you do what we say, if you want us to deliver the goods."

"What are these goods and where do you have them?"

"We have something precious to give you, but you will have to answer our question. Why are you acquiring such a load of sin, robbing people and causing pain to all God's creatures? What do you hope to gain thereby?''

"I have eight children, and the ninth is coming. I have to find food or the means for them; also there are always one or two guests when we eat.''

"Poor fellow, have you ever thought at what price you are keeping your dependents alive?''

"What do you mean?''

"The life that you now enjoy or suffer is a result of your actions in previous lives, and now you are acquiring more sins every hour, instead of seeking liberation at least in a future life. Go home and ask your wife and children if anyone is willing to share this burden with you. Since they are so ready to share your loot, ask them if they are willing to share your sins too. Now go and bring us their answer and we will give you everything we have.''

"This is a dodge, perhaps,'' he said.

"You have our solemn word that we shall await, at this same spot, your return with their reply.'' They took their seats convincingly on a little rock under a tree.

The hunter commanded, "Don't move. Stay there. I will be back.''

He was gone quite a while and returned, panting with excitement; he found his seven victims still waiting for him. He came up and stood before them with bowed head.

"What is their reply?'' they asked.

"Not one is prepared to accept a share of my burden. I had never thought of it all these days. They will not help me in any way. My children treated my question as a joke and laughed, and my wife said I was getting mad notions in my head.''

"We promised you a precious gift. Do you want it?''

"Yes.''

"Very well, then. Here in the shade of this tree, sit down on the bare ground, shut your eyes, and repeat, 'Mara, Mara,' without ever stopping. Let this word be like the breath that goes in and out of your nostrils, as natural and constant. Empty your mind of all other thoughts except the sound of the word 'Mara.' ''

"What does it mean?''

"You will understand as you repeat.''

After they left, the bandit flung away his weapons, squatted under the tree, and uttered the word "Mara" with every breath.

"Mara, Mara," through repetition fused together and became "Rama, Rama," the hero of *Ramayana*, the very sound of whose name is said to deepen one's being.

Years passed. We cannot normally measure this passage of time, which must have been thousands of years according to the stories, perhaps long enough for the nature of the country to be changed, for forests to become cities, kingdoms to become deserts, for mountains to change their contours and rivers their courses. From behind a vast mound of earth one heard constantly repeated the word "Rama," sounding like the endless murmur of an ocean. Passers-by heard the unceasing sound, felt baffled, and passed on.

In the fullness of time the Seven Sages came that way again, and they alone knew where the sound emanated from. They broke open the crust of earth and the anthill which had grown over the old hunter, who was lost in the trance of muttering the name of Rama. His body had grown emaciated, long hair covered his head and face, but he sat unmoved until they woke him up. Since he emerged from an anthill,* he was known as Valmiki.

He was a *rishi* now, one on whom grace had descended. He was beyond hunger and thirst and the needs of the body. Presently he established his hermitage on the banks of the Ganges.

At this stage of the narration Valmiki explained to Rama himself: "Owing to the potency of your name, I became a sage, able to view the past, present, and future as one. I did not know your story yet. One day the sage Narada visited me. I asked him, 'Who is a perfect man—possessing strength, aware of obligations, truthful in an absolute way, firm in the execution of vows, compassionate, learned, attractive, self-possessed, powerful, free from anger and envy but terror-striking when roused?' " Narada answered, "Such a combination of qualities in a single person is generally rare, but one such is the very person whose name you have mastered, that is, Rama. He was born in the race of Ikshvahus, son of King Dasarata . . ." And Narada narrated the story of Rama.

Rama was unaware of his godliness in this life, although he was actually an incarnation of Vishnu come to redeem the world from the ten-headed demon Ravana. When he took human form

---

* *Valmika* in Sanskrit.

he forgot his godly origin and was subject to the pain, pleasure, and joys of life at the human level. He was born the son of Dasarata, who had three wives—the oldest of four sons. At a very young age Rama exhibited all the great qualities that made him an ideal man, an ideal son, and an ideal husband. His reputation for courage and excellence in archery was great.

One day the sage Viswamitra arrived at the court of Dasarata, and said, "I want a favour of you."

Dasarata said, "Granted," immediately.

Viswamitra said, "We are performing a sacrifice at Siddhasrama and we want your two sons Rama and Lakshmana to accompany me and protect the sacrifice from the *rakshasas* who are disturbing the *rishis* by putting out the sacrificial fires, throwing offal on the sacred spots, and frightening the performers themselves. I can't think of anyone with the courage and competence to stand up to them, except Rama."

Dasarata was distraught; his favourite son, brought up so tenderly in the comforts of the palace, to go out on this dangerous mission. He began, "They are so young . . . Rama is not even sixteen years old, and Lakshmana . . . What can these children do?"

Viswamitra was not a man to tolerate counter-suggestions. "Are you afraid or are the boys afraid?" he asked grimly.

The boys' teacher, Vasishta, Viswamitra's perpetual rival in spiritual strength, said merely, "Let Rama go, he and his brother will manage." Rama was already off to take leave of his mother, and, followed by Lakshmana, started out with Viswamitra.

At the sacrificial ground the demons were, as usual, active. Rama and Lakshmana stood guard, shot numerous arrows into the sky in such a manner as to weave them into a gigantic umbrella above the sacrificial ground, and slew every *rakshasa* who approached. After the performance of the sacrifice, Viswamitra was greatly pleased and surrendered to Rama all the spiritual merit he himself had acquired. He taught him certain rare feats of archery and took him and his brother to Mitila for the Swayamwara of Janaka's daughter Sita. There Rama lifted and strung a gigantic bow and qualified himself to be chosen as a husband for Sita.

After his marriage to Sita, Dasarata wanted to make Rama his deputy and heir and seek gradual retirement, but the whole ceremony took a different turn when Kaikeyi, Dasarata's third wife, insisted on exercising her privilege of asking the crown for her son Bharata, and that Rama be banished to the forests for fourteen years. Kaikeyi had saved Dasarata's life on the battlefield once; out of gratitude the king had promised to grant her two major favours any time she demanded them. Kaikeyi, advised by her old nurse, found this the best moment to put forward her demands.

Although Dasarata was shattered by this turn of events Rama took it calmly, without resentment. He accepted the situation out of a sense of duty and felt it an honour to be able to help his father fulfil his promise. He took himself off, followed by Lakshmana and Sita, to the forests.

Bharata, who had been absent at the time, returned home and followed Rama into the forest in order to persuade him to come back, but Rama resisted his plea. Bharata succeeded only in taking Rama's sandals with him to the capital, where he placed them reverently on the throne and ruled only as a regent until Rama should return from his exile.

Deeply stirred by this tale about Rama, told him by Narada, Valmiki could hardly find room for any other thought in his mind and spent his days in meditation at his *ashram*. One day, on his way to bathe in the Tamasa River, Valmiki stopped to admire a pair of *krouncha* birds as they were fondling each other on the branch of a tree. All of a sudden the male fell down shrieking, shot down by the arrow of a hunter, and the widowed bird lamented pitiably. Valmiki was moved to the core by this experience. A mixture of rage and pity overwhelming him, he burst into a *sloka*, or poetic composition, cursing the hunter for his callousness. The verses ran: "Man, the destroyer, who cannot let innocent birds mate in peace. May you perish!"

This was the poet's first composition, which actually welled up from the depth of his soul, possessing a jewel-like perfection of form although expressing grief and resentment. Valmiki went back to his *ashram,* repeating the stanza, and began to feel uneasy at the thought that he had composed a stanza which was negative, violating the first principles of composition, which decreed that poetry should exalt and construct rather than destroy. He was in deep anguish; the pain of perpetrating a negative composition was no less keen than the memory of the dying bird.

He was in this state of profound grief when Brahma the

Creator himself came down to help him. He cheered the poet by giving his stanza a different interpretation.*

After Brahma left, Valmiki saw the whole of Rama's life in one grand vision as he sat cross-legged on a mat of wild grass, his eyes closed. His disciples sat around and listened as he recited the entire twenty-four thousand stanzas of the composition, beginning with the conception of Rama and ending with Rama's once more becoming a god after his earthly mission. Valmiki looked for a worthy repository for his composition and selected two youths, Kusa and Lava (sons of Rama himself, who had never met their father), for the task. How it all came about, how these two youths came to reside with the author of the story, will be understood if we go back a moment to the story of the *Ramayana* itself.

At Lanka, Ravana had been slain by Rama (who undertook the expedition in order to recover his abducted wife Sita), thus ending a chapter of demoniac oppression of the world. After the death of Ravana, Rama sent his emissary Hanuman to fetch Sita. Sita was overjoyed. She had been in a state of mourning all along, completely neglectful of her dress and appearance, and she immediately rose to go out and meet Rama as she was. But Hanuman explained that it was Rama's express wish that she should dress and decorate herself before coming to his presence.

A large crowd pressed around Rama. When Sita eagerly arrived, after her months of loneliness and suffering, she was received by her husband in full view of a vast public. Sita felt awkward but accepted this with resignation. But what she could not understand was why her lord seemed preoccupied and moody and cold. However, she prostrated herself at his feet, and then

---

* The Sanskrit language is so highly evolved that the same word can be made to give more than one meaning by varying the stress or the syllabification. For this reason it is impossible to understand the language unless one has mastered the rules of grammar.

    Brahma explained to Valimiki that the poem echoed the lamentation of Mandodari, the wife of Ravana, on the death of her demon husband. The death of Ravana implied hope again for mankind and fulfilled the purpose of God's incarnation as Rama, which was to be the conclusion of the epic germinating within the mind of the poet.

stood a little away from him, sensing some strange barrier between herself and him.

Rama remained brooding for a while and suddenly said, "My task is done. I have now freed you. I have fulfilled my mission. All this effort has been not to attain personal satisfaction for you or me. It was to vindicate the honour of the Ikshvahu race and to honour our ancestors' codes and values. After all this I must tell you that it is not customary to admit back to the normal married fold a woman who has resided all alone in a stranger's house. There can be no question of our living together again. I leave you free to go where you please and to choose any place to live in. I do not restrict you in any manner."

On hearing this Sita broke down. "My trials are not ended yet," she cried. "I thought with your victory all our troubles were at an end! . . . So be it." She beckoned to Lakshmana and ordered, "Light a fire at once, on this very spot."

Lakshmana hesitated and looked at his brother, wondering whether he would countermand the order. But Rama seemed passive and acquiescent. Lakshmana, ever the most unquestioning deputy, gathered faggots and got ready a roaring pyre within a short time. The entire crowd watched the proceedings, stunned by the turn of events. The flames rose to the height of a tree; still Rama made no comment. He watched. Sita approached the fire, prostrated herself before it, and said, "O Agni, great god of fire, be my witness." She jumped into the fire.

All the gods appeared. From the heart of the flame rose the god of fire, bearing Sita, and presented her to Rama with words of blessing. Rama, now satisfied that he had established his wife's integrity in the presence of the world, welcomed Sita back to his arms and expressed the wish to return to his own capital, Ayodhya. Vibhishana, the good successor to Ravana's throne, lent him the use of his flying chariot, Pushpak, in which Ravana had flown over Kailas and which he then had used for abducting Sita; Rama ascended it with Sita now.

Ayodhya celebrated Rama's enthronement, and an era of peace and joy commenced for the citizens. Rama and Sita were after all united again and found time to live a peaceful domestic life.

Years passed, and Sita was with child. Rama took her about the gardens of the city and the banks of Sarayu to keep her in good cheer. They were enjoying the sights of the countryside when Sita expressed a sudden desire. "I am feeling homesick for the forests and the *ashrams* where we spent so many happy years. I would love to go back to them for a while, away from all the palace comforts, and to live for a few days with those saints in the forests."

Rama smiled and understood that this was but the craving of a pregnant woman, not to be questioned or explained, and so said, "Tomorrow I will arrange to send you down to the forests." It proved a prophetic statement.

After Sita had retired for the night, Rama, as was his custom before closing his day's affairs, sent for his chief of intelligence, who was to report to him every night what the public thought and said. The intelligence chief reported routine matters and then hesitated. "What is your hesitation?" asked Rama.

The chief said, "Forgive my mentioning it, my lord, it is but my duty to report fully everything I hear. In the market place a group of men were standing around and chatting away. I mixed with them to hear what they were saying. Forgive my repeating their words."

"You are only doing your duty. Fear nothing. Tell me."

"They said, 'If our king Rama can take back home his wife who was lost to him for months and months, all of us can do it. Any wife who runs away can always return home with impunity. Why, then, quarrel with your wife?' "

After the officer left, Rama sought Lakshmana and told him, "Tomorrow before daybreak you will take Sita in a chariot to the banks of the Ganges and leave her there."

"And then?"

"That is all," said Rama.

"When is she to be brought back?"

"Never," said Rama and explained. "I have to set an example to my people. I cannot afford to indulge my personal feelings."

"But she is in a delicate state," said Lakshmana.

"She will be well," said Rama. "Take her to the *ashram* of sage Valmiki and leave her there. The sage will look after her."

And so next day Lakshmana escorted Sita out of the palace. She only thought that Rama had arranged to satisfy her craving for a change. "May I not see my lord and take his leave?" she asked.

Lakshmana replied awkwardly, "Let us go before the city wakes up. We have a long way to go."

Sita noticed that Lakshmana was gloomy and silent throughout the trip. When they reached their destination Sita asked, "You have not spoken a word all the way, what is on your mind?" At which Lakshmana burst into tears and Sita grew quite anxious. "Is Rama well? Is there any calamity that I have not known?"

Still Lakshmana could not bring himself to explain, at which Sita said, "Why are you unhappy, especially at this moment when I feel so happy, revisiting these beautiful spots? If you feel unhappy to be away from the capital, let us cut short our stay. Please take me to a few nearby *ashrams:* I have brought gifts for the persons whose hospitality we enjoyed long ago. We will rest for the night with one or another of those noble souls and start back at dawn. I have also a feeling that I cannot be away from Rama too long."

At this Lakshmana braced himself to tell her the truth. "People may speak ill, and Rama knows there is nothing in what they say. But still . . ."

When she recovered from the first shock of this blow, Sita calmly said, "I really do not know what to do with myself now. Perhaps I could fall into this river . . . but then, I have to think of the child to come! I have to live so that Rama's line may continue. Anyway, go back and tell Rama that I do not mind being sacrificed if it helps him. However, let him be considerate at least to those who were born with him—his brothers, I mean. Let him care for them unflinchingly and at no time sacrifice any of them for a cause."

Lakshmana left her within sight of Valmiki's *ashram* and started back for the capital. Sita sat at the edge of the river and wept.

At Valmiki's *ashram* some men reported to the sage, "A woman of divine aspect is at the river's edge. She seems to be in grief."

Valmiki came out, introduced himself to Sita, and said, "You do not have to explain anything to me. I know who you are and everything that has happened to you. Come to my *ashram,* for that is Rama's intention." He escorted her to his *ashram.*

She felt revived the moment she stepped into the hermitage.

Valmiki presented her to the other inmates of the *ashram*. "Here is one who deserves not only your respect but your love."

Kusa and Lava, the twins, were born in the *ashram* and grew up there. Valmiki became their mentor, trained them in their studies, and made them the repository of his great composition *Ramayana*, when they were barely ten years old.

Rama was performing a special sacrifice and had sent an invitation to Valmiki, who sent Lava and Kusa to represent him. He instructed them, "Go to Ayodhya, but don't enter the sacrificial ground. Stay in the woods and sing the story of Rama loudly enough for those inside the palace to hear you. Don't accept money or other rewards that they may offer, for you will not need them. You alone are fit to recite the *Ramayana*, for you are both gifted with music."

Lava and Kusa set forth on this mission. They reached the vicinity of the hall, where thousands of guests and priests had assembled to witness the sacrifice. Over and above the chanting of hymns and the ritual prayers came the twin voices, reciting the *Ramayana*, gripping the attention of the entire crowd. All other thoughts went into the background, all activities were suspended, as people listened to the song. Rama dropped everything and went forward to meet the source of this great song. The personalities of the twins, when he saw them, exerted an unconscious power over him, and he invited them in. Thereafter he mustered various scholars, poets, and literary experts and made the young men recite Valmiki's composition, a certain number of stanzas each day. He analysed and studied the lines with the greatest delectation; he was thus not only the hero of the story but its first reader.

As soon as the identities of the twins were established, Rama sent his messengers to fetch Valmiki and Sita. When Sita arrived, he welcomed her back warmly. But now it was her turn. All that she said was: "O Mother Earth, take me back to your bosom; heed my words if I have been pure at heart," and the earth cleaved under her feet, and she vanished into it.

Rama was seized with anger (as we have seen him on another occasion when he wanted to reach Lanka and the sea would not give way to him). He cried, "O Earth, give me back my wife; otherwise I will wipe you out, with your mountains, rivers, sea, forests, and everything. Take care!" He had never been seen in such a rage before. Everyone trembled at the sight of him.

At this moment Brahma appeared and said, "O Rama, you are an incarnation. You are Vishnu, and not Rama the mortal; don't let the illusion carry you away and make you forget your real identity. You are the great god Vishnu, who existed before *Ramayana*, and will continue beyond its conclusion. You incarnated yourself as Rama for a purpose, that is to save humanity from extinction. Sita is not lost. She is Lakshmi, your eternal spouse, who, having fulfilled her role, will await you in your own world. And now the mission on which you came to the earth has been fulfilled."

Rama was appeased. He made preparations for retirement now. He divided his kingdom among his sons, brothers, and their sons and retreated from public view. It was said that he proceeded to the banks of Sarayu, performed oblations to it, stepped into the water, and was not seen again.

The author, Valmiki, watched rather helplessly the conclusions that the characters of his epic were working out for themselves. He had a hope that he might be able to bring his hero and heroine together, help the family reunite, and thus round off his tale. But the characters managed their affairs in their own way. At the moment when Rama was eager to take Sita back, Sita decided differently. Rama himself decided on a great renunciation. The characters, as they would in any perfect work of art, got out of control. Valmiki let them act in their own way, watched the conclusions as an outsider, and returned to his life of contemplation.

DRAUPADI

THE STORYTELLER WAS in a loquacious mood. He sat me
on his mat as usual, brought me a plateful of sweets, and said,
"I collected these at weddings I attended today, quite a lot of
them, I tell you. For weeks I seem to have been doing nothing
but officiate at weddings, and everyone gives me a packet of
sweets; if I eat all of it at my age . . . And so I have kept them
for you. This has put me in mind of the whole business of
marriage. At the officiation I recite and make the bride and the
bridegroom recite before the holy fire their promises, but secretly
watch with interest the couple measuring each other slyly; in our
society husband and wife learn to understand each other after
marriage—unlike the Europeans, who, I hear, allow boys and
girls to move freely and settle their own marriages. When a girl
in our society consents to marry, she naturally accepts the judgment of her elders, but she also attempts to gauge the situation
for herself at the first chance. While I recite the mantras I also
watch with amusement the look of apprehension mingled with
hope in the eyes of the bride as she sits before the holy fire; and
it has always brought to my mind the situation Draupadi must
have found herself in when she had to accept five husbands in
one marriage!

"I hear that it is not unusual in the Western world, especially in the cinema world, for a woman to be married to five
persons—but one presumes it is always one after another and not
all at the same time. But Draupadi had the experience of being
married to five brothers at the same time. It sounded quite
impossible and outrageous even in those times. The whole thing
arose from a misunderstanding."

* * *

Kunthi, the mother of the Pandavas*, was inside her house when the brothers arrived, bringing home a hard-won trophy, the beautiful Draupadi, whom Arjuna, the third brother, the gifted archer, had won by performing an extraordinary feat of marksmanship. I'll come to that story presently, but first let me explain how the five-husband situation came about.

Earlier, the five brothers had gone out, as was their daily habit, to collect food and alms. When they came home they brought with them not alms but a bride. Bhima, the second son, the strong man, wanting to sound lighthearted, cried from the doorstep, "Mother, come out and see; we have brought home a *bhiksha*, a gift of alms."

Without coming out, Kunthi answered from the kitchen, "All right, share it among yourselves."

"Oh!" exclaimed Bhima. "Oh! Oh!" cried everyone, and the loudest exclamation was from Arjuna, who had won the bride.

The mother came out to see why there was an uproar and cried, "Oh! Who is this? You have won? Arjuna!" She was full of joy and clasped the girl's hand. "Oh, Arjuna, you have won this bride, this princess, this lovely creature! So you entered the contest after all. I never believed that you seriously meant to go there. What a risk you took of being discovered by your enemies! How happy I am to welcome this daughter-in-law. Tell me . . . What was the . . . Come in, come in." Her joy was boundless, her son had won in the greatest contest and had come through it safely and gloriously. "Come in, come in. . . ."

They trooped in behind her. She spread out a mat and told the girl to be seated, but, like a well-mannered daughter-in-law, Draupadi would not be seated when her husband and mother-in-law were standing. Moreover, her mind was all in a whirl. So was it for everyone, including Kunthi, who seemed to overlook it momentarily.

There was an awkward pause as the five brothers stood around uncertainly and Draupadi stood with downcast eyes, trying not to stare at the five men who were to share her, if the mother's injunction was to be obeyed. What a predicament for

---

* The five brothers who are the heroes of the epic *Mahabharata* and of the present story.

the girl, who thought that she was marrying one man and found four others thrown in unexpectedly!

The eldest of the brothers was there—Yudhistira; tall, graceful, a man of absolute, uncompromising idealism, peace, compassion, and justice. The next brother was Bhima—the outsized man, at whose birth the kings of the earth trembled; Bhima rolled over, when an infant, and dropped onto a rock; people went down to pick up the child, fearing great injury to it, only to find the rock on which he had fallen split and pulverized by the weight of the baby; Bhima could root out a tree by tugging at it and by a sweep of his arms knock down a multitude. After him came Arjuna, the greatest warrior born, beautiful and resplendent as Indra himself, and after him the twins, Nakula and Sahadeva, men of learning, handsome youths. Each one of them was endowed with an aspect of the god to whom Kunthi prayed at conception. Yama, the god of justice and Death, was the father of Yudhistira; Vayu, or the god of wind, was the father of Bhima; Arjuna was begotten by a mental union with the chief of gods, the powerful Indra; and the twins were born of the Aswinis, elves of paradise.

I will pause for a brief while to explain why the Pandavas were born to so many fathers. Kunthi's husband, Pandu, could not have union with his wife for two reasons: one, he was a sick man destined to live out his life in the forests; and two, a curse hung over his head that he would die on the day he went to bed with his wife. Once, while hunting, he had killed a female deer engaged in loveplay with its mate, and the dying deer cursed him that he would die when he made love to his wife. But as Pandu advanced in years he began to worry about progeny. He called his wife Kunthi and permitted her to invoke the gods by appropriate sacrifices and prayers, and to attain motherhood. She begot the three older brothers one after another, and the twins were born in the same manner to Pandu's second wife.

Now Draupadi studied the five brothers as unobtrusively as possible, wondering what freak of fate had brought her to this pass. Kunthi tried to make light of her own advice and said with a simper, ''Of course I did not know what you meant when you said you had brought *bhiksha.* I thought it was the usual gift of alms. . . .'' Her voice trailed away.

Bhima the strong, incapable of the subtleties of speech,

struggled to explain himself. "I . . . meant to be jocular, I meant . . ."

It was Arjuna who broke the awkward moment by becoming explicit; he said, "Mother, your word has always been a command to us, and its authority is inescapable. How can it be otherwise? We will share Draupadi as you have commanded."

"No, no, no . . . ," said the mother.

You may well imagine Draupadi's reaction to this situation. She sent up a silent prayer to the gods to solve this problem and edged closer to the only woman in the house, feeling relieved at the thought that whatever might be the number of husbands, she would have only one mother-in-law. (At this the storyteller permitted himself a smile.)

The eldest brother, Yudhistira, said, "What preposterous suggestion are you making in jest? A woman married to one man is a wife, to two, three, four, or five, a public woman. She is sinful. Whoever heard of such a thing!"

The mother said, "Don't make too much of an inadvertent bit of advice. You make me feel very unhappy and guilty, my son. Don't even suggest such an outrage."

Arjuna pleaded, "Please don't make me a sinner; it isn't fair to condemn me to suffer the sin of disobedience to a mother's word. You, my eldest brother, you are a man with a judicious mind and a knowledge of right and wrong. We four brothers and this girl will be bound by your words. You must advise us as to what is good and fair. Advise us, and we shall be bound by your words, but bear in mind that we cannot go back on the command of a mother. . . ."

When he said this, all the brothers studied the face of the girl, and their hearts palpitated, for already Manmata the god of love was at work, stirring their blood and affecting their vision.

Yudhistira brooded for only a moment, recollected the words of a seer who had already prophesied this situation, and, deciding to avoid heartburn amongst the brothers, declared, "This rare creature shall be wife of all of us."

The king of Panchala, father of Draupadi, summoned the Pandavas to discuss the arrangements for the wedding. The five brothers with their mother and the girl were invited to the palace and were honoured and feasted. They were taken through the palace and its grounds, where fruits, souvenirs, rare art objects, sculpture, paintings, carvings, gold-inlaid leather, furniture of rare design, agricultural implements, chariots, and horses were displayed. When they passed through the hall where swords, arms, shields, and equipment of warfare were kept, the five brothers picked up the articles, admiring them and commenting among themselves, spending more time in this part of the palace than anywhere else. Observing this, the king suspected that they might be warriors, although they were disguised as Brahmins. When they repaired to the chamber and were settled comfortably, the king point-blank said to Yudhistira, "I know you will always speak the truth. Tell me who you are."

And Yudhistira declared his identity and that of his brothers, and explained their trials and tribulations since the time of their leaving their kingdom, a year before, to escape the machinations of their cousins, the Kauravas.

Now the king said, "Let us rejoice that this day your brother Arjuna, the man with the mighty arm, will marry my daughter, and let us celebrate this union of our families in style. Let us make everyone in this world happy today."

Yudhistira said, "I am the eldest and still unmarried. I must be the first to marry, according to our law. Please give me your blessing to be married first."

"So be it," said the king, little dreaming of the implication. "You are the eldest, my daughter now belongs to your family. If you decide to marry her yourself, you will be free to do so, or you may give her to whomsoever you like among your brothers. I have nothing more to say."

"Now," said Yudhistira, simply and quietly, "Draupadi will have to be married to all of us." He explained how it had come about and concluded, "We have always shared everything and we will not deviate from the practice ever."

The king was stunned on hearing this. When he recovered his balance he cried, "One man can take many wives, but one woman taking several husbands has never been approved anywhere, either in practice or in scriptures. It is something that can never receive approval from any quarter. A man of purity like you, one learned and well equipped in knowledge—what evil power has brought this to your mind?"

Yudhistira said, "The right way is subtle and complicated. I know I am not deviating from it. O conqueror of the worlds, have no misgivings, give us your permission."

The king said faintly and desperately, "You and your ven-

erable mother and my daughter . . . Please talk it over among
yourselves and tell me what should be done"—and left them.

At this moment the sage Vyasa* arrived. They honoured
and seated him. When all the formalities were over, the king
asked, "Give us your guidance. Can a woman marry five men?"

"Not always. But now, in this particular instance, it is
correct. Now listen . . ." He got up and walked into the king's
private chamber; the others followed at a distance and waited
outside. "Your daughter," said Vyasa, "was Nalayani in her
last birth. She was one of the five ideal women in our land. She
was married to a sage called Moudgalya, a leprous man, repul-
sive in appearance and habits, and cantankerous. She was, however, completely indifferent to his physical state and displayed
the utmost devotion to him as a wife. She obeyed all his erratic
commands, accepted his fickle moods, submitted herself to all
his tyrannical orders, and ate the scraps on his plate. All this she
did without hesitation or mental protest, totally effacing her own
ego. They spent many years thus, and one day the husband said,
'O beautiful one, perfect wife on earth, you have indeed passed
through the severest trial and come through unscathed. Know
you that I am neither old nor diseased, nor inconsiderate; I
assumed all this vicious and disgusting appearance in order to
test you. You are indeed the most forbearing partner a man could
hope for. Ask of me any boon you may fancy, and I will grant
it.'

"She said, 'I want you to love me as five men, assuming
five forms, and always coming back to and merging in one
form.' And he granted her the wish. He shed his unpleasant
appearance in a moment and stood before her as an attractive,
virile man, and he could assume four other forms too. The rest of
their life was all romance; they travelled far and wide, visited
beautiful romantic spots on earth, and led a life of perfect union,
not in one but several worlds. They lived and loved endlessly in
every form, mood, shape, and circumstance.

"She never tired of it, but he did. He told her one day that
his life of abandon was at an end and that he was retiring into
loneliness and introspection, at which she wailed, 'I am still
insatiate. I have lived a wonderful life with you. I want you to
continue it forever.'

---

* Author of the *Mahabharata*.

"Moudgalya rejected her suggestion, warded her off as a drag on a man's spiritual progress, and departed. Whereupon she came down to earth from the dreamy Elysium in which she had dwelt and prepared herself to meditate on Iswara the Almighty. She meditated with great rigour, and when Iswara appeared before her, she muttered, 'I want my husband, husband, husband. . . .'

" 'You will soon end this identity and will be reborn as a beauty and marry five husbands,' said the god.

" 'Five husbands! God! Why five? I want only one.' 'I cannot help it. I heard you say "husband," and that five times,' said Iswara, and that proved the last word on the subject. A god's word is unretractable."

The god apparently spoke in jest, but he had his purpose. In the vision of a god there is no jest, everything works according to a scheme and towards a fulfilment. Justice and goodness had to be reinstated in this world. The Kauravas, the cousins of the Pandavas, were evil incarnate, powerful, clever, and accomplished. For the good of mankind, they were to be wiped out, and Draupadi was to play an important role in this. It was finally Draupadi's anger that brought about the downfall of the Kauravas.

Vyasa explained how Nalayani was reborn as the daughter of the king of Panchala; how she was not conceived in the womb normally but appeared out of a sacrificial fire when the king was performing a powerful sacrifice. She was known as Draupadi because she was immediately adopted by the king, whose name was Draupada. Her complexion was dark, her eyes scintillated like the surface of a lotus pond, her tresses were long and fell in ringlets.

She grew up in the palace, and when the time came for the king to think of her marriage he announced to the whole world that his daughter was about to choose a husband through a Swayamwara. A suitor, to qualify himself for her attention, would have to accomplish an extraordinary feat of archery. A target in the shape of a fish would be hoisted on a column beyond layers of revolving discs, each with a hole in its centre. The suitor must first string an enormous bow, and hit the target with one of five arrows, not looking up but looking down at the reflection of the target in a pool of oil. Whoever succeeded would be acceptable to the princess.

The announcement went out far and wide. On an auspicious

day, princes from all corners of the country assembled in Panchala. A special pavilion was built to accommodate the hundreds of competitors, visitors, and spectators; decorated, caparisoned elephants and horses of the visiting princes and their followers were tethered in all open spaces. On learning of this contest the Pandavas, disguised as Brahmins, also arrived, and unobtrusively occupied a few back seats. The other competitors preened themselves and examined each other with haughty envy and suspicion.

At an appointed hour Draupadi arrived at the centre of the pavilion with a garland in her hand, and the competition began. The announcer called upon the contestants in the assembly to approach the huge bow placed at the centre of the hall, lift it, and shoot. The princes from the warrior class were the first to approach, but most of them withdrew after one look at the bow. One or two dropped it on their toes. Some could not even stretch the steel coil forming the bowstring.

The king's daughter watched the process of elimination with relief. She saw the princes, wearing decorations and imposing battle-dress, coming on haughtily and retreating hastily, and galloping away on their horses. Comments, jokes, and laughter filled the air.

The Kauravas were in a group at one corner of the hall, watching contemptuously the arrivals and departures. Karna, the most gifted master of arms and archery, was there, and Duryodhana, the King of Hastinapura, the chief moving spirit in the rival camp—expert warrior, man of hate, gifted, strong, and merciless. His brothers and henchmen occupied the seats of honour and jeered at the candidates who failed. A lull fell on the assembly when their turn came, and the girl shivered instinctively and prayed to the gods to be saved from them.

She watched with apprehension as Karna approached the bow and lifted it as if it were a toy; he stood it on its end and stretched out the bowstring; the ends almost touched, but when there was still the width of a walnut to go the string snapped back, almost knocking him down. He withdrew. Next came Duryodhana; he held the bow firmly and stretched the string, but recoiled when it still had to cover a gap the width of a black gram; he had dislocated his finger, and dropped the bow and withdrew with a groan. The crowd bellowed with excitement.

There was a stir as one got up from the Brahmin group.

There were shouts of protest. "How dare a Brahmin enter this contest, which is open only for the warrior class? Let Brahmins stick to their scriptures." But the king made a ruling that, as he had mentioned no caste in his announcement, anyone was free to try his luck.

Arjuna approached the bow—being the son of Indra, he was auspicious-looking, strong, and beautiful. One look at him, and Draupadi became anxious lest he should fail. He not only strung the bow but hit the target again and again, five times. Draupadi approached him with the garland of flowers and slipped it about his neck. At that moment they were betrothed. Arjuna took her hand and led her off.

There was at once a commotion. "We have been cheated! How can a Brahmin be allowed to win a Kshatriya bride? We'll not allow it. We'll kill this king and carry away the girl." Fighting broke out, and the king's bodyguard met the threat with appropriate action. Bhima, the strong brother among the Pandavas, was seen guarding the girl, armed with the trunks of two huge trees, which he had plucked out of the park. The five brothers, accompanied by the girl, went home to the potter's cottage where they lived and where their mother awaited their return. It was there that Bhima announced from the doorstep, "Mother, we have brought home a *bhiksha*," and she answered from inside, "Share it among yourselves."

Draupadi was wedded to the brothers according to the strictest ritual. The first to clasp her hand for the god of fire to witness was the eldest, Yudhistira; next came the mighty Bhima, and after him the actual winner of her hand, Arjuna; and lastly the twins, one after the other. She was to live with each brother for one full year as his wife, and then pass on to the next. When she lived with one, the other brothers had to eradicate from their minds completely the image of her as a wife. It needed a very special kind of detachment and discipline of mind to practise this code. Anyone who violated it, even in thought, exiled himself from the family and had to seek expiation in a strenuous pilgrimage to the holy rivers.

At Hastinapura, the capital of the rival cousins, the Kauravas, whose king was Duryodhana, there was much uneasiness at the realization that the Pandavas were still alive. The Kauravas had planned several schemes to exterminate the Pandavas, who came through them all unscathed. Lastly they had devised a masterly scheme to house the Pandavas in an inflammable wax mansion, which was calculated to go up in flames at a certain moment and destroy the inmates. There was a fire, of course, but the one to perish in it was the hireling architect who had designed the wax mansion, and not the Pandavas, for whom the elaborate trap was laid. All the five brothers escaped and wandered in the country disguised as Brahmins—wearing sacred thread, clothed in deer-skin, their faces covered with hirsute growth.

The Kauravas had taken it for granted that their enemies were no more. When they learned that the Pandavas were intact and, what was more, had won the hand of Draupadi, they were filled with rage and consternation. Hasty consultations were held to decide how to ward off this menace to their security. "A cobra which you have hit and not killed will pursue you until it destroys you," they said, speculating on various schemes to kill the Pandavas—starting with the hiring of assassins to creating jealousies over the possession of a single wife.

The Kauravas speculated on this last with relish. "Five men to possess one wife? Unheard-of sin. They will be ridiculed and castigated by all mankind!" With all their speculations, they could do no more than come to the conclusion that for the moment the only practical course for them would be to let the Pandavas rule their half of the kingdom and bide their time.

The Pandavas established themselves on a deserted piece of land, built their capital, and called it Indraprasta, a city of splendour. Their palace was enormous. They had created a paradise out of ashes and mud. To celebrate their re-establishment they held a *rajasuya yaga*,* and, as a matter of propriety, invited their enemy cousins to it. Duryodhana with his brothers and henchmen arrived in great style, mostly to spy on the prosperity of the Pandavas, of which they were hearing so much.

The capital, with its parks, gardens, and mansions, and above all the palace with its pillared halls, was impressive. Duryodhana saw it and was consumed with envy. "They are

* A *rajasuya yaga* is a "royal sacrifice," an elaborate ceremony performed to mark the installation of a king or the consolidation of his conquests, to mark his supremacy over all other kings.

efficient, competent, and the gods favour them,'' he reflected bitterly.

Duryodhana as the head of the Kauravas received a special invitation to visit the palace. While on this special visit he committed several grotesque *faux pas*. Stepping over a courtyard paved with shining marble, he tucked up the hem of his robe, mistaking it for a pool of water; his hosts laughed at this. His next blunder occurred when he passed through a hall with paintings on the walls and attempted to pluck a fruit painted on a cornice piece. His hosts, conducting him through the palace, permitted themselves unrestrained laughter at this mistake. The third awkward moment occurred when he tried to walk through a glass panel. The Pandavas roared with laughter, the loudest peal emanating from Draupadi. Duryodhana withdrew from the scene, his nerves all aquiver, swearing to himself, ''If I do not humble the five brothers, and especially that woman, I'll change my name. They created the whole situation in order to insult me.''

Later, Duryodhana invited Yudhistira to play a game of dice. In the hall of games in the Hastinapura palace Duryodhana sat before the dice board, flanked by all his supporters; on the opposite side sat Yudhistira and his brothers. The stakes were light at first—a few pieces of jewellery and money. By evening the fever had risen high. Yudhistira was continually losing. Excitement ran high in the camp of the Kauravas. They began to taunt and tease Yudhistira until he became desperate to win back something.

''What have you left? Your palace? I'll stake this palace where we are now playing. Will you stake yours?'' asked Duryodhana.

''Yes, of course,'' said Yudhistira. He had become blind to all consequences, and presently lost his palace, horses, elephants, arms, and finally his capital and his half of the kingdom. His brothers watched him helplessly. He was the eldest, and they could not order him to stop, although they tried to restrain him. Finally all that was left was his own person—he staked it and again lost.

''Do you still want to play? Have you anything left?'' asked Duryodhana and answered the question himself. ''You have nothing left, and you are my slave. You may still make a last bid. Who knows? Your luck may turn and you may recoup everything that you have so far lost. Why not try? I want you to have a last chance, who knows?''

It was a subtle suggestion, falling on fertile ground. Yudhistira was in the right state of delirium for it, and all that he said was, with a final desperation, ''I've nothing left to stake.''

''You have forgotten your wife,'' said Duryodhana. A cry of protest arose from the Pandavas. Ignoring it, Duryodhana elaborated his thesis.''Isn't it a wife's duty to help her husband when he is in trouble? Is a wife only for good times? Play the game with some seriousness and who knows?''

Yudhistira thought it a good solution and staked Draupadi as a last effort and lost her. A shout of victory went up from the assembly of evil men. Sakuni, the uncle of Duryodhana, had an evil, powerful mind. He had ingeniously suggested this gambling bout as a possible means of putting down the Pandavas and had directed the entire game for Duryodhana, practically moving his fingers along the game board.

Duryodhana ordered a messenger. ''Go and tell that slut that she must present herself before us.'' Being slaves now, the Pandavas were ordered to remove themselves to a far corner of the hall and not to be seen standing so near the king.

The messenger came back—without Draupadi—and reported, ''She wanted to know whether she had been staked last or as last but one, Your Majesty, and when I told her that Yudhistira lost himself first and then lost her, she had the temerity to reply that the loss could not then bind her, as Yudhistira had no authority to stake her when he was no longer a free man. My lord, I warned her of Your Majesty's anger, but she was adamant. Such an obstinate woman!''

''Obstinate? She will get over that soon enough. Tell her she is to obey our command and no argument about it. Tell her she is our slave now.'' He looked about triumphantly.

The five brothers stood far away. Bhima whispered, ''I will smash them,'' and ground his teeth. ''Quiet,'' commanded the eldest brother. Arjuna said, ''One arrow from my bow . . .'' Yudhistira whispered, ''Be quiet. Don't do anything.''

The messenger soon came back—but again without Draupadi. This time he said, ''Your Majesty, she pleads that she cannot come before men for three days.''

''Why?''

There was an embarrassed silence, and he whispered, "She is in her monthly retirement."

"\ That so? As if no other woman has her month!"

"She pleads she is not well and is not dressed properly."

"How many excuses! Go and tell her she must come whether she is half clad or fully clad, we don't care.¸ . . . At once!" he cried.

Draupadi arrived and stood aside, half concealed in the passage, feeling ashamed to appear before this big assembly of men. Duryodhana sent his wild brother Dussasana to fetch her to his presence, but he came back and said, "She resists."

"Does she? Drag her here!" he commanded, twirling his moustache haughtily.

The wild brother reappeared in the hall, dragging Draupadi by her hair. Her husbands watched the scene helplessly. Duryodhana and his men—his blind father, his kinsmen and allies—found it extremely amusing. They laughed at her. Duryodhana felt avenged for the laughter he had heard resounding through the halls of Indraprasta when he mistook a marble surface for water. Draupadi demanded of the assembly how any civilized men could perpetrate this savagery.

This only provoked more mirth among the men. "You are now our slave," Duryodhana said. "You will join the other slaves in the palace and learn your tasks, what to wash and where to scavenge. Forget that you were ever a princess. Ah, what a fuss your father made with that monstrous bow, you five-husbanded one!"

Draupadi averted her eyes, bowed her head, and tried to cover with her outstretched palms her body exposed to public view.

"Take your hands away!" commanded Duryodhana. "A slave has no business to conceal any part of herself when her master desires to inspect her. You feel you are not dressed for the occasion. You are overdressed, take off every bit on you!"

A groan escaped from Bhima and the rest, but as usual Yudhistira restrained them, and then Draupadi let out a wail as Duryodhana commanded Dussasana to disrobe her. Dussasana was already tugging at her sari. Bhima cried, "I can wipe out all these men; give me permission," and Yudhistira said, "We are slaves. We are not entitled to protest in any manner."

"My husbands in this hall are not moved to protect me?

You elders assembled there, you are wise and experienced. After all, I am married to your nephews, how could you be so indifferent and callous? Is there no one here who can save my honour?'' cried Draupadi and looked around. No one made any move to help her. "Oh, Krishna, God incarnate, help me!'' she cried in the end.

And now the miracle happened. As Dussasana tried to snatch away her sari, it kept growing. Draupadi could not be disrobed. She shut her eyes and remained in meditation.

This episode concluded when the elders of the family, who had found it all amusing at first, became repentant at the signal of God's help and came up to Draupadi and said, "What can we do for you?''

Draupadi briefly replied, "Give me back my husbands, and give them back all that they have lost in foolish gambling.'' It was granted.

Once more Duryodhana did not quite like the compromise. He felt defeated and consulted his evil uncle Sakuni as to how he could harass and neutralize the Pandavas again. Sakuni suggested another bout of gambling and promised even greater help.

Duryodhana again invited Yudhistira to a game, and once again that inveterate gambler accepted the challenge and lost everything. This time Duryodhana consolidated his gains and acted more practically. He made a condition that the Pandavas should leave their capital and exile themselves to a forest life for twelve years, and that in the thirteenth year they should live incognito anywhere—but if they were recognized by anyone at that stage, the penalty would be another period of twelve years' exile and one year incognito, and so forth. If they lived through this period they could claim their kingdom at the end of thirteen years, or a further period of thirteen years.

In a hut in the forest the six of them dwelt, leading the life of nomads. Draupadi, with her tresses untied as on the day she had been dishonoured, accepted the situation in dead silence and resignation.

Krishna, who was in human form god Vishnu in his eighth incarnation ("For the protection of the good, for the destruction of the evil-doers, . . . I am born from age to age,'' he explained later to Arjuna), arrived at this camp, and Draupadi burst out, "See what I am reduced to! Married to the most renowned warriors of the world! They exposed me to the greatest shame!

Here was this great Yudhistira, who looked on. He was so non-violent, so peace-loving and an incarnation of goodness, that he would not lift his little finger to save his wife's honour! Not only that, his philosophy of mildness affected his brothers too! Where was Bhima? What happened to his strength that could shift a mountain? Was it not said that kings wet their beds on the day they heard Bhima was born? Where was he? What happened to Arjuna, the bearer of Gandiva?* What terrible weakness had come over this cream of mankind? Just my fate! My fate!''

Krishna appeased her in the godliest idiom he could muster.

She said, ''Now my husbands must redeem my honour and theirs by fighting and winning back everything they have lost. If they die in the attempt, I will not be sorry. They must win back their kingdom, for they lost it through foul play, through Sakuni's deceit and the Kauravas' cunning. This is the time to wage a war.''

Her passionate eloquence drove Yudhistira to answer, ''Why should we fight? They have only won the stakes we lost.''

Enraged, Draupadi said, ''Neither the elders nor my husbands want to help me in any way; perhaps fate wills it that I should suffer. Fate wills it that we should lose the kingdom through unfair trickeries.''

Krishna said, ''If I had been free I should have come to Hastinapura and stopped the gambling whether they wanted me there or not. But I heard you cry when they attempted to shame you in public. I will help you. We will fight and win. Have no fear.''

Draupadi said, ''When Dussasana tugged my hair, it fell loose on my back, and I have left it thus. I shall never do it up again until I am able to dip my hair in that monster's blood. This is my vow, and I beg my valorous husbands to help me achieve it.''

Thirteen years had to pass before this vow could be fulfilled, years of agonizing exile and travail. But Draupadi's refrain never ceased. ''Wage a war and kill Duryodhana and his men, or let us die in the attempt.''

The Pandavas lived in the kingdom of Virata in their last year of exile, being compelled to remain incognito for the whole period. The spies of their enemy cousins were searching

---

* Arjuna's famous bow.

for them everywhere, but they remained undetected in the palace of Virata under assumed names. Yudhistira became a courtier and gambling adviser to the king; Arjuna in the guise of a eunuch guarded the precincts of the women of the court; Bhima worked as the chief of the cooks in the kitchen; and the other two brothers looked after the horses and the cattle in the palace stables. Draupadi became a handmaid to the queen.

It was an eventful year, as they were always on the point of being found out. Near the end of this period the Kauravas discovered the identity of Arjuna during a minor battle in which, still in disguise, he was helping Virata's son. The Pandavas finally had to declare a war in order to regain their kingdom, for when, after thirteen years of exile, they laid claim to their rights, Duryodhana refused to hand back their kingdom. This brought them to the last phase of the struggle, and urged by Krishna, they were finally arrayed on the battlefield of Kurukshetra. Arjuna arrived in his chariot, raised his famous bow, but lost heart at the last moment. Seeing all his cousins and uncles and blood relations, he quailed, wavered, and cried that he could not destroy his kith and kin. Krishna, who had assumed the role of his charioteer, lectured to him on the philosophy of detachment and action, explained the nature of time and immortality, good and evil, and duty (all of which form the contents of the famous scripture *Bhagavad Gita*) and revealed himself in all his divinity and stature, all-embracing and filling the entire universe with his immanence. Arjuna was overwhelmed by the vision, recovered his spirit, plunged into the battle with a free mind, and wiped out the evil-doers, enabling Draupadi to fulfil her lifelong vow.

Their earthly mission over, in due course, perhaps a few thousand years later, the Pandavas and Draupadi moved towards heaven, all of them hoping to be admitted in their mortal forms, as the shastras promise for perfect beings. But at various stages, one by one, each fell back, owing to subtle, unsuspected short-comings in their earlier records.

Draupadi was the first to falter and step off the road to heaven. Bhima asked how a person of her qualities and perfection could fail to reach heaven, whereupon Yudhistira explained that, although she was equally married to the five brothers, she always had a secret, unconscious partiality to Arjuna the warrior, who had won her hand and heart at her Swayamwara, and that flaw in her nature was enough to deny her entrance to heaven, until she passed through purgatory.

The only one to reach heaven unhindered was Yudhistira, and even ahead of him was an insignificant mongrel that had somehow attached itself to him during his exiled wanderings. When the gatekeepers of heaven refused admission to the dog, Yudhistira declined to accept his own privilege of entering. Whereupon they had to open the gate for both the man and his pet.

FOUR

NALA

SAVITRI

THE MISPAIRED ANKLET

SHAKUNTALA

In each of these stories, which depict the heroine according to Indian tradition, a wife is shown overcoming formidable obstacles in order to regain a lost husband. In "Nala," the daintily bred Damayanti undergoes many hardships while searching the world for her husband. Savitri tenaciously follows Yama, the stern god of death, until her pleading persuades him to yield back the life of her husband. In "The Mispaired Anklet," Kannagi, hitherto gentle as a fawn, becomes a fury when she learns of her husband's unjust execution and sets the city literally aflame with her indignation. Shakuntala undertakes an arduous journey in order to revive the memory of a man who married and forgot her, and waits with a godly patience to be reunited with him.

NALA

NALA WAS THE ruler of Nishadha, a kingdom of the utmost prosperity and beauty, where the citizens lived a life of peace and contentment, reflecting the qualities of their ruler, who was young, brave, and good. He was a bachelor. Why such an accomplished personality should have remained unwed remained a mystery to everyone, but the gods had other plans for him, as we shall see. He remained unthinking of a wife until an itinerant poet arrived at the court one day and recited:

> "Tree without bark,
> House without walls,
> Gold bowl without food or wine—
> What do they remind you of?"

The king, who was in his audience chamber with a select group of courtiers and scholars, answered, "They remind one of a tree without a bark, that is all."

At which the poet became serious and said, "They are not unlike a man without a wife—a life wasted in solitude and pining; whatever may be the glitter and the shine outside, inside it's all just bare and unprotected, without content. So is a man without a wife; so is a woman without a husband. In a week I've seen two such—Your Majesty's good self and Damayanti, the daughter of Bhima,* the king of Vidarbha, where I sojourned eight days ago. You are made for each other, but yet have let cruel distance separate you. . . ."

The poet described Damayanti. "Fashioned by the Creator in His best mood; I stammer and grow incoherent when I try to

---

* A different Bhima from the one in the *Mahabharata*, who figures in "Draupadi."

describe her eyes, lips, complexion, and figure, for I at once reject every known epithet as being inadequate.'' The propitious moment for which Manmata, the god of the sugar-cane bow, had been waiting seemed to have arrived.

The king said, ''Poet, go back to Vidarbha and tell her . . .''

''O king, that I cannot do. When I move, I move in a forward direction and never turn back. Forgive me, sire. Send a messenger.''

So the king fell in love with the unseen Damayanti. His interest in sports, administration, and court life dwindled. He could not shut his eyes without being haunted by her image. All day long he kept wandering in his garden, idly watching the lotus pools and the fountains. It was a total and absolute love-sickness, which deprived the king of taste for food, sleep, company, and solitude alike.

At the lotus pond one evening he saw a family of swans gently paddling along; he envied their poise. He shot out his arm and caught one and lifted it up. The swan struggled in his grip and said, ''King, let me go, I have not harmed you in any way. You are sick in mind. I am not, but that is hardly my fault.'' All the other swans paused in their perambulation, and watched their companion.

Nala apologized to the swan. ''I didn't know what I was doing. I'll let you go. I envy you, that is all.''

The swan said, ''Wing-flapping, water-soaked creatures like us to be objects of a king's envy!''

''You can fly, I can't,'' said the king. ''I am earth-bound. . . .''

''But you have fast chariots, and your horsemanship is known in all the worlds. You can make a horse fly by a mere touch.''

''But still I am not able to go where I most wish to go. Oh swan, go to Vidarbha. Fly over and beyond those high walls where the princess dwells; descend into her garden and tell her that I am desperate and dying.''

All the swans in the flock crowded around eagerly. They cried with one voice, ''O king, we'll all fly off together and help you. We will plead your cause.''

''You can fly over moats and battlements—lend me your wings for a day,'' said the king. He stroked the back of the swan and let it go.

The swan said, "King, I'll never forget your kindness. We'll lay our lives at your feet."

The swan got back into the water and made preparations for travel—whatever preparation a swan would normally make before a long flight—perhaps pecked the backs of the fledglings to say good-bye, and asked an aged relative to keep an eye on the young ones—and the company of swans flew off.

The king looked suddenly cheerful, but he had a tendency to stay near the lily pond. His ministers, who were now emboldened to pace around with him, noticed the pond and asked, just to make conversation, "Where are all the swans one used to see here?"

Nala ignored the question as if to indicate that he had more important subjects on his mind than swans. He had a suspicion, the usual one that besets lovelorn men and women, that all his plans were sacred and secret, and likely to be spoiled by others.

The brood of swans arrived back in due course, at dusk one day. The chief swan said, "Our mission has been succesful," and explained how they had met Damayanti, given her the message, and bore her reply, that she also had been pining for him, ever since she had heard his name mentioned, and that Nala should have his chariot ready to come flying to Vidarbha the moment a Swayamwara was announced.

Damayanti began her preparations. No girl could ever go to her father straight away and declare that she was anxious for a Swayamwara; it was not done in such an elementary, blunt manner. The idea had to be conveyed by signs and in code. Damayanti's maids often went to the queen and bewailed that the princess was losing weight, her bangles were slipping off her wrists, her eyes were becoming dark-ringed, and that she seemed to have a burden on her mind.

A busy father like Bhima hardly ever noticed anything until he was told, but now he took the hint and sent out heralds far and wide to announce that as the princess would soon be selecting her husband, all eligible bachelors (and others too!) were welcome to come to Vidarbha and try their luck. Soon the traffic on the road to Vidarbha noticeably increased, as suitors converged on the capital on horseback, in chariots, and by elephant.

Nala was one of the earliest to start, although he could have been the last, considering his equestrianship as well as his chances. While on the road he was joined by four others. They were all gods in human form: Indra, the chief of all the minor gods; Varuna, the god of rain, air, and ocean; Agni, the god of fire; and Yama, the lord of death. The sage Narada, that supreme intellectual who moved with ease among all the worlds, conveying news from one world to another, and relishing the twists and interplay of human and divine situations, had taken the trouble to visit Indra in his world and inform him and the other gods of Damayanti's Swayamwara. He gave an edge to the news by adding that the gods' chances were nil, as Nala was already predestined to be the bridegroom, and that the whole of the Swayamwara was just a formality. This stirred the gods to undertake a trip to the earth. They came down precisely where Nala was resting his horse, revealed their identities, and asked, "Will you help us?"

"In what way?"

"How can you ask? What will it be worth if the help is circumscribed and limited? Will you help us or not?"

"Yes, I promise you my help," said the mild king, intimidated by their manner.

"Do you promise?"

"Yes, I do," he said unthinkingly.

At once the god Indra said, "You must go ahead of us and persuade Damayanti to choose one of us as her husband."

Nala replied, "How can I do that? I'm myself going there hoping to be chosen."

"You promised us your help, are you backing out on it now?"

"O gods, forgive me. Take pity on me. How can I do something against my own interests? I have waited for this chance all my life."

"Why did you say you would do anything? Break your word if you dare," said the gods grimly, hinting at eternal consequences.

Nala tried a little diplomacy now. "Most of the approaches to the palace will be blocked, except the one leading straight to the pavilion where the Swayamwara is to be held. I know that the most rigorous steps are being taken to keep out intruders."

The gods smiled as if to say, "Everyone is going to be an intruder except you!" and rose to the occasion by promising, "We will help you to get past all barricades, barriers, and battlements. We will help you to get within whispering distance of Damayanti, provided you plead our cause."

Nala was thrilled at the prospect of an approach to his beloved and cried enthusiastically, "Yes, I'll go."

By their magic powers the gods helped him stand face to face with Damayanti in her private garden. They met like long-lost lovers, having held each other in vision, dream, and thought for months. Nala explained his mission. Damayanti declared without hesitation, "It is impossible. Let them do their worst. I'll not even glance at anyone. You are my lord."

Nala went back to the gods swiftly, the same way by which he had come, and happily explained to them, "Damayanti will not garland anyone except me."

The gods remarked, "You kept your word, but failed in your mission. You should have been more persuasive; you have kept to the letter of your promise and little else."

"I did my best," replied Nala.

At the assembly all the princes had gathered, resplendently dressed and decorated, and measuring each other with haughty side-glances. At an auspicious hour, chosen by the learned astrologers, the princess entered and picked up a garland from a tray set in the middle of the hall. Every candidate in that vast hall stared at her longingly.

Damayanti looked around, searching for Nala. He sat in a back row, unobtrusively, so that the competing gods might not blame him for spoiling their chances. Damayanti's eyes smiled, but, glancing to the side, she found, to her bewilderment, four others—all looking like Nala. The gods had each assumed the form, features, and dress of Nala himself.

Distrusting her eyes, Damayanti came nearer, and there she saw arrayed five Nalas all in a row, like quintuplets on display. She stared hard, but there was no way of detaching the real Nala from the rest. So she did the only thing she could under the circumstances, that is, pray to the very gods who were taunting her. With the garland in her hand, she appealed in a silent prayer to Varuna, Indra, Agni, and Yama to help her solve this conundrum.

When she opened her eyes again, her prayer had been answered—the four gods looked on with unwinking eyelids (which is the sure mark of a god), while the human Nala's eyes fluttered normally. That was enough. Damayanti went forward and garlanded him. The gods, having enjoyed their little diversion, were satisfied, and now blessed this couple and vanished.

Two other gods were rather late in coming, and were told by Indra and Agni, while on their way to Bhima's country, that they might as well go back. "It is all over," said Indra. "Don't waste your time."

These two gods, Kali and Dwapara, who presided over the cycle of Time, felt snubbed and swore. "They had no business to make a farce of the Swayamwara. Nala has played a trick on all of us. No one is going to feel happy over it."

After Nala had settled down to a happy married life with Damayanti as his queen, Kali and Dwapara entered his capital. Kali got into the mind of Pushkara, brother of Nala, and made him challenge Nala to a game of dice. Nala accepted the invitation. In their private chamber the brothers rolled the dice, as a big circle of courtiers stood around and watched in silence.

Kali stirred within the younger brother's bosom and made him win aggressively. The other god animated the dice by entering their core. First the little diamond on the king's finger changed hands, and then the necklace on his chest, and then his chariots, horses, palace, and finally his kingdom itself. Nala played on as though in a trance, pinning the usual hopes of the gambler on the next chance.

Pushkara became dynamic with evil intentions. He presently suggested, "Brother, you have lost everything in this world. The only possession that you are left with is your wife. Why not stake her as a last chance? It may be the turning point."

Nala thought for a moment. "No," he said, and rose to his feet. He was stripped of his ornaments and dress, and was left with only a piece of cloth around his loins. Damayanti was shorn of all her jewellery and was permitted to leave with the one sari she wore.

Now the brother reached the acme of his evil purpose by ordering Nala and his wife out of the country. He made it known through the beat of drums that anyone offering shelter to this couple would invite severe punishment, and the announcement went forth to the people under the seal and authority of their new ruler.

The only place where Nala could stop without upsetting the order of the new ruler was on open ground at the edge of the forest. Damayanti followed her husband blindly and dumbly.

Fatigued by the tramping, and by the shock of the day's events, they sat down to rest. A large white bird alighted nearby— perhaps once again it was inspired by the twin gods out to torment Nala. An idea struck Nala that he ought to catch it. He had no bow or arrow with which to attack it. He approached it strategically, took off the single piece of cloth he had been wearing, and threw it at the bird. He had calculated that under the weight of the cloth the bird would be pinned to the earth and then he could just stretch out his hand for it. In his mental state it seemed a perfectly feasible plan, but the moment he threw the cloth the bird took off with it, and the king was left with no sort of cover for his body. His wife, as ever, came to his aid. She unwound the end of her sari and wrapped him in it.

They progressed through the forest, feeding on edible roots, and reached a hilly eminence. Nala pointed out to her a distant town. "That's your father's capital, where you lived happily as a child."

"It doesn't interest me," she replied firmly. "I won't go back to my father. I won't leave your side."

That night, when Damayanti was asleep, Nala edged away, having resolved to leave her within sight of her father's city. He reproached himself bitterly for deserting her, but the dangers that faced her in his company were grave, and if she was left behind, there was a chance that she might turn homeward, especially when the glow of her father's capital invited her. He gently cut off his portion of her sari and stole away, taking care not to rustle the dry leaves under his feet.

In the morning Damayanti's only prayer to the gods was that they grant her feet the strength to tramp in search of her husband. She made her way through the forests, averting her face from her father's capital, which seemed to beckon to her tantalizingly. She addressed the mountains, trees, and birds, as she went along. "Did you see my husband pass this way?"

She came upon a group of saintly men in a remote hermit- age, who received her kindly and told her to stay on for the night. She fell asleep, lulled by their gentle conversation and laughter; when she woke up in the morning to find her helpers gone, she realized that she had spent the previous evening in the company of celestial beings who were perhaps guarding her.

As she set out on the road again to resume the search for her husband, she found a caravan of traders passing and begged the leader of the caravan to let her join them. They asked her where she was bound, and she could only say, "Wherever you may be going."

Later, while the caravan was crossing a valley, a herd of wild elephants swooped down on it and caused panic and destruction. The survivors in the caravan turned upon Damayanti and declared, "You are an evil creature in a woman's shape." Noticing her ragged dress and dishevelled appearance, they cried, "You are a witch. Don't come with us, we'll kill you if you follow us."

They surrounded and heckled her, until the leader of the caravan intervened. "Silly men, leave this woman alone, don't you see that she is helpless?"

"If she is a normal woman, why should she be wandering in lonely places?"

The leader said, "Let us leave her at the next town, don't trouble her now."

They left her in a city called Chedi* and passed on. Watching the caravan go, she felt desolate, as even the false lull of security that she had experienced in their company was now gone. The last man in the caravan cried, "Stay back, woman."

One of the street-loungers asked, "Why do you leave her behind?"

"God help us! We have had enough trouble. She is . . . I don't know what she is, but our leader softens at the sight of women. Five minutes after she joined us, we were attacked by elephants. She is . . ." They said something lewd and passed on. Damayanti had support at the head of the caravan but not at its tail.

Now she stood alone in the market place. One or two loafers jeered at her. She was dishevelled, in rags, and her face was caked with mud and distorted with suffering. A shopman cried to her, "Get out, don't block the way. You have an evil face, don't spoil my business standing there. Here, take this coin and begone." He flung a coin at her.

Some urchins, noticing from a distance the gesticulations of the shopman cried, "The shopman is stoning that madwoman!" And, following his supposed example, they picked up a couple of pebbles and threw them at her. Other boys joined. It seemed

---

* Not the same as the capital in "Viswamitra."

quite an accredited activity for boys to throw stones at mad persons and monkeys. Presently Damayanti was running down the street with a howling mob pursuing her.

Just then the royal chariot passed that way. The king, returning from the temple on the hill, had noticed the yelling crowd and, the moment he reached the palace, dispatched his horsemen to the market place to rescue the woman. One of the guards came back to report. "She is in the rest house, being guarded by our men. They said she was mad, but she has explained that she is looking for her husband, lost in the forests."

The king ordered, "Fetch her."

When Damayanti was brought before him, he ordered her to be sheltered in the women's section of the palace. The king's mother took charge of her.

Nala, clad in the cut-off piece of his wife's sari, wandered far and wide. At one spot he came upon a conflagration of leaves and bamboo and put it out. A serpent which had been encircled by the fire now emerged from hiding and said, "You have saved me from the fire and absolved me, this moment, from a curse which had condemned me to the existence of a serpent, with constant threat of being clubbed to death." The serpent continued, "I'm grateful for your help, Nala. I want to show you my gratitude before I assume my real shape. Now take ten strides, counting each step aloud."

Nala obeyed the serpent and when he took the tenth step, counting aloud, *"Dasa,"* which in Sanskrit means "ten" and also means "bite," the serpent acted on its second meaning and immediately darted up and plunged its fangs in his veins, emptying all its venom.

"Is this the return for my help?" Nala asked.

The serpent said, "This is my last bite as a serpent. All the poison will now circulate in your veins, and Kali, who has entrenched himself within you, watching and relishing all your travails, will now leave you, unable to stand the venom. This poison will also affect your appearance."

And Nala found himself growing dark as a cinder and short and deformed. He could hardly recognize his own hands and legs. "What is happening to me?" he cried in alarm.

"This disguise will help you. You will not be recognized. Now listen carefully. Keep these two pieces of cloth; wrap yourself in them when you wish to resume your original personality. But don't do so until you achieve your purpose. If you walk southward for five days, you will reach the kingdom of Rituparna. He is a good king. Teach him horsemanship. Learn from him the science of gambling, in which he has mastery; and await further developments. Do not reveal yourself to anyone until you get back your kingdom and your wife. God be with you. . . ." The serpent assumed its original celestial form and vanished.

At the gate of the palace of Rituparna stood a dwarf, sounding the bell which meant that he wanted an audience with the king. The gatekeepers laughed at him. But he was adamant and the rules did not permit anyone to be turned away arbitrarily. So they said, "The king cannot set eyes on so deformed a creature. We will consult his aides and come back, if you will wait here."

An officer of the palace household came to the spot and, making a wry face, demanded, "What do you want?"

"I must speak to the king."

"The king is busy. You may tell me what you want."

"Are you the king?"

"No, no."

"I want to speak only to the king—that is, if this bell means anything."

So the courtier went back and the king appeared on the balcony; the deformed man said, "There are many things I can do, king, only admit me in your palace. I can make you happy, serving you in a hundred ways unquestioningly."

"What can you do?"

"Don't be misled by my looks. God has chosen to give me this guise, but Your Majesty will be pleased with me when you have tried me. I'm an adept at managing horses. Let me work in your stables, and you will see how I can make the tardiest horse fly like a whirlwind. I can look at a horse and tell you what he'll be like in five days or five months or five years."

The king was impressed with this man's talk. He found him, in due course, extremely valuable. Any horse responded to his touch, and the king enjoyed nothing more than a drive in the chariot with the deformed man holding the reins. During those outings they became friendly. Nala also threw a hint that as a cook he could prepare food fit for the gods.* The king's love of food being very marked, Nala soon became the chief creator of good food in the royal kitchen. Between the kitchen and the stables, Nala captivated the heart of the king, much to the envy of all the court.

Damayanti longed for her husband secretly and realized that, in spite of all the comfort that surrounded her in the palace at Chedi, she ought to slip away and resume her quest. She felt so oppressed by this thought that one evening she quietly walked off through a gap at the back garden of the palace. A guard at his post cried, "Who goes there?" and Damayanti got confused and attempted to hide herself in the shadows of the rampart. The guard led her back to the queen mother, who comforted her and said, "Tell me what is troubling you. I will help you."

Meanwhile, Bhima, Damayanti's father, had sent search parties far and wide, and one of his emissaries was at Chedi, following the trail of Damayanti through various clues. At the Chedi bazaar, having heard of a madwoman sheltered in the palace, he managed to reach the presence of the queen mother and begged, "Please summon the refugee. Let me see her face."

"I hope you will find out who she is and tell me," replied the queen. "She won't speak about herself. Last night she wanted to run away, but we brought her back. How can I let her go unless she is able to say where she wants to go?"

When Damayanti was brought before him, the man rose to his feet, made a deep bow, and said, "I've come to the end of my quest. This is our princess. I cannot be mistaken. I have known her since the day she was born."

Immediate arrangements were made to send Damayanti to Vidarbha, although she demurred and protested.

Back in her father's house, she sent emissaries far and wide. She selected special men for this mission and said, "Wherever you come upon one who may possibly be my husband, repeat this message: 'What is the measure of manliness of one

---

* In the years of his early training a prince was taught all kinds of arts, crafts, and accomplishments. Nala had gone through this training like others; he became such an expert in culinary arts, as well as in horsemanship, that the term *Nala paka*, "Nala's cooking," has passed into usage, signifying the tastiest food.

who steals away from his wife, at dead of night, with half her clothes?' and bring me his answer.''

A few days later, one of the messengers came back to report, ''At the stables of the king of Rituparna I found one who retorted, 'It was a dark night and the path was lonely and wild creatures snarled, but the man thought it was the only way to make a foolhardy woman go back to her father's house.' ''

''What made you seek out this stable boy?''

''Because I had heard of his horsemanship and his cooking.''

When the man described the stable boy's appearance, Damayanti became unhappy. Still, in order to draw him to Vidarbha, she sent out an announcement that, having despaired of finding Nala and having allowed sufficient time to elapse, she was now proposing to choose another husband by holding a Swayamwara, and all those aspiring to her hand might come forward. The announcement was directed especially to Rituparna and his entourage, and the notice was so short that none but the fastest horsemen could hope to reach Vidarbha in time for the Swayamwara, which Damayanti organized with her mother's help.

The moment Damayanti's Swayamwara became known, Rituparna ordered, ''Bring the fleetest-footed horses, we must reach Vidarbha before noon tomorrow. I want to try my luck there.''

Nala presently brought his choice of four horses, which did not look imposing in the least—they were scraggy. The king said, ''You call yourself an expert. You are sure these horses can reach Vidarbha intact, let alone in time?''

''Yes,'' replied Nala. ''Don't be discouraged by appearances.'' He explained his technique of horse-judging and assured the king, ''We will reach Vidarbha an hour before you want to be there.''

They left the capital and Rituparna realized, as the horses galloped on, what an expert his charioteer was! At one point a gust of wind suddenly blew off Rituparna's scarf. ''Oh, stop, go back and recover the scarf.''

''Impossible,'' said the charioteer. ''Not if you want to reach Vidarbha at noon. Can you guess what distance we have covered?'' And he gave a calculation of the speed of the horses by observing the foam at their mouth and the distance traversed since the scarf blew off.

Rituparna was impressed but, wishing to show off his own knowledge in another line, said, "If you rein in the horses for five seconds, I will tell you how many leaves that fig tree has on its branches, by a glance at the leaves fallen on the ground."

"That's worth stopping for even if it means missing the Swayamwara by five seconds," said Nala. "However, I'll goad the horses and make up the time." He brought the horses to a stop.

The king chose a particular tree, made his calculations in a split second, and proved correct to the nearest bud! Nala was stupefied. "Your Majesty, if you will teach me this art, I will teach Your Majesty the secrets of horsemanship."

"It's a gift I possess," said the king, "and few in the world can challenge me in any game."

From her balcony Damayanti listened to the sound of the horses' hoofs and declared, "He is coming. No one else can gallop horses in that style."

After Nala had arrived she sent a girl to the guest-house with the message, "What is the measure of manliness of one who steals away from his wife, at dead of night, with half her clothes?"—and received the same reply as before. The girl added, "Oh, Princess, it is someone . . . a horrible-looking man. . . ."

But Damayanti asked, "Is he also cooking the food for Rituparna?"

"Yes, madam, the king, it seems, will not eat any other food." .

Damayanti begged, "Please, somehow, manage to bring a sample of his preparations."

"But we are forbidden to bring edibles into the palace, madam."

"Please, somehow smuggle in a thimbleful of anything he has cooked, and I'll give you a necklace."

"It may be unsafe," the girl said.

"If it is poisoned, so much the better for me, you will be helping me either way."

The girl was gone for a while and came back with a small bowl filled with some fragrant tidbit. Even before tasting it, Damayanti cried, "It can't be anyone else."

"But madam," protested the maid, "one can't bear to look at him; don't be hasty. . . ."

Damayanti decided to see him for herself, nevertheless. This caused a commotion in the palace, but Damayanti was adamant. She merely said, "When I was lost in the forests, mountains, and strange cities, encountering strangers, and facing dangers every minute of my life, who was there to protect me? I was stoned, chased, strange men taunted me with their attentions, who protected me then? My life is dedicated to searching for my husband. If I do not succeed in finding him, let me die in the attempt. . . ."

"But this man has not the slightest resemblance to your husband!"

"I will take my chance. Nothing will happen to me." When she saw the deformed man, she burst into tears. She could hardly muster the courage to talk to him; yet the horses flew, food tasted divine. Above all, he answered the question she had phrased in code.

"How do you know about the man who deserted his wife?" she asked.

Nala taunted her for a little while. "When a bird flies off with the only garment a man possesses, what's left for him but to rip an edge off his wife's sari?"

Damayanti grew more and more bewildered until he declared, "And if the wife has thought fit to have recourse to finding a new husband for herself, when the old one is lost . . ."

"It was a last desperate measure to entice him back," she replied.

Nala chose this moment to drape over him the cloths given him by the serpent, and assumed his original form.

"You have no doubt found your husband," said Rituparna, "but I have lost a wonderful horseman."

"You will continue to be my master until I regain my kingdom," said Nala. "Teach me the purest form of gambling, and I'll play it for the last time."

"It'll be a privilege to help you. I'll stay with you and make you an adept."

After one month of intensive training, Nala sent a challenge to his brother Pushkara. "This is really the final phase of the game," he declared. "The stake this time is Damayanti."

Pushkara was tempted. He was a happy usurper, but he had always felt that his conquest would be complete only if he attained his brother's wife as well. He accepted the challenge.

The jealous gods who had wanted to punish Nala were no longer malevolent and they no longer inspired either Pushkara or the dice. Soon the usurper lost everything. Nala, strengthened by Rituparna's guidance, reduced his brother to the state of having to walk down the street in a loincloth, but at the end he relented and gave him a portion of his kingdom, advising him to turn over a new leaf.

SAVITRI

ASVAPATI WAS THE ruler of Mudra, an ideal king devoted to the happiness and welfare of his subjects and all living creatures on earth. But as with all such good men, he was childless. He devoted all his hours to praying for issue, offered rare sacrifices, and practised all kinds of austerities for eighteen years single-mindedly. The goddess Savitri, whose hymn he recited a hundred thousand times as a part of his prayer, appeared before him and conferred on him the boon of a daughter (although he prayed for a son), and in honour of the goddess she was named Savitri. She was a darling child in every way.

When she reached the age of marriage, her father had high hopes of her being courted by eligible young men, but none came forward, in spite of her beauty and accomplishments. It was not difficult to find out why. The king sent his secret-service messengers abroad to sound out the eligible princes in the neighbouring states as to why they were not coming forward to ask for Savitri's hand. The messengers came back in due course to report, "They are afraid to ask for her hand. They think that she is a goddess incarnate and cannot be asked to be a wife."

The king felt both flattered and pained. By a strange twist of circumstances the very perfections of the maiden were acting as a handicap. He asked, "Would it not have been useful to tell them that she is really human? Very well. We will remedy it."

He sent for his daughter, who was playing the *veena* in her own chambers. He told her, "My daughter, you will now go out into the world and find yourself a husband, my only condition being that he must seem as good to you as you are to me."

"How can I ever measure myself or others, Father?"

"When the time comes you will understand," he said. He

selected one of his trusted ministers and a band of courtiers to escort her during her quest. He warned them, "You will go where she goes, and you will in no way attempt to influence her mind."

She went far and wide and returned one day when the king was sitting in his court, conversing with the sage Narada, who had stopped by on one of his interstellar journeyings. When she came in, Narada asked, "Where has she been? How is it that you have not thought of finding her a husband?"

The king explained, "She has just returned from her quest. Let us hear what her luck has been."

The daughter, at her father's invitation, came forward and said, "I have found my . . ." She hesitated for half a minute before uttering the word "husband," but then she overcame her shyness and said, "I have found the man who will be my husband—not in a palace but in a hermitage hidden away in the forests from prying eyes. It was my good fortune that led my steps there. His name is Satyavan. There he is tending his aged father, who is blind."

At this stage the all-knowing sage Narada interposed, "He is the son of the king of Salwa. Through ill luck this king lost his eyesight when his son was born. An old enemy who had been waiting to attack him most cruelly chose this moment, and the king had to flee into the forest, carrying his child. I know all about it. Savitri, am I right?" Savitri felt happy when the sage added, "Your daughter has chosen a worthy husband. Satyavan is brilliant, strong, mighty, graceful, and generous, and is handsome like the twin Aswinis. But . . . Permit me to speak frankly, my child, because I see the future as I see the present and the past. His earthly existence will last for only a year more, until exactly one year from today. . . . My child, go out again and choose another person for a husband."

Tears came to Savitri's eyes. Her father trembled with apprehension. Savitri drew herself up resolutely before uttering these words: "O great sage, forgive my disobedience. I will not think of anyone else as my husband; it matters little to me how long or how short is Satyavan's life. My mind is made up. To adore someone or marry someone is an action like birth and death. It can happen only once in a lifetime and cannot be repeated or corrected at will. Satyavan alone will be my husband."

Narada was pleased. "It is spirit like hers that conquers

death,'' he said. "King, help her to join her husband. It is your duty. Love like hers mocks at death.''

After Narada left, Asvapati started out in search of the forest where the blind king lived, introduced himself, and offered his daughter to his son. The blind king said, "Life in a hermitage is strange, lonely, and hard, and unsuited to a delicate creature like Savitri."

The king cut short his talk with "Say no more. There is no alternative. She will marry Satyavan and none else."

"And Satyavan will marry her and no one else, I have known it ever since she came here. So be it. Heavens bless their union."

It turned out to be a happy marriage. Satyavan found Savitri attentive and courteous to his aged parents also, at all times observing the courtesy of restrained speech, cheerfulness, helpfulness, and all other codes of good manners prescribed for an ideal daughter-in-law. Savitri performed these tasks not as a mere duty but with all her being, because she experienced supreme joy as both wife and daughter-in-law.

However, through all the happy hours in the forest hermitage, Savitri was secretly gnawed by the thought that each moment was taking Satyavan nearer his last one. When just four days were left of Satyavan's tenure on earth, Savitri undertook a severe penance and continuously fasted for three days and nights. Her father-in-law, puzzled by the severity of her prayers, said, "Savitri, you are a princess, how can you undertake such severe penances? Let me not presume to advise you to give up your plan, let me content myself by saying, 'May your vow, whatever its nature, be fulfilled!' "

She was fatigued by the fast, but she looked unperturbed, unmoved, and firm, like a block of wood.

On the fourth day, the fateful day, she counted the hours. She performed the climax of her observance by offering oblations to the fire, prostrated herself before an assembly of elders, and took their blessings in reverent silence. Then her parents-in-law advised, "You have completed your penance now, please eat your food."

"Yes, after the sun sets," Savitri replied and noticed her husband Satyavan leaving for the forests, bearing an axe on his shoulder. She rushed up, crying, "I am coming with you."

Satyavan said, "Why? Rest here and nourish yourself; you

have put yourself through a lot of hardship the last four days. I am going deep into the forest, and the paths are rough; you can't walk so far."

Savitri said, "I am not tired after the fast. I must go with you."

"Very well," said Satyavan. "Please explain it to my parents so that they may not think that I am forcing you to go with me."

She approached her parents-in-law and said, "I wish to go into the forest with my husband. I want to watch him gather fruits and firewood. I have been here almost a year and have not seen the forest in bloom."

Her father-in-law said, "Savitri has never made any request. Let her enjoy herself."

Savitri walked through the forest, clasping her husband's hand as he explained the finer points of forest life to her. All through those hours, while watching beautiful scenes or enjoying beautiful moments, Savitri was racked with the thought that the hour of doom was approaching. She helped Satyavan gather fruits, and then he went off to cut wood. Resting, she watched him without batting an eyelid as he wielded his axe and the forest resounded with steel hitting wood.

Suddenly he dropped the axe and came to her, muttering, "I am not feeling well. My head throbs; perhaps I have exerted myself too much." She sprang to her feet, took him in her arms, and gently helped him lie down on the grass, resting his head on her lap. Gradually he seemed to fall asleep.

Hardly had he ceased to stir when she sensed a strange presence hovering about close by. She concentrated all her powers of observation and espied the formidable figure of a man with red eyes, blood-red robes, holding a noose in his hand. He stood over Satyavan and stared at his recumbent figure. On seeing him, Savitri gently laid down Satyavan's head, rose to her feet, and, saluting this presence, said, "You are not an ordinary being. You must be divine. Tell me who you are and why you are here."

"You are a rare person, Savitri. Your austerities have made you extraordinarily sensitive. I would normally not converse with any being, but I will talk to you. Good woman, I am Death. My name is Yama, as you well know. I am here because your husband's earthly time is over. It is my duty now to extract his subtle life with this noose and carry it away, leaving his gross self there on the ground for you to burn.''

Savitri asked, "How is it, my lord, that you have come yourself, when ordinarily you would only send your messengers to perform this task?"

"Because Satyavan is not an ordinary mortal; he is a distinguished one. I wanted to have the honour of calling him away in person." He extracted from Satyavan his subtle personality by means of his noose and moved off south, for in the south lies Yama's kingdom.

Savitri saw the inert body lose its gloss gradually; she laid it away in a safe place and started after Yama. Yama noticed her determination, and stopped to say, "Don't follow me into my realm. Perform the obsequies for your husband's welfare in the other world and dispose of his physical body in the proper manner."

"I cannot go where my husband is not. No other path is open to me," Savitri said, persistently following him. "We have been taught that a good married life, with discipline and self-control, is the highest form of existence. I have no other life, nor any intention of following a life of renunciation or asceticism. Married life is the highest goal attainable by me, as taught to me by my elders; and so I have nowhere to go except where my husband goes."

"You cannot follow your husband any further, but I am pleased with your outlook; ask for a boon and I shall grant it. Ask for anything except the life of this person."

Savitri promptly asked, "Please restore the sight to my father-in-law."

"It is granted. Tomorrow when he wakes up, he will see the light. Now turn back and go before you get very tired."

"I cannot feel any tiredness where my husband is," she said. "In good company one attains salvation, and therefore should one always stay where good people are found."

Yama was pleased with this sentiment also and said, "Ask for a second boon, my dear girl, anything except the life of Satyavan."

"Please restore to my father-in-law his kingdom, which he lost years ago."

"I gladly grant it. Now go back before you feel fatigued."

"I have often speculated on what is a good life. To my way

of thinking it seems to consist in the eradication of malice in thought, word, and deed, and in positive, active benevolence and in giving without acquisitiveness. Correct me, O Yama, if I am wrong. I want to learn the verities from you. Good men make no distinction between friends and enemies while exercising mercy or kindness.''

Yama was again pleased with her words and said,''Your words and sentiments have again moved me. Ask for another boon, excepting the life of this husband of yours.''

Savitri said, ''It has long been a secret sorrow for my father that no son was born to him. Please grant him the birth of a hundred sons.''

''He shall have a hundred sons,'' said Yama. ''Now, go back, you have come a long way.''

Ignoring the advice, Savitri still followed him, explaining, ''While I follow my husband there can be no such thing as distance or fatigue. All right, if you insist, I will stay behind, but will raise my voice so that you may hear my words as you go. You are the son of the sun god, and the wise call you appropriately Vaivaswat. The subjects of your kingdom enjoy absolute, unblemished justice, and that is the reason why you are called king of dharma.* In the company of good people one enjoys a sense of confidence and security, which is not experienced even in one's own company. Therefore, anyone, naturally, prefers to remain in the company of the good.''

Yama was visibly moved by this speech of hers. ''I am one dreaded, and no one speaks such words as you have just spoken. I am moved by your words. You may ask for a fourth boon, excepting the life of this man.''

''Then grant that a hundred sons be born to me.''

''Gentle lady, you will have a hundred sons, valiant and

---

* Dharma may be defined broadly as the ultimate code in thought, word, and deed for each individual—that which alone is right for him. The word also carries the meaning of duty, as well as the code, at all levels. Evil arises when one deviates from the path of dharma. All stories and parables taken together illustrate the eternal importance of dharma. Although it varies from one individual to the next, according to birth and mental equipment, there is a dharma for everyone, whether he be a king or a Chandala, and he must live according to it.

strong, to make you happy. Now you must turn back, you have come too far.''

"The company of good people is never fruitless," began Savitri and expounded the worth of the company of the good, and went on to explain rather intricately how the sun in its orbit moved and the earth sustained life as a direct result of the goodness of the good people.

Yama was again impressed with this philosophy. "When you speak, my steps lag in order that I may listen to you and get the full import of your words; I revere you, O lady, for your understanding of righteousness. Ask of me a unique boon, O chaste one.''

"My chastity is unassailable. If your granting of the boon of a hundred sons is to be fulfilled, you have to give me back my husband. You cannot take away my husband and yet leave me with the boon of a hundred sons.''

"Yes, I recognize that," said Yama and loosened the noose that held the life of Satyavan in his hands. He blessed Savitri and her husband with longevity and went forward alone, for the first time in his career yielding back a life.

Savitri hastened back to the spot where Satyavan's body had been laid. She lifted him gently onto her lap and revived him. He opened his eyes, murmuring, "I have slept too long. How patient you have been! Why did you not wake me? I felt someone else was nearby, or was it a dream? I was going somewhere. . . . Tell me, have I been here all along?''

Savitri said, "The night is far advanced. It is dark and your parents will be anxious. Let us go back to the hermitage, if you are able to walk.''

"Oh, I feel quite refreshed. Let us go back.''

At the hermitage a crowd had gathered because the old king was worrying about his son and daughter-in-law, who had not returned home. They crowded around the couple as they entered the precincts of the hermitage and demanded, "Where were you, out so late?''

Savitri replied, "We were on a far-off expedition and are happy to be back.''

THE MISPAIRED ANKLET

After the chronicles of the activities of gods ranging through millennia and acted out on a stage of cosmic proportions, we now come to a tale whose events occur within a comparatively human compass, the happenings dating no further back than the second century A.D. This story has its beginning in Puhar, capital of one of the southern Indian kingdoms mentioned by Ptolemy in that century.

PUHAR WAS A flourishing seacoast town where the river Cauvery joined the sea. When this story begins, the marriage of Kovalan, the hero of this tale, with Kannagi was being celebrated, with the whole town rejoicing and feasting, every citizen having been invited by an announcer riding on an elephant up and down the streets of the city. Kovalan and Kannagi lived a happy married life in their comfortable home until the day when Madhavi, a young *danseuse*, gave her first dance recital before the king.

In recognition of her talent the king presented her with a garland of green leaves and one thousand and eight pieces of gold. According to custom, Madhavi could now select a lover for herself. She passed the garland to a hunchbacked woman who stood in the city square, where wealthy citizens passed or congregated, and announced, "This garland is worth one thousand and eight pieces of gold. Whoever buys it also becomes the husband of the most accomplished dancer honoured by our king." Kovalan became a ready customer for this garland, and gained admission to Madhavi's bridal chamber and forgot all his problems and responsibilities in life. When he was not making love to her, he spent the time listening to the music of her steps.

The city was celebrating Indra's festival. There were music, dancing, and entertainment everywhere; special prayers were said in the temples; people moved hither and thither in gay dress, and the air throbbed with speech and laughter. Kovalan and Madhavi went about together and enjoyed the festivities. At the end of the day, Madhavi went home, freshened her body with a bath in a cool, scented fountain, put on a new set of ornaments and dress, and in Kovalan's company passed again through the illuminated city to the seashore, which twinkled with lamps hoisted on poles around groups of merrymakers and gaily lighted ships anchored off shore. Madhavi had her own corner on the beach, with canopy and screens set up for privacy, away from the tumult of the waves and the din of the crowds. When they had settled down, Madhavi took her lute out of its silken cover and tuned it. Kovalan took it from her, casually ran his fingers over the strings, and burst into a song in praise of the river and the sea and then addressed to a beauty tormenting a lover with her slender waist and weighty breasts, "who walks like a swan in the shade of *punnai* trees, where the waves break on the shore."

"O foolish swan, do not go near her, your gait cannot rival hers," another song said. "Your father kills the living things of the sea by catching them in the meshes of his net. You kill living things by catching them in the net of your long eyes."

"She is a goddess who dwells there in the sweet-smelling groves of flowers," ran another. "Had I known of the existence of this goddess, I would not have come here at all."

Madhavi pretended to appreciate the songs, gently took the lute from his hands, and began a song of a lovelorn girl pining for her vanished lover. "Through the swamps, fenced by the park . . . someone came and stood before us, saying, 'Make me pleased!' and we could not take our eyes off him."

"Seeing the swan playing with its mate, a godlike one stood looking on all yesterday. He would not leave our minds, even as the gold-tinted moss cannot leave our body. . . . O crane, come not near our park, for you will not speak of my present lovesickness to my lord of the sea-tract. Do not approach our park. . . .''*

---

* The songs are quoted from V. R. R. Dikshitar's translation of

Kovalan muttered, "I merely sang a good composition, but she has her mind on someone else who inspires her." He withdrew his hands from Madhavi's, saying, "The day has come to a close, let us stir ourselves." She did not get up. But he hurried home.

After he was gone, Madhavi got into her chariot and went home. She dressed and decorated herself afresh and moved to the upper terrace and sang more songs, danced, and fell into a languor. Thereafter she wove a garland with several flowers, and, taking the pale inner petal of the screw-pine, etched a message of love on its smooth surface: "This moon, who has risen with the love-anguish . . . should kill the poor lonely ones with his sharp darts. . . . Please understand this." She called one of her maids and sent her off with this message to Kovalan; she was to repeat the message orally, and then give him the garland wherein he would see it written.

The maid came back to say that Kovalan had rejected the message and the garland. Madhavi felt unhappy and sighed, "If he does not come tonight, he is certain to come tomorrow morning," and spent a sleepless night.

Meanwhile Kovalan said to his wife Kannagi, "We must leave this town."

Kannagi knew that Kovalan's funds were fast dwindling, through his buying presents and fineries for Madhavi. Kannagi had parted with her ornaments one after another in order that he might find the money for spending. She had been complaisant and unquestioning. She replied now, "I have still a pair of anklets," leaving unexpressed the thought, "which you may pawn to buy presents for Madhavi."

But he said, receiving the anklets, "This very night we will slip out of this place, go to Madurai, and start a new life in that city with the little money we may get by selling these. I will not be seen by my parents until I have redeemed my integrity. One becomes defiled to the very core through association with low, mercenary women, and by the time one learns the truth of the matter one is too far gone in damnation. This is no occasion for leave-taking. Let us slip away quietly."

At dead of night they packed their clothes in a small bundle

the "Epic of the Anklet," *Silappadhikaram*, published by the Oxford University Press (1939).

that could be slung over the shoulder, shut their house, and started out. The festive crowd had dissipated out of sight and all the noise of merriment had died down. They passed along the south bank of the river, which was deserted; on the highway they became merged with groups of minstrels and mendicants and wandering scholars and saints, travelling in the same direction, and forgot their own troubles listening to their talk. "We missed all this staying at home," Kovalan said.

They reached the ferry and crossed over to the north bank of the river and ultimately came to a town called Uriyur. Kovalan left his wife in a rest house and sought a tank for his ablutions. As he stood waist-deep in the water, scrubbing himself, a stranger accosted him and said, "I want to speak to you."

"Who are you?" asked Kovalan. .

"My friend, don't you recognize me? I am from Puhar. I have worn out the soles of my feet tracking you, inquiring everywhere, 'Have you seen such-and-such'?"

"Why did you follow me?" asked Kovalan sharply.

"Madhavi has sent me, she is dying of grief at the separation. She begs a million pardons of you for any pain she may have caused. She begs you to return home—begs your forgiveness for her mistakes."

Kovalan brooded for a moment and said, "Go back."

"I saw your parents too, and they are heartbroken."

"Tell them that I'll seek my fortune and return to them as a worthy son some day. I have been living in a sort of fantasy all along; now I see the realities. Tell Madhavi that I have no grudge against her, but I have definitely turned my back on the past."

When Kovalan returned to his wife, they were ready for the road again. He did not mention his encounter with the messenger from Puhar, for fear of disturbing Kannagi's mind. They trudged along and finally reached the bank of the Vaigai, which skirted the boundary of Madurai, the capital of Pandyan kingdom. They viewed the soaring temple tower and the mansions of Madurai city and felt happy and relieved that they had reached the end of their quest. Kovalan stood on the edge of the river, propitiated the river god, crossed it, and reached the city boundary.

In the city the couple were received into a colony of cattle-tenders. They were lodged in a cottage, surrounded by a green hedge, a cool inner courtyard and walls splashed with red mud, and a kitchen stocked with rice, vegetables, buttermilk, jack fruit, cucumbers, pomegranates, and mangoes. Kannagi felt happy to be running a home again after weeks of tramplike existence. She washed the floor of the house. When food was ready Kannagi spread a grass mat for her husband to sit on, and a green plantain leaf for him to dine on. After he was fed, she gave him betel nuts and leaves to chew.

With his lips red with betel juice, Kovalan sat back and said, "You have been forbearing; how your parents would grieve if they knew of the hardship you have gone through." He became regretful at the thought of his misdeeds. "I have wasted my life in the society of an easy-going woman and scandalmongers, wasted my time talking loudly and guffawing at bawdy jokes."

Kannagi said, "Why speak of the past again and again? I was unhappy, no doubt, but no one could have guessed how I felt in those days. Your parents were kind and considerate."

In the end he said, "I will now take one of your anklets to the city, sell it, and come back with money, and then we will start a new life. Who knows? We may return home soon with riches and re-establish ourselves honourably." He embraced her before leaving, averting his eyes to conceal his tears; he felt depressed at having to leave her alone in the midst of strangers. As he briskly walked out, he was so preoccupied that he failed to notice a humped bull in front of him, indicating a bad omen.

He passed through various parts of the city. At the bazaar he noticed walking past him an imposing man in a brocade coat, flourishing a pair of pincers to indicate that he was a master goldsmith, followed by a company of minor goldsmiths. At the sight of him Kovalan thought, "This must be the famous goldsmith of the Pandyan court. I am fortunate to come across him so easily."

He approached him and said, "You are the prince of goldsmiths, I presume. Your fame is known even in Puhar." The goldsmith smiled patronizingly.

Kovalan now asked, "May I trouble you to appraise for me a piece of jewellery, an anklet fit for the queen's feet?"

The goldsmith said pompously, "I'm generally concerned with the making of crowns and sceptres for our kings, but I am not totally ignorant of feminine adornments."

Whereupon Kovalan produced the anklet. The goldsmith examined it with minute care and delight and declared enthusiastically, "This is not an anklet that an ordinary woman could aspire to, it is fit only for our queen. Let me speak to her and come back. Stay in that hut. Don't go away, I will be back soon."

The king and the queen had had a lovers' quarrel recently. The queen had left his company on the pretext of a headache. The king transacted some business with his councillors and left for the queen's chambers at the earliest possible moment in order to pacify her.

As he approached the portals of the queen's chamber the goldsmith crossed his path and after formal courtesies of address said, "Forgive my interrupting Your Majesty, but the matter is urgent. One of the queen's anklets has been missing. I have managed to catch the thief and have shut him in my humble hut. He is a subtle thief who does not operate with daggers and crowbars but with black magic."

It was a fateful moment, and as the king was in a hurry to meet his wife, he summoned the city watchman and ordered, "If you find the anklet in the possession of the thief, execute him and fetch the anklet." He was in a hurry, and the fates were gearing their engines for a tragedy, so the king spoke thoughtlessly, although normally he would have said, "Bring the thief before me." He uttered the sentence of death without giving the matter thought, and hurried on to the queen's apartment.

The goldsmith returned with a company of men and said to Kovalan, "These men have come to examine the anklet at the command of our sovereign."

Kovalan, pleased that he was coming so near a transaction, messed about with his bag again while the goldsmith explained to the executioners the minute details of the anklet about to be displayed. "It has workmanship of the highest kind; grooves at the neck; a slight depression with silver garlands entwining, and two leaves. It has a peculiar polish at the stem that has given it the facet of a crystal, reflecting off a diamond-shaped cutting."

As he described it further, Kovalan's eyes shone with pleasure; he took it as a recommendation from the goldsmith and remarked, "What an observant eye you have, you great artist in gold!"

"True, true," said the crafty goldsmith. "Otherwise how could I have progressed in my profession? I am known for my searching eye, which can find out a lot of things.'' He glanced at his companions and smiled wryly.

When the anklet was produced, the chief executioner took it in his hand and examined it in detail. ''Yes, it is the same anklet that you have described,'' he said.

''Now let the man pay the price accordingly,'' said the goldsmith; and the men stepped forward, encircling Kovalan.

Kovalan looked about in bewilderment. More bewilderment when the chief cried, ''This man does not look like a thief.''

''A thief who has mastered his art will look least like one,'' said the goldsmith. ''The science of thieving mentions eight methods that may be employed by an expert thief: drugs, illusion, control of mischievous spirits, and so forth; he can pick up your valuables and walk right into your presence while you watch him helplessly; he can make himself invisible, he can look like a good and saintly one and extract worship from you. . . .'' The goldsmith expatiated on this theme.

Kovalan listened to it and said, ''Let us come to a decision; if you noble men approve of this piece of jewellery—''

''Spend no more time,'' said the goldsmith. ''Finish your errand and let us go back.''

A young man with a lance said, ''Do you know what once happened when I drew my sword—it jumped into the thief's hand and suddenly I found myself at his mercy. Some are so crafty and deft! Our king's order must be carried out.''

''No more talk,'' said a drunken man in their midst, and he hurled his scimitar at Kovalan, practically cutting him in two.

Blood flowed from the fallen man. The goldsmith and executioners withdrew. The goldsmith looked back as if gratified that he had had divine assistance in his crime. He had stolen the queen's anklet earlier in the day and felt it a peculiar good fortune that he should have come across someone to take on that crime with appropriate evidence.

At the cowherd's colony, a matron said to her daughter, ''The milk in the pot has not curdled; tears dim the eyes of our cattle; the butter in the store is all hardened, lambs are dull, cows shudder and bellow, and their bell ropes have snapped. What calamity has befallen whom?'' They thought it over and pronounced the usual remedy for warding off evil and turning the mind to cheerful subjects. ''We shall dance the Kuruvai, for our guest, for our beautiful guest watching us.'' An elaborate dance was organized in their midst.

Kannagi felt worried. Why was her husband gone so long? It was diverting to watch her hosts sing and dance as they depicted episodes from the life of the god Krishna, who was the patron god of milkmaids.

After the dance the matron went to bathe in the river, heard rumours about Kovalan, and hurried back home. Kannagi cried at the sight of her, ''Friend, why won't you speak? Where is my husband? Every particle of air in my lungs seems fevered. I can hardly breathe. Where is my husband? I feel restless. Help me, are people saying anything about him? Don't hide anything from me.''

''They said he was a thief who had stolen the royal anklet, and executed him,'' said the matron.

Kannagi fell in a faint, recovered, and raved against the fates, the country, and the king. ''The Pandyan king, reputed to hold a righteous sceptre, has committed injustice. My husband a thief!'' She shouted at the top of her voice and called up all the women and the girls who had been dancing and addressed them. ''Could my husband be a thief, thieving my own anklet! O sun god, you are witness to all things of this world. Is my husband a thief? Answer!'' she cried commandingly.

Kannagi gathered herself, her stature seemed to swell; her eyes blazed with anger. She cried, ''Here is my anklet, the widowed one. They have killed my husband, unable to pay the price for the one he had with him. Now who is the real thief?''

Followed by a sympathizing crowd, Kannagi strode through the streets of the city with authority in her gait and fire in her speech and looks. People trembled at the sight of her. Some persons led her to where her husband's body lay; and the sun (as the poet who composed this tale explains) set behind the hills, in order to draw a curtain over the sad spectacle.

Night came on. Kannagi mourned. ''Is it right that you should be lying there in that bloody pool while I . . . while I . . . Are there no women in this city whose purity could prevent such an injustice? Are there no good people in this country or women of purity and devotion to their husbands? How can such an injustice happen where there are good men and good women? Has God forsaken this town?''

While she lamented thus, hugging the inert body of her

husband, strange things seemed to happen. She thought that she saw the body stir and her husband stand up and wipe the tears from her face and mutter, "Stay here," and go heavenward.

Kannagi cried, "What is happening? Is it some mischievous spirit that is deceiving me? Where can I find the truth of all this?" She left the spot and ran towards the palace, saying again and again, "I must get an explanation from the cruel king himself. . . ."

The king was in the company of his wife. The bell at the gate tolled furiously. Over the sounding of the bell Kannagi screamed "Go and wake your king who has put his conscience to sleep, whose heart has become granite, and tell him that a wretched woman bearing a widowed anklet is at his gate."

The gatekeepers were cowed by the appearance of the woman and ran to the king's presence and announced, "Your Majesty, a woman of frightening aspect seeks audience. Is she Kali, the Goddess of Destruction? Is she . . . ?"

"Let her in," commanded the king. When she was brought in, he asked, "Who are you? What do you want here?"

"You have murdered my husband. We came from Puhar only to seek our fortune here."

"Oh, my most revered sister, is it not my duty to execute a thief?"

"My anklet has been stolen," added the queen. "And it was found with your husband, who was trying to sell it."

"Here is another one, take it also," said Kannagi. "All the anklets in the world are yours, O queen, spouse of the embodiment of justice." She tossed her anklet in the queen's lap.

The queen, looking at it, said, "This also looks like mine, but how is it there are three anklets now? I had only two."

"Does a thief take away or add? Do you know?" asked Kannagi with bitter laughter. "What you are wearing on your left anklet is not yours, it belongs to the thief who lies in bloody dust."

The king seemed to lose in a moment his regality, and the queen was panic-stricken. "My evil dream of last night—" she began.

Kannagi asked, "Do you at least know what it is inside that rattles and tinkles when your anklet is shaken?"

The queen took time to understand the purport of the question and said, "Pearls, yes . . . Pearls inside."

"Break open my anklet, which is on your left foot, and see what is in it."

The queen handed her the anklet without a word. Kannagi broke it open, and sparkling gems spilled out of it.

The king faltered at the sight. "What king am I to allow a goldsmith to sway my judgment?" He tottered and fell from his seat, and the queen broke into a loud lamentation.

Kannagi watched the scene coldly and strode out of the palace, loudly shouting the virtue of her town Puhar and all the good things that had happened there since she knew it, in contrast to this city where evil flourished. She walked round the city thrice with unceasing laments, declaring, "If I am a chaste woman, I shall not let this city flourish." Then she tore her robes, twisted off her left breast, and flung it over the city. Immediately the god of fire, in the shape of a Brahmin of blue complexion, appeared before her and asked, "I will, of course, destroy this city as you command, but is there anyone you would spare?"

"Spare only the innocent, the good, the learned, the infirm, and the children, and all dumb creatures."

The city was enveloped in flames immediately. Those who could escape from the city poured out of its gates. The rest perished. The presiding deities of the town left. Kannagi roamed through its streets and alleys restlessly, bewildered and in a state of delirium.

The presiding deity of the city, with her head decorated with a crescent and her matted locks, white radiant face, half of her body dark blue and the other half golden, with a golden lotus in her left hand and a sword in her right, unwilling to face the sorrow-stricken wife, approached her softly from behind and murmured gently, "Blessed lady, listen to my words. I understand your suffering. I see the havoc that your rage has wrought on our city. Please listen to my words for a moment. The king has never committed any injustice in his life; he comes of a long line of righteous rulers who have observed strictly the laws of justice and humanity. But what has happened to your husband is unparalleled and is a result of fate. Listen, fair lady, to the history of his previous life. Your husband, Kovalan, in his previous birth was called Bharata and in the service of his monarch caught hold of an innocent trader who was selling his merchandise in the streets of Sangama and denounced him as a spy and had him executed. The trader's wife was grief-sticken and wandered as a madwoman for fourteen days, raving and cursing, until she climbed the hill and jumped off a cliff, uttering her curse on the man responsible for her husband's death. As a result of it, now you have to go through this agony. You will have redemption in fourteen days.''

This was consoling, and as Kannagi's heart softened with understanding, the fire in the city abated gradually. She passed the fourteen days wandering and waiting. She walked along the river's edge and reached the northern mountain tracts. A group of country girls while bathing and sporting on the mountain roads saw an extraordinary being who had only one breast appear before them. Her presence was electrifying, and the women worshipped her at first sight. Presently they saw her husband come to her in spirit form and take her heavenward.

The spot became sacred as that of the godly wife. A latter-day king built a temple on the spot and installed the image of Kannagi in it for public worship. The image was carved out of a slab of stone hewn from the Himalayas and bathed in the water of the Ganges, and it came to be known as Pattini Devi—meaning ''the wife who became a goddess.''

SHAKUNTALA

SHAKUNTA MEANS "BIRDS," and Shakuntala meant one who was brought up by the birds in a forest. As an infant, Shakuntala had been abandoned by her parents. She was left on a bed of leaves, beside the Malini River, and all the birds protected her. After some time the protective birds waited upon the sage Kanva, whose hermitage was nearby, on the banks of Malini, and begged him to give the child shelter. He was a man of compassion, and although he was leading an ascetic life he adopted the child and brought her up amidst birds, butterflies, trees, and animals. In these tranquil surroundings even wild animals were at peace with each other and with all creatures.

To understand how Shakuntala came to find herself thus abandoned we must delve into an earlier episode.

Viswamitra, that great purposeful sage, once sat in a rigorous penance. Indra, the chief of the gods, endowed with limitless power, splendour, and riches, trembled whenever anyone meditated intensely, ever afraid that he might be displaced. As a measure of self-preservation, he always devised distractions for anyone in meditation. Now he called upon Menaka, the most accomplished beauty in his world, and told her, "Go down to the earth and tempt that man Viswamitra out of his meditation. Otherwise the fire of his concentration will soon scorch us."

Menaka was aware of her own potency, but she was hesitant. "How can I go before that sage? Have you forgotten how powerful he is? How many thousand years he prayed to rival the ancient Vasishta himself, how he could create a river, if one was needed for his wash; how he could force it to turn back and flow against its normal course if he so chose, how he created a world for Trisanku, with stars and solar system all his own, in order to challenge the Creator himself?''

''But the world of Trisanku remained in mid-air and upside down,'' sneered Indra.

''At the time he performed the feat, you were in a panic,'' Menaka reminded him.

''Why go into all that now?'' asked Indra.

''Because it is important to remember with whom one has to deal now,'' replied Menaka. ''He may curse me and reduce me to ashes if he finds that I am attempting to disturb his meditation,'' she wailed.

''Not if you employ your gifts properly,'' Indra said, and finally promised, ''I will ask the god of love and his minions to help you. Have no fear.''

''Please also send the god of wind to help me,'' said Menaka. Thus fully armed, she set out on her mission.

She went down to the earth, where the sage had been performing his penance for thousands of years, and awakened him by the sound of her anklets. Vayu, the god of wind, lent his cooperation by hitting her suddenly in a gust; then he loosened and disarrayed the clothes off her person and carried them away in a lump out of sight, reducing Menaka to the necessity of chasing her clothes desperately, stark naked, just as Viswamitra opened his eyes.

Vayu blew the cool breeze of spring that induced languor and charged the air with the teasing fragrance of rare flowers. Manmata, the god of love, found this an opportune moment and poised his shafts. Viswamitra came fully out of his trance and approached Menaka with the intent of helping her retrieve her clothes, and enjoyed her company for a thousand years, completely indifferent to every other purpose in life.

A child was born of this union. It was said that the child came into the world fitted with every adornment and all nature sang a symphony of joy at her birth.

Nature may have expressed happiness at her birth, but not her father. When Menaka presented him with the baby, he rejected it outright. ''Go away, woman, you and your baby. I am not here to tend a bawling infant, begone, both of you, I have better things to do. Take that child away with you.''

Menaka said, ''I have been away from my own world too long,'' deposited the child on the bank of the Malini, and vanished. And Viswamitra resumed his austerities without wasting further time in pleasure or regret.

One morning some years later a king, Dushyanta, set out from his capital with a retinue of a thousand hunters carrying all kinds of weapons and cudgels. When the army of hunters had marched through the streets of the capital earlier in the day it was watched by all the women standing on terraces and balconies. All of them commented, "How divine-looking the king is!" By afternoon the hunters had maimed and destroyed hundreds of wild animals and were lunching in groups on meat roasted over the fire.

The king, leaving those who wanted rest, went forward with a small band. While chasing a deer, he was led to Kanva's *ashram* in the depths of the forest. "No animal in this place can be attacked. This is a sanctuary," someone reminded him.

"I'll go in and pay my respects to the hermit who lives here," said the king. The place was serene, and groups of scholars sat under tall trees, absorbed in their studies; novices were chanting music or verse, and the smoke of the holy fire rose in the air on the banks of the Malini. "It may disturb the hermit if all this army turns up here, and he may mistake our intentions," said the king, ordering his followers to stop at a distance; he removed his badges and decorations and entered the gate of the *ashram* itself in the guise of a commoner.

He stood at the gate of the hermitage and called, "Who is there?" in an authoritative voice. Shakuntala, tending the plants in another part of the hermitage, came forward. She felt drawn to him.

He looked at her with rapture in his eyes, only hoping that she would not turn back and send someone else to speak with him. But she advanced towards him and asked, "You want to see my father? He is away. Come in and rest." She went into the hermitage and brought out a pail of water and a tray of fruits, and placed them before him.

After refreshing himself, he did not leave but stayed on, talking, and before long he proposed that they should be married.

Shakuntala said, "At no stage can a woman act independently—as a child she is guided by her father, as a wife by her husband, in old age by her son. You must seek my father's permission before you speak to me."

"Father! May I know how this sage has come to have a

daughter, being the most confirmed celibate?'' He wished to linger on and talk to her, without letting the conversation lag. She explained her birth and adoption by the sage.

At the end of her narration Dushyanta declared his love for her. ''At first sight I loved you and felt that you must be a princess, and no less than that. I now know you are a princess and fit to be my wife, being the daughter of Viswamitra, who was once a king.'' And he proposed that they marry then and there.

Shakuntala replied, ''My father will have to give me away. He is a man with great spiritual powers, and if his anger is roused he can reduce the whole world to ashes.''

''I am doing nothing that should anger him. I am a king wanting to marry you, that is all. It is perfectly legitimate for a loving couple to marry according to Gandharva rites, whereby, with the gods as witnesses, the bride can give herself away. It is the most sacred form of marriage.''

Shakuntala pondered over this and said, ''Even if it be a Gandharva marriage, I would like certain formalities to be observed, so that if a child is born of the marriage it should be absolutely free from all blemish. I attach great value to sacred rites. Another condition—if a son is born to us, you must declare him to be the heir to your throne.''

The king agreed and sent one of his followers to fetch a priest who was in his retinue. With the priest's help a sacred fire was lit, holy verses were chanted, and the couple clasped each other's hands over the fire and became husband and wife, their union sealed for all eternity.

Later the king returned to his company. Shakuntala was distraught at this parting. But he said, ''I cannot take you away in the absence of your revered father. But I will send a decorated chariot for you, and palanquins for your maids and attendants, and elephants and footmen and all the honours due to a queen moving to her own palace, and then we shall never be separated.'' She was comforted and watched him go, and felt lonely when the darkness and silence of the forest came on.

When the sage Kanva returned to the hermitage, Shakuntala attended him as usual, washed his feet, and set his prayer mat and trays of flowers. But she felt uneasy in his presence. He noticed this and asked, ''What is this change I notice in you today?''

She stood before him shyly and explained how she had become a wife and perhaps a mother-to-be. He blessed her. "May you be a happy queen, begetting a son who will protect this land and preserve its glory."

On the day following the departure of the king, Shakuntala dressed herself, ready to leave the moment the chariot should arrive. But the noon passed, the evening came, and still there was no sign of anyone from the city.

She asked her father, "How far is the capital from here?" Kanva understood the purport of her question and said something comforting to her mind. She went on calculating. "He must have reached the palace late at night, perhaps after a tiring day, must have gone straight to bed, forgetting to tell the palanquin bearers and others that they should be here."

Shakuntala reclined in the shade of a tree and involved her mind in deep and intricate calculations of time and distance: how long the king was going to sleep before giving his orders to the charioteer and others, who, if they didn't dawdle on the way, should arrive at sunset; if they arrived so late her father would let her go only on the following morning; and if they started at dawn . . . She was lost in speculations. But no sign of any message or messenger from the city.

Each day it became more unbearable. She could not understand why. Was the king faced with a sudden war or revolt, or was he suddenly sick? She was full of anxiety. Day by day she hoped, straining her ears for the chorus of palanquin bearers and the sound of chariot wheels. She began to lose the lustre in her face, wasted away in secret anxiety and bewilderment.

At the proper time a son was born to her, when flowers showered from the heavens, and god Indra spoke aloud his blessing: "Shakuntala, your son will be the greatest emperor on earth." When he was six years of age, this child could handle with ease all the wild animals of the forest, and the members of the hermitage watched him with wonder and named him Sarvadaman, Tamer of All Creatures. But when he came of an age to ask about his father, Shakuntala felt anguished.

Kanva noticed the declining spirits of Shakuntala and said one day, "I know what is troubling you, my child. Tomorrow is an auspicious day. I have arranged for a band of my disciples to escort you to the capital. Go and join your husband, and may you always be blessed."

He clasped his grandson in his arms and said, "You will go with your mother. A new life opens before you; and you will leave behind all your pranks with animals and birds and the climbing of trees, and live in a palace worthy of your status as the crown prince. When you become king, give a thought to your grandfather. . . ."

At this the little fellow fell at his feet and cried, "You are my father, you are my mother, and you are everything to me. I know none else. Let my mother go to the palace if she desires so, but I will stay with you here. I do not want to live in a palace."

The sage was moved by this innocent attachment, and tears came to his eyes. He called his disciples who were to escort Shakuntala and said to them, "Shakuntala was born in the forest and grew up here in my hermitage, she knows nothing of the world. Take her and her son up to the capital at the confluence of the Ganges and the Jumna. You don't have to go into the palace yourselves; she and her son can go forward on their own right into the palace. . . ."

After a painful parting, the party started out, and, crossing rivers, forests, and hills, they reached the capital of the king. The sages took leave of Shakuntala at the confluence of the rivers. "It is forbidden for us ascetics to step into the city, and so we'll turn back, if you do not mind." And Shakuntala with her son went towards the palace all alone, bewildered by the city, its buildings, shops, and crowds.

The king was in his seat in the assembly hall, surrounded by petitioners, visitors, courtiers, and ministers, when Shakuntala arrived. She was overwhelmed by the grandeur of Dushyanta's surroundings and for a moment had a misgiving whether this was the man who had held her in his arms at the *ashram* or someone else.

Shakuntala whispered to the child, "Make obeisance to the king your father."

She felt weak and clung to a pillar as she cried, "We seek your grace, O king, be good to us. . . ."

The king looked at her and asked, "Good lady, explain the object of your visit. I will help you, the more so since I notice you are a mother with a child to support."

Shakuntala said point-blank, "This is your son, born to us. You promised that evening that you would crown him the prince.

Now the time has come. Remember Kanva's hermitage, where you married me."

"I do not remember ever meeting you, good lady. I do not understand what you are trying to say now."

Shakuntala was overcome with anger. She said, "Why do you speak like a rustic, saying, 'I do not know'? You do know, and your heart knows, and your soul witnesses everything. The gods know. Why don't you observe this boy—his gait, appearance, colour, limbs—every inch a replica of the great sovereign occupying that throne? . . . Don't reject your son. He has come from afar to be received by his father. Don't break his spirit. You came that noon into my father's hermitage, and I was a virgin until you took me in your arms. Did you not say that we were married according to Gandharva rites? Where is that priest whom you brought along with you that day? I have come to you for refuge. Don't be false to yourself. All right, cast me out if you choose, but your son you must accept."

The king said, "You are a lowly woman come with a false claim. I do not know you at all. Begone. Go where you please, but don't ever come here."

"My birth is not lowly. It is superior to yours who are false. I am the daughter of Menaka." And she explained her history.

"Oh, I do not doubt that you are! You have inherited and learnt much from that celestial courtesan; but your speech, actions, and aims are unworthy of the sage whom you mention as your father. However, we have no time to talk to you. You may ask for gifts and take them away. You may take what you like. But don't ever again mention your stories."

Shakuntala said, "King, you hurt me. You talk like a licentious, irresponsible man. Never mind, if in the depth of your being you cannot believe me, I will go away. I only speak what I have lived through, but there is no witness to it. I will go away. But this child . . ." She looked pathetically at her son, in whom she read all the childish hope and puzzlement, and cursed herself for being so helpless. "I have no witness," she cried to the stunned assembly. The king fidgeted in his seat. No one dared to say anything.

Into this grim silence a voice from heaven cried, "O good king, let her not endure this trial any more. She spoke the truth, and this is your son, accept him." At these words flowers were showered on the assembly. The voice further said, "He shall be called Bharata,* and from him will arise and spread fresh fame for the entire line of kings."

This transformed the whole situation. The king at once rose in his seat and addressed the suffering lady. "Welcome, my wife, welcome, my son." All problems were now solved. He explained with his arms about his wife and son, "I had to pretend to forgetfulness because I wanted this august assembly to understand fully the whole episode and its background! I did not want them to think that someone had come in and was making a claim and that I had accepted her because she was attractive. I wanted my wife, the queen, to speak for herself fully and explain." A rather lame excuse for his grave lapse and rudeness, but Shakuntala rose to the occasion and apologized for her speech. In due course Dushyanta, like all good rulers, handed over the kingdom to his son and, accompanied by his wife, sought the seclusion of a hermitage in the forests.

This story as narrated above is basically true to the source in *Mahabharata*. Taking that as an outline, Kalidasa, in the fifth century A.D., (very much as Shakespeare utilized Plutarch's *Lives*), wrote his famous poetic play *Abhijnana Shakuntalam. Abhijnana* means "signet" or "token"; the episode turns on a token and lapse of memory. *Abhijnana Shakuntalam* may be called the earliest story written around the theme of forgetfulness.

In Kalidasa's version the whole near-tragedy arises from a curse uttered by that ill-tempered, sharp-tongued sage Durvasa, who had come to the hermitage of Kanva on a certain day and found Shakuntala preoccupied with thoughts of Dushyanta, who had just left her. The arrival of this august visitor passed unnoticed by her. The sage shouted his curse, "Whoever is the object of your thoughts now will forget you."

His utterance was loud enough to shock Shakuntala's companions Priyamvada and Anasuya, who were nearby, and who ran after the departing sage with apologies on behalf of Shakuntala. But Shakuntala herself heard nothing and saw no one, her mental state being one of the utmost confusion. She had just given herself in marriage to Dushyanta on her own responsibility, and

---

* Bharata is said to be the founder of India, which is also called "Bharat" in Sanskrit.

the king had parted from her, promising to take her home within three days. Her father was away, she had married without his sanction, and she felt guilty and very lonely after the departure of the king. In this state of mind she overlooked the arrival of the august visitor. She was totally unaware of the curse as well as of the mitigation the angry sage pronounced on the appeal of Shakuntala's companions: "The man's memory will revive when he sees a memento."

After waiting for a few months, with pregnancy advancing, Shakuntala starts off for the city with escorts from the *ashram*. The escorts take her into the presence of the king and explain the object of their visit. The king shows concern for the girl, but has no recollection of ever meeting her. At a critical moment of their effort to revive his memory Shakuntala dramatically tries to flourish the signet ring that was given her by Dushyanta after their secret marriage.

SHAKUNTALA *(searching her finger)*: Alas! Where is the ring?

GAUTAMAI *(one of her escorts)*: Perhaps it slipped off when you dipped your fingers in that river.

KING: Ah, ready-witted women!

SHAKUNTALA: The fates are playing a prank. Let me explain.

KING: Yes, yes, I am all attention. What next?

SHAKUNTALA: One day, you remember, when we were in the bower of *vetasa* creepers, you held water in a cup of lotus leaf.

KING: Go on, I am listening.

SHAKUNTALA: Just then Dirghapanga—do you remember the name?

KING: No. How can I remember a name I never knew?

SHAKUNTALA: Dirghapanga was my pet deer. You were fond of it. You tried to make him drink the water you held, but he shied away. Later, when I took the lotus cup to his lips, he drank the water. Then you said something in jest—

KING: False women attempt to achieve their ends with honeyed anecdotes.

SHANKUNTALA: Ignoble man, you wrong me by such remarks!

Her escorts argue with the king, but he firmly rejects her claims; finally they just abandon Shakuntala then and there and leave, saying that if Shakuntala speaks the truth her place is with her husband, irrespective of what he says or remembers; on the other hand if she is making a false claim, following moral transgressions, she can have no place in their *ashram* and will have no reason to follow them back there.

The king is in difficulty. His priest and mentor advises that he let the lady stay in his house until she is delivered of her child. All that Shakuntala can now do is to follow the priest in tears, appealing aloud in desperation to Mother Earth, "Mother Earth! Take me!" Later they report to the king that as the girl followed, crying and lamenting her fate, a celestial being floated down from the skies, took her in her arms, and vanished. It was none other than her mother, Menaka, who had heard her appeal and responded.

That seems to be the end of all this unhappy episode, leaving the king bewildered, apologetic, and with an indefinable uneasiness at heart. But one day the police chief brings up for disposition the case of a thief found in the market place trying to sell a ring which seems to bear the royal seal. At the sight of the ring, memory returns. The king orders the thief to be rewarded. The "thief" is actually a fisherman who had caught a fish in the river and, opening its belly, found the ring in it.

The king, now fully aware of his obligations, becomes hopelessly contrite and longs to join his wife but does not know in which world to seek her. The Dushyanta of Kalidasa is not a philanderer but an ideal king, a protector of sacrifices. His reputation in all the worlds is so high that god Indra once sends over his chariot to fetch him and courts his help in destroying certain demons infesting his world. While returning victoriously from this expedition, Dushyanta stops at a mountain retreat called Hemakuta, the dwelling place of certain ethereal beings.

In a thick wood, in this peaceful sanctuary, he notices a young child of about twelve years holding down a lion cub by its mane, having tugged it away from its mother's side, while his nurses remonstrate with him to leave the lion alone. Struck with wonder at this demonstration of precocious valour, the king approaches him, feeling greatly drawn to this boy. He observes him and engages himself in a conversation with him until the boy says, "My father, indeed, is Dushyanta, not you." Soon Shakuntala, emaciated by rigorous vows, comes on the scene, and there is a happy reunion of the family, with the gods blessing the meeting.

FIVE

HARISCHANDRA

SIBI

The central character in both these stories is a king, each illustrating a different aspect of the ideal ruler. Harischandra demonstrates the extent of human endurance when faced with a challenge to his kingly principles, and Sibi carries to an extreme the role of the king as protector.

HARISCHANDRA

ALL THE TROUBLE (said the storyteller) for Harischandra started on a higher plane, when two sages discussed the man in a spirit of gossip. The name Harischandra had become synonymous with steadfastness and adherence to truth at any cost. Such fanaticism always invites a challenge. It is human nature to protest against too much perfection; at least as a debating point one likes to controvert it.

The human mind feels at home only when it can detect slight imperfections. It was in such a mood that the two saints came to talk about Harischandra, in an upper world, while that king, unaware of his being the subject of a debate, was happily ruling his country down below on the terrestrial plane. The argument arose between the greatest of the sages, Vasishta, and his perpetual rival, closely following on his heels, Viswamitra. Vasishta had just arrived at Indra Loka from a visit to Ayodhya, Harischandra's capital. While all the celestial beings lounged around on their golden seats, Vasishta was welcomed and asked where he had come from.

Vasishta replied, "I was in Ayodhya attending the *rajasuya* sacrifice of Harischandra. In gifts, in the versatility of sacrificial offerings, in the divinity that he manages to invoke with his devotions and sacrifices, in the kingly showering of gifts on guests and visitors, and in every way, few have I met in any of the worlds above or below, to equal Harischandra. . . ."

A clicking of tongues and an exclamation of the utmost deprecation was heard at this moment and arrested everybody's attention. The exclamation proceeded from where Viswamitra was seated. Everybody turned to him. He quietly said, "You found it all overwhelming, I suppose. You must be easy to please.''

Vasishta looked at him and said without acidity, ''Anyone would agree with me. Anyone who is aware of the qualities of Harischandra.''

The assembly held its breath and waited, for any clash between these two minds always produced interesting results.

Viswamitra pursued the subject further. ''And pray, what are those qualities?''

''Should you ask?''

''Yes,'' said Viswamitra, ''because I'd like to be enlightened.''

Vasishta knew that Viswamitra was spoiling for a fight, yet answered with a casual air, ''If there is one sentient being who has utterly consecrated his existence to truth, it is Harischandra. It is a fact known in all the worlds and, I think, needs no repetition.''

''What is the meaning of 'truth'? Is there none else in all creation who cares for truth? Pray explain.''

''In thought, word, and deed, he is the most truthful man. He will keep his word, whatever may happen.''

''Oh! Oh!'' laughed Viswamitra. ''Are you aware that this Harischandra remained without issue until he prayed to Varuna and performed sacrifices to please that god to give him a son, promising him that son as gift? But when the time came, you know what he did? He became too fond of his son and did not have the heart to fulfil his vow. And so that son himself went round to find an acceptable substitute. They finally got hold of a poor boy, who would have been surrendered to Varuna had I not rescued the child from the sacrifice. . . .''

''Could not be this Harischandra. He is not the one to go back on his word.''

''Should we not put it to the test?'' asked Viswamitra, and all the gods and the assembled sages murmured an enthusiastic assent—a promising show was coming off, in their view. Viswamitra swore, ''I will prove that he will back out of his promises. Otherwise I will surrender all the merits I have so far acquired.'' And so Viswamitra set about his task with zest, and tried in various ways to provoke a conflict between himself and Harischandra.

Now the scene of action shifted to Ayodhya, which was

being ruled by Harischandra in an exemplary manner, with the peasants, artisans, traders, and learned men of the city happy, contented, and loyal. While making the rounds of his capital, Harischandra found a woman in deep grief. He got off his horse, stood before her, and asked, "What makes you so unhappy?"

"My name is Siddhi," she said. "There is one Viswamitra who is doing deep and severe meditation to conquer me, that's why I'm unhappy," she said.

Siddhi means attainment of extraordinary powers, explained the storyteller. When one has attained the *siddhis*, one can walk on water, float in air, travel through various planes, transmute, transmigrate, and so forth. Here the name is symbolic of the goddess presiding over those powers, whom Viswamitra was trying to conquer through his austere meditations. Don't ask me why Harischandra took it literally and not symbolically. I'm only a storyteller, and I narrate it as I've heard it, that's all.

Harischandra was completely shaken by this woman's grief (he continued), and told her grandly, "I'll help you, do not grieve any more." He undertook a search for the meditating sage and found him in a far-off cave, sitting stiff without food or respite, concentrating on the powers he wished to attain. It was almost impossible to get him out of his abstract state, but the king took the risk and made enough noise to rouse Viswamitra.

Whenever a man like this is awakened from contemplation, no human being should come within the range of his immediate vision. He must take care to keep aside and emerge gradually into his notice. Harischandra stood away until the thunderous challenge rang forth, "Who is it that has chosen to disturb me now?"

Harischandra came before him humbly, offered his salutations, and said, "Burn me up, O sage, but your torment of the woman Siddhi must stop. No person should create unhappiness for any other."

This suited Viswamitra, who with all the pugnacity in him wished to have a specific cause for declaring war on Harischandra. "Burn you up!" thought the sage. "Not so fast," he thought, and said aloud, "I am happy that you care so much for the welfare of your subjects. All right; go in peace." He added, perhaps, "If you can."

The king saluted him and returned to his capital, pleased with the success of his mission. But hardly had he set foot within the gates of the city when messengers came hurrying to him and cried, "Your Majesty, we have been searching for you. A strange beast has invaded the city and is wrecking everything in its way."

"Beast! Beast! What sort of a beast is it?" asked the king.

"Looks like a boar with tusks sharp as a sword, runs and jumps and moves like lightning. It is reckless and fast and destroys everything, whether human beings, trees, or cattle; gardens, orchards, and fields have been devastated. Not a single stalk of corn stands anywhere."

The king was disposed to treat their speech as an exaggeration. But when he went round and saw the devastation he was appalled. The unseen menace was here, there, and everywhere, and people came running in with fresh reports. Children were shut in, women were afraid to come out to the river for water, men with sturdy limbs carried heavy weapons, such as axes, sticks, and rods, and moved about casting cautious glances over their shoulders.

The king did not like the atmosphere. He ordered, "Summon all our hunters, let them be ready with their weapons. . . ." Harischandra hurried back to the palace, took leave of the queen, refreshed himself, and was ready in a moment with his armour, lance, sword, bow and arrow, and every kind of equipment for cutting, stabbing, piercing, and destroying this unseen enemy.

After half a day's search he detected the beast emerging from under a bridge at the northern limits of the city. It was a boar, apparently of a special kind, dark as rock, high as an elephant, with tusks gleaming in sunlight and a grunt that sent shivers through one's nerves. Its skin stretched over its muscles shone black and gave it the air of a geological specimen.

The king sent his fastest arrow, and it rebounded. He threw a javelin; it glanced off. The boar started a game of hide and seek, with all the army of huntsmen in pursuit, on foot, on horseback and in various ways. It wove its way in and out of the city, blindly crushing and damaging everything in its path. For all its might, it was elusive and extremely cunning. It was not hurt in the least by the chase, as the variety of missiles aimed at it fell away from it. It seemed to possess a charmed life. Only its pursuers were exhausted; one by one and in groups they fell back, and finally the king found himself all alone, charging along, separated from his companions.

He became obsessed with the dark mass moving ahead of him through thicket, upland, and valley; it led him on and on and finally vanished from view. He sat on a boulder, under a blazing sun, footsore and thirsty and fatigued beyond words, having lost even his mount, as the beast's movements had compelled him to follow it on foot. He felt defeated; now he craved for a little shade and a drink of water. Time to bother about other things later. He did not even know his bearings—although he had been familiar with all the intricate passages and pathways in the forests and hills around. He had forgotten his quarry in the exhaustion of the chase. He sat and mopped his brow with a corner of his scarf, sighing and panting.

Now appeared before him a venerable old man, radiant and saintly, at the sight of whom the king made an instinctive obeisance. Without waiting for the king to speak, the venerable man said, "O king, I understood how thirsty you are. Go up and turn to your left, where you will find a deep grove . . ." and then he gave him directions for reaching a pool of water tucked away in the rocks.

The king reached the pool, impressed with the beauty of the place; the water was so transparent that he could see white pebbles on its bed. He quenched his thirst, and the venerable man also appeased his hunger by setting before him a basketful of fruit; he sat on a stone, watching the king refresh himself, and remarked, "It proves that one who has faith can never get lost. If you have to follow a wild boar, you do it best by changing yourself into a wild boar for the time being," said the saintly man and expanded the theme into a subtle philosophical disquisition.

There, sitting on the cool slab of stone, watching this saintly man, with his thirst and hunger quenched, the king was overwhelmed with a profound sense of gratitude and veneration and said, "When I despaired after the chase, you appeared as if sent by God, and you have revived me in this wilderness and given me food for my body and my soul. I do not know if you know who I am. . . ."

"It is immaterial," said the saint.

"Whatever it may be, please give me a chance to show my gratitude to you, not only for what you have done but for what you are and for deigning to appear before me."

This was the chance that the saint had been waiting for: he was none other than Viswamitra. It was a culmination of a series of attempts that this sage had been making to ensnare the king. First he set Siddhi, next he set the wild boar, his own creation, and now he appeared in the splendour of his sagelike personality. He was a man of tremendous attainments and powers and could create anything anywhere. Harischandra's troubles began.

The sage said, "O king, I know who you are. I appreciate your effort to show me your gratitude. What can I ask of you?"

"Anything," said the guileless king.

"All right, I will let you know what I want, but first prepare yourself properly to offer the gift: bathe in that tank and come back after your evening prayers."

"As you command," said the king, completely under the spell of this grand personality. He got into the tank, took a holy bath, said his prayers, and stood beside the sage as he sat on the stone with his eyes shut in meditation. Harischandra said, "O master, I am ready to do your bidding. What can I give you?"

"Your kingdom, with the entire contents of your treasury; all the ornaments and dress on you, and all the ornaments on your wife and son. You may keep your wife and son with you, but must leave the capital at once."

"I will," said the king.

Now when he returned to the capital it was only to wind up his affairs as a king. He soon divested himself of every possession; his wife, Chandramati, followed suit, and his son was stripped of his earrings. Viswamitra loomed over them, watching that the minutest treasure was not carried off. The populace was in grief and followed their king through the streets.

Viswamitra now said, in addition to his other demands, "Do you know, Harischandra, that all you have given away is worth nothing unless it is properly presented? A gift must be accompanied with *dakshina* to make it complete."

"Yes, that's true," said the king. "But since I possess nothing at this moment, please grant me time to earn the amount and give it to you, whatever it may be."

"Yes, I grant you exactly thirty days to make good the amount."

The wailing populace followed their king to the gates of the city and returned. Harischandra with his wife and son set his course in the direction of Kasi (Benares), a neutral city owned by god Iswara himself, where he could live in the charity houses that abounded all along the river course, and on alms distributed at the temple gate. Needless to add, his wife and son shared his trials without a murmur.

Twenty-nine days passed uneventfully in Kasi. As they sat on the river steps, gazing on the brilliant stream, Viswamitra appeared again, reminding, "Tomorrow will be the last day I could give you for the payment of your *dakshina*. How do you propose to manage it?"—and mentioned after due calculation a figure that stunned the king, but it was really a tenth of what the king had for years collected as revenue in his kingdom.

Close on the heels of Viswamitra appeared a Brahmin, saying, "I am on the lookout for a good woman who can do my household work and keep my house clean. I can buy this woman if she is available."

Chandramati said, "O my husband, sell me for what I am worth, if it will help you pay off your debt."

Now the son added his little voice. "Please take me too, for what I am worth. Let me to some extent help my father."

Harischandra steeled himself to sell his wife and son, and thus collected eleven crores (over a hundred million gold pieces) and handed it to the creditor, who waited beside him with a ruthless determination. After receiving the eleven crores in gold, the sage said, "There is still a balance left. Will you be able to pay it before sunset tomorrow? If you are unable to fulfil your promise, you may say so."

Harischandra said, "If it is due, it must be paid, and there can be no question of offering excuses."

At this moment there appeared a fierce person of the Chandala caste who said, "I am the chief of the Chandalas; all the cremation grounds are in my charge, and all the butcheries, and it is my men who sweep the streets and the drains and remove corpses and burn them at the river's edge. I want a man to do my bidding. If you agree to serve me, I will pay you. . . ." He offered a sum which was just enough to complete the payment due to Viswamitra.

Viswamitra accepted the money and left. The gods in heaven who were watching this drama were so pleased that flowers were showered on Harischandra and invisible voices blessed him for his devotion to truth. The Chandala master assigned Harischandra various tasks at the cremation ground.

Chandramati went away, her only consolation being that her

son was with her. The Brahmin who bought her, a rich man with numerous dependents and a large household, got his money's worth in service. Chandramati's tasks were varied and unspecified. She had to get up at four in the morning, clean and scrub the floors, polish the vessels, attend to the cattle in the yard, water the garden, light the fire for the day, and get hot water for everyone's bath, and wash their clothes at the well. She took care of the numerous children in the household, and if one of them cried or grumbled she was taken to task immediately. She was the last to dine and was seated in the passage and served her food on a dry leaf. Her son was allotted a number of duties, and she could find the time to have a word with him only late at night as they lay on their mats, which they were allowed to spread out in the servants' quarters next to the cattle shed. Sometimes she was severely scolded for some shortcoming in her service. Sometimes they left her alone for days, and sometimes they threw at her a word of encouragement. The son was often out of sight, as he was mostly used as an errand boy.

One afternoon the boy was sent to the forest to gather banyan twigs for the sacrificial fire, and he had not come home by evening. A couple of shepherd boys came to say, "We were in the forest grazing our cattle and saw a boy dead under a banyan tree, bitten by a cobra; his body was blue. Perhaps it was your son. Sorry."

Chandramati burst into a loud wail involuntarily, and it brought to her side immediately her master, who said hysterically, "What is this lamentation at this hour? Don't you know that this is a Friday, and that especially at this hour of dusk there should be no inauspicious sound? It will bring ruin on my family if you persist thus. Stop it, woman. I was wrong in accepting a woman with such an inauspicious horoscope into my house." When he understood the cause of her lamentation he merely said, "It is a pity, but one should be careful while walking in the forests. That boy must have been careless."

She asked for permission to go with the cowherds and see if the dead boy was her son. The man said, "Yes, after you finish your work for the day. Nothing is to be gained by your going there now. What can you do? Tomorrow we have sacred rites to perform; we can't put it off. Finish all your work and then go. . . . But be sure to be back for work at five in the morning." She accepted this condition also as a part of her trial and performed her arduous tasks until midnight and then was guided by the cattle grazers to the forest where her son's body lay.

Attracted by the lamentations proceeding from within the forest, a group of night patrolmen followed the sound and came to where Chandramati was crying over her son's body. They approached her and asked, "Who are you, woman? Why are you here at this hour? What is your explanation for bringing a dead body here?"

She did not hear their words and did not vouchsafe them an answer. She merely looked up and continued her lamentations. They whispered among themselves. "Must be a supernatural creature who has kidnapped some poor child and sucked its blood. Must be pretending to be in grief to put us off. . . ."

They approached her again and got no answer. "No normal human being would dare to be here alone at this hour. Must be a witch."

One of them stood at a distance and prodded her with the sharp point of his lance. She did not even wince; she had become oblivious of her own physical pain. This only confirmed their suspicion that she was supernatural. They suddenly fell on her, bound her with ropes, and took her before their chief, who happened to be the Chandala, Harischandra's master.

He heard the complaint of the patrolmen, questioned her, got no satisfactory answer as to the dead body that she was hugging, and declared, "This is a bad sort, I know. We must make an example of her. We don't want creatures like this in this holy city. Call that man." Harischandra was summoned and told, "Take this woman to the cremation ground and cut off her head."

Harischandra said, "Killing a woman! Oh, ask me to do anything, I will conduct a war and annihilate your enemies if you have any. I will do anything, but not harm a woman."

"Obey my order," said the Chandala. "I have not bought you at an exorbitant price in order to hear your argument about things. Take her away, I say."

"I beg of you, spare me this ordeal," pleaded Harischandra.

The Chandala said, "I accepted you only on your undertaking to obey me implicitly. You remember? Obedience is the first condition of our contract. Do you realize it? Obey my orders. Surely we don't want more children in this city to be devoured by this witch?"

"Yes," replied Harischandra gloomily, "I'll obey you." He ordered the woman to be taken to the cremation ground, where she might be beheaded and cremated simultaneously. She was asked to carry her burden along with her—the dead body of her child.

Harischandra went through his duty blindly, shutting his eyes, literally, to the person before him, benumbing his mind to everything around him with a deliberate effort. To the appointed spot he went with his sword sharpened. Chandramati knelt before him. It was a dark hour and he could not see clearly. He wept at heart and prayed to the heavens to forgive him, and at once corrected himself. "Forgive? Why should I be forgiven?"

The woman pleaded now. "This is my own child. Let me cremate his body before I die. Give me time, help me with this task."

"Yes, you may," Harischandra said. "But my master collects a tax for every body that is burnt in this ground. You will have to pay it before proceeding further."

The woman said, "Alas, I possess neither money nor any valuables."

"But I see a gold chain around your neck. Give that as the tax."

Chandramati looked up and scrutinized him in the flickering torchlight. For she had been given a boon at birth that the sacred gold *thali* around her neck would not be visible to anyone except her husband.

When they recognized each other, they decided to burn themselves together on the same pyre built for their child; there was no meaning in existence any more. Hardly had they set foot in the fire when the gods in heaven realized that the limits had been reached in the trial of this hardy soul. Flowers rained from the heavens, the fires were put out with a rain of nectar, and voices in the heavens said, "Your trials have ended. May victory be yours."

Viswamitra, the great tormentor, appeared on the scene. "Harischandra, you have proved me wrong every time. No other creature could have borne the trials as you have. All your tormentors, the Chandala, the Brahmin, the cobra that bit your son, the wild boar, and Siddhi have all been my creations, and only acted my part or spoke my words—all intent on making you break your promise at least once. You have borne much from me.

Now I give you back your son.'' The son rose to his feet as from sleep.

"Go back to your kingdom and rule it, as the great king that you are,'' said the sage. "I accept defeat gladly. I will begin my spiritual training and the acquisition of merit all over again from nothing, because I am surrendering all the merit and powers of my spiritual life to you, with all my heart.''

SIBI

THERE IS A half-moon in the sky today which will disappear shortly after midnight, said the storyteller. I'll select a tale which will end before the moon sets, so that you may all go home when there is still a little light.

The tale concerns a king and two birds. The king was Sibi, who had just performed a holy sacrifice on the banks of the Jumna. The guests were resting in the tree shade after partaking of a feast. The air was charged with the scent of flowers and incense. Sibi went round to make sure that everyone was comfortable. A cool breeze blew from the south, patches of clouds mitigated the severity of the sun in the blue sky, the embers of the holy fire subsided into a soft glow under the ash.

The king, satisfied that all his guests were happy, dismissed his attendants and proceeded to his own corner of the camp to rest under a canopy. He had closed his eyes, half in sleep and half in prayer, when he felt a gust of air hitting him in the face and some object suddenly dropping on his lap. He awoke and noticed a dove, white and soft, nestling in his lap. Its feathers were ruffled in terror and its eyes were shut. It looked so limp that he thought it was dead, but then he noticed a slight flutter of breath. He sat still in order not to frighten away the bird, and looked about for a servant.

Just then a hawk whirled down in pursuit, and perched itself on a low branch of the tree beside the canopy. The hawk exclaimed, "Ah, at last! What a game of hide and seek!"

"What do you want?" asked the king.

"I am addressing myself to that creature on your lap! Never been so much tricked in my life! If every mouthful of food has to be got after such a trial, a nice outlook indeed for the so-called king of birds! As one king to another, let me tell you, the dove nestling in your lap is mine. Throw it back to me.''

The king thought over the statement of the hawk and said, "I am indeed honoured by a visit from the king of birds, although I had thought till now that the eagle was the king!''

"I am a hawk, not a kite. Know you that the hawk belongs to the kingly race while the kite is a mere caricature of our family, pursuing a career of deception by seeming no bigger than its victim and then attacking it. How often one mistakes a kite for a dove!''

Sibi wanted to divert the attention of the hawk from the subject of the dove and so said, "The kite also goes out of sight when it flies, so don't be offended if we land-bound creatures imagine that the kite floats in the same heaven as the hawk.''

The hawk sharpened his beak on the tree-trunk and lifted one leg to display his talons and said, "I'm sorry to see the mistakes you human beings make. The kite no doubt flies—but not beyond the back of the lowest cloud. And you think that it sports in the heavens itself! The only common element between us is that we both have pointed, curved beaks, that's all; but the kite has a taste for helpless little creatures such as mice and sparrows—creatures which we would not care to notice.''

The king realized that the subject was once more drifting towards food and diverted the hawk's attention again by saying, "The general notion is that the eagle is the king of birds.''

The hawk chuckled cynically. "Ignorant mankind! How the eagle came to be so much respected, I shall never understand; what is there to command the eagle? Its wingspread? You people are too easily carried away by appearances! Do you know that the hawk can fly just as high as the eagle? And yet you have no regard for us!''

Sibi said, "You can't blame us, we take things as they seem from here! I now know better.''

The hawk looked pleased at this concession and said, "Have you ever seen a mountain eagle walk on the ground? Is there anything more grotesque? Don't you agree that the first requirement for kingliness would be grace of movement? Only we hawks have it.''

"True, true," said the king. "When I move from my bed to the bathroom, even if alone at night, I catch myself strutting along as in a parade, I suppose!'' The king laughed, to entertain the hawk; he thought it might please the bird to be treated as a fellow king. The hawk looked pleased, and the king hoped that it would take itself off after these pleasantries.

The dove slightly stirred on his lap, and he hastened to draw over it his silk scarf. The hawk noticed this and bluntly said, "King, what is the use of your covering the dove? I will not forget that my food, which I have earned by honest chase, is there, unfairly held by you."

The king said, "This bird has come to me for asylum; it is my duty to protect it."

"I may brave your sword and swoop on my prey, and if I die in the attempt the spirits of my ancestors will bless me. We have known no fear for one thousand generations, what should we fear when the back of our prime ancestor serves as the vehicle of the great god Vishnu?"

Again the king was on the point of correcting him, that it was a golden eagle that Vishnu rode, not a hawk, but he checked himself.

The bird emphasized his own status again. "You who are reputed to be wise, O king, don't confuse me with the carrion birds wheeling over your head. I know where I stand," said the bird, preening its feathers.

The king felt it was time to say something agreeable himself, secretly worrying that he was reaching the limits of his wit. The dove nestled within the silk scarf. There was an uneasy pause while the king dreaded what might be coming next.

The hawk suddenly said, "All the world speaks of you as one who has the finest discrimination between right and wrong. And so you have a serious responsibility at this moment. You must not do anything that goes contrary to your reputation. Remember, I am in the agonies of hunger, and you refuse me my legitimate diet. By your act you cause me suffering, you injure me every second that you keep your hold on that parcel of meat. You have attained immeasurable spiritual merit by your deeds of perfection; now this single selfish act of yours will drain away all your merit and you will probably go to hell."

"O infinitely wise bird, does it seem to you that I am holding this dove out of selfishness so that I may eat it myself?"

"I am not so simple-minded," said the bird haughtily. "By selfish I meant that you were thinking of your own feelings, totally ignoring my viewpoint."

"When I recollect the terror in its eye as it fell on my lap, I feel nothing ever matters except affording it protection."

"O prince among princes, food is life, out of food all things exist and stir. Between life and death stands what? Food! I am faint with hunger. If you deny me my food any longer I may die. In a cranny of yonder rock my wife has hatched four eggs, the little ones are guarded by their mother, and all of them await my return home. If I die here of hunger, they will keep peeping out for my return home until they perish of the same hunger. And the sin of ending six lives will be on you. O maharaja, consider well whether you want to save one doubtful life, which is probably half gone already, or six lives. Let not the performance of what seems to you a rightful act conflict with bigger issues. You know all this, king, but choose to ignore the issues. And all this talking only fatigues me and takes me nearer to death. So please spare me further argument."

Sibi said, "I notice that you are an extraordinary bird. You talk wisely, knowledgeably; there is nothing that you do not know. Your mind journeys with ease at subtle heights of thought. But, bird, tell me, how is it that you fail to notice the sheer duty I owe a creature that cries for protection? As a king is it not my duty?"

"I am only asking for food; food is to life what oil is to a lamp."

"Very well. You see all these people lying around, they have all rested after a feast in which nothing was lacking to satisfy the sixfold demands of the palate. Tell me what you want, and I will spread a feast before you in no time."

"King, the nature of food differs with different creatures. What you call a feast seems to me just so much trash. We observe from our heights all the activity that goes on in your royal kitchen and ever wonder why you take all that trouble with spice, salt, and fire to ruin the taste of God-given stuff. King, I do not want to speak at length. I am famished and I feel my eyes dimming. Have consideration for me too."

"If it is flesh you want, I will ask them to get it for you."

The hawk gave an ironical laugh at this. "See where all this leads you! How are you going to get flesh without killing something else? When you interfere with what God has ordained, you complicate everything."

"What is God's plan, actually? Please enlighten me."

"The dove is intended for me; God has no other purpose in creating it and letting it multiply so profusely. Are you not aware of the ancient saying that hawks eat doves?"

The king thought it over and said, "If you spare this dove, I'll guarantee you food every day in my palace all your life."

"I have already told you, my lord, that your food is inedible. Your assurance of daily feeding does not appeal to me. I hunt for food when I want it. I do not see why I should bother about tomorrow. Hoarding for generations ahead is a human failing, a practice unknown to us. I repeat the ancient saying that hawks eat doves."

The king brooded over the words of the hawk for a moment. "Ask for anything, except this little bird on my lap. I won't give it up, whichever way you may argue."

The hawk tilted its head, rolled its eyes, and said, "So be it. I will ask for the next best thing. I want warm flesh, with warm blood dripping, equal in weight to the dove. We are used to eating only fresh meat, we are not carrion birds, let me remind you. You will have to cut it out of your own body, as I know you will not choose to kill another creature for it."

The king brooded over this. "Yes, but I must consider which part of my body will yield the flesh you want without destroying my life. Give me a little time. Bear your hunger for a moment." And he added, "A ruler has no liberty to die. Many depend on him."

"In the same way as my family," said the hawk.

The king beckoned to an attendant. "Bring a pair of weighing scales."

The attendant was nonplussed. "Your Majesty, how can we find one here, in this remote place?"

The king repeated, "I want a pair of scales for accurate weighing."

"May I send a messenger to fetch one from the city?"

"How long will he take?" asked the king.

The courtier made a swift reckoning and declared, "If he rides a galloping horse, he should be back tomorrow at dawn."

The king looked at the hawk, who already seemed to droop. He did not want to hear again about his family on the mountain. It was also time to clear up all this situation and feed the refugee on his lap. He said to the courtier, "Construct a balance immediately with whatever is available here. I'll give you ten minutes!"

"Whoever fails will have his head cut off, I suppose?" sneered the hawk. "That would be truly kinglike, but let me tell you straight away that I am not interested in a cut-off head."

"You shall have my flesh and nothing less," said the king.

They bustled about. By now the whole camp was astir, watching this incredible duel between the king and the hawk. They managed to dangle a beam from the branch of a tree. Suspended from either end was a plate from the kitchen; a pointer, also improvised, marked the dead centre of the beam.

The king looked at the hawk and said, "This is the best we can manage."

"I understand. A little fluctuation should not matter in the least. Only I do not want you to lose more flesh than is necessary to balance the dove."

The king did not let the bird finish his sentence, but rose, bearing the dove in his hand. He walked up to the crude scales in order to test them. He addressed the hawk, "Will you step nearer?"

"I can watch quite well from here. Also I can trust you."

The king placed the dove on the right-hand side of the scale pan, which immediately went down, making the king wonder how a little bird which had lain so lightly on his lap could weigh down the balance in this manner.

He wasted no further time in speculation. He sat on the ground, stretched out his leg, and, after a brief prayer, incised his thigh with a sharp knife. The courtiers and guests assembled groaned at the sight of the blood. The king gritted his teeth and tore out a handful of flesh and dropped it on the scale.

The pan became bloodstained but the pointer did not move. Someone cursed the dove, "It has the weight of an abandoned corpse. It looks dead, see if it is dead."

Another added, "Just pick it up and fling it to that hawk and be done with it, the miserable creature."

The king was too faint to talk; he gestured to them to stop commenting. He had now only the skin on his right thigh. Still the scales were unbalanced. The king went on to scoop the flesh from his other leg; the pointer was still down.

People averted their eyes from the gory spectacle. The hawk watched him critically.

"O hawk, take all that meat and begone!" they said.

"I have been promised the exact equal weight of the dove,"

insisted the hawk, at which all those assembled cursed the hawk and drew their swords. The king was faint with pain now, but mustered the last ounce of his strength to command his followers to keep away.

He beckoned to his chief minister to come nearer. "One has no right to end one's life, but this is unforeseen. Even if this means hell to me, I have to face it," he said. Everyone looked at the dove with distaste. "My brother shall be the regent till the prince comes of age."

With this he struggled onto his feet and stepped on the flesh-filled pan. At once the other pan went up and equalized.

The hawk now flitted nearer and said, "This is more than a mouthful for me and my family. How am I to carry you to the mountain?"

The king mumbled feebly, "I did not think of that problem," and added, "You wouldn't have been able to lift the dove either! So bring your family here."

The hawk flapped its wings and rose in the air and swooped down as if to peck at the king's flesh. People shut their eyes, unable to bear the spectacle. But presently they heard divine instruments filling the skies with music. The hawk was gone, but in its place they found Indra, the god with the dazzling crown, armed with the diamond spear, seizing Sibi's hand and helping him down off the weighing scales. A flame rose where the dove had lain, and from the heart of it emerged the God of Fire.

They said, "O king, we put you to a severe test. We challenged your integrity; and we happily accept defeat. You are indeed blessed, and as long as human beings recollect your tale, they will partake of the spiritual merit that you have yourself acquired"—and vanished. The king recovered his energy in a moment, while the pieces of flesh in the scale pan turned to fragrant flowers.

A NOTE ON COSMOGONY

THE WORLD OF Indian mythology consists of seven islands and seven seas. The islands are known as *dwipas*, of which Jambu Dwipa is considered the central one. At its centre is the golden mountain named Meru. It rises 84,000 *yojanas** above the earth and extends 16,000 *yojanas* below it; its diameter is 32,000 *yojanas* at the summit and 16,000 at the base, so that it has the shape of a seed-cup of lotus. On the summit of Meru is Brahma's city, covering 14,000 leagues, and surrounding it, at its cardinal points and the intermediate quarters, is the city of Indra.

The earth is said to go down to a depth of 70,000 *yojanas* and to consist of seven layers of worlds below, called Patala Lokas. Each one of these layers has a name (Atala, Vitala, Nitala, and so on) and is inhabited by *asuras*, and also by certain semi-divine beings, among them *yakshas* and *dhanavas*. Below the seven worlds extend the coils of a dark snake, on whose thousand heads rests the entire world. The snake is called Sesha, and his coils form the couch on which god Vishnu stretches himself in rest. Below the earth and the waters and all the worlds are twenty-eight layers of hells, the province of Yama, full of instruments of torture and fire into which sinners are cast.

The earth, called Bhurloka, with its oceans and mountains, extends to the frontiers of the illumination cast by the rays of the sun and moon. The sphere of the sky extends above it up to the planets. The solar orb is situated a hundred thousand leagues from the earth, and beyond it are the spheres of Venus (Sukra), Jupiter (Budha), and Mars (Kuja). The sphere of the Seven Sages (Ursa

---

* A *yojana* is the distance traversed by a horse in one harnessing, as much as nine miles.

Major) lies a hundred thousand leagues beyond Saturn, and at the same distance from that point is Dhruva (the Pole Star), the pivot of the whole planetary system. Above Dhruva, ten million leagues away, lies the sphere of the saints, called Mahar Loka. At twice that distance reside the sons of Brahma, in Janar Loka. At four times that distance is Tapo Loka (the Sphere of Penance), inhabited by the deities; at six times that distance is Satya Loka (the World of Indestructible Truth).

All the worlds are protected by a divine cosmic shell. Around the outer shell lies water equal in extent to ten times the diameter of the earth. The waters in turn are surrounded by fire, fire by air, air by mind, and mind by the origin of the elements. Enclosing the whole is the Supreme Principle, which guides all these, and which is infinite and measureless.

Of course the cosmic arrangement, as it may be deduced from the puranas, is impressive in its variety and vastness; but it is not susceptible to being mapped on any rational basis of cartography.

GLOSSARY

ashram—a sanctuary, or hermitage

astra—weapon

asura—demon, anti-god

bhiksha—alms

Brahmin—member of the priestly caste

Chandala—a member of the lowest caste

dakshina—fee

danda—staff of authority (mace)

dasa—ten; also means kite

deva, devi—god, goddess

Dharma—established order, rule, duty, virtue, moral merit, right, justice, law (in an eternal sense)

dhoti—sarong-like garment

durbar—court

Gandharva marriage—a marriage consummated without ceremony, by mutual consent only

guru—teacher, preceptor

jivan mukta—one who has attained salvation

Karma—action; the law of Karma is the result of action and reaction in a series of births.

Kshatriya—member of the warrior class

Kuruvai (Tamil)—pastoral dance

loka—world

Mahabharata—the epic composed by Vyasa

mantra—incantation

Pandya (Tamil)—a ruler of Madurai, a Tamil country

patala—nether

puranas—source books of mythology, said to be older than the *Vedas*

rakshasa—a demonic being

Ramayana—the epic composed by Valmiki

rishi—saintly man, highly evolved

sadhu—an ascetic

samadhi—state of deep meditation, when one becomes unaware of one's normal surroundings

Sanskrit—classical language of ancient India

shastras—scientific treatises or codes

Swayamwara—a ceremony by means of which a princess chooses a husband

Tamil—a Dravidian language

tapas—concentrated meditation over prolonged time for a spiritual growth, spiritual powers, or purpose; penance

thali—a sacred thread or necklace, which is knotted around a woman's neck by the husband at the time of marriage

vahana—vehicle

vajra—diamond, or diamond-like hardness

Vedas—revealed scriptures, which are timeless

veena—an ancient stringed instrument

vimana—flying chariot

yogi—a spiritual adept

Bantam Classics bring you the world's greatest literature—books that have stood the test of time—at specially low prices. These beautifully designed books will be proud additions to your bookshelf. You'll want all these time-tested classics for your own reading pleasure.

☐	21109	BEOWULF AND OTHER OLD ENGLISH POEMS	$1.95
☐	21082	CANTERBURY TALES, Geoffrey Chaucer	$2.95
☐	21179	THE PRINCE, Niccolo Machiavelli	$1.75
☐	21076	COMPLETE PLAYS, Sophocles	$2.95
☐	21169	THREE COMEDIES, Plautus	$3.95
☐	21041	THE AENEID, Virgil	$2.95
☐	21182	FAUST, Johann W. von Goethe	$3.50
☐	21166	CANDIDE, Voltaire	$2.25
☐	21164	COMPLETE PLAYS, Aristophanes	$3.50
☐	21219	TEN PLAYS, Euripides	$3.50
☐	21151	GREEK DRAMA, Hadas, ed.	$3.50

Dante: THE DIVINE COMEDY

☐	21069	INFERNO	$2.50
☐	21133	PURGATORIO	$3.50
☐	21204	PARADISO	$4.95

Look for them at your bookstore or use this handy coupon:

Bantam Books, Inc., Dept. CL, 414 East Golf Road, Des Plaines, Ill. 60016

Please send me the books I have checked above. I am enclosing $_____ (Please add $1.50 to cover postage and handling.) Send check or money order—no cash or C.O.D.'s please.

Mr/Ms _____

Address _____

City/State _____ Zip _____

CL 8/86

Please allow four to six weeks for delivery. This offer expires February 1987. Price and availability subject to change without notice.